I0818989

AMERICA, U.S.A.

ALSO BY EDDIE S. GLAUDE JR.

An Uncommon Faith: A Pragmatic Approach to the Study of African American Religion

Democracy in Black: How Race Still Enslaves the American Soul

African American Religion: A Very Short Introduction

In a Shade of Blue: Pragmatism and the Politics of Black America

African American Religious Thought: An Anthology (edited with Cornel West)

Is It Nation Time? Contemporary Essays on Black Power and Black Nationalism (editor)

Exodus! Religion, Race, and Nation in Early Nineteenth-Century Black America

Begin Again: James Baldwin's America and Its Urgent Lessons for Our Own

We Are the Leaders We Have Been Looking For

AMERICA, U.S.A.

HOW RACE SHADOWS THE NATION'S ANNIVERSARIES

EDDIE S. GLAUDE JR.

CROWN
NEW YORK

CROWN
An imprint of the Crown Publishing Group
A division of Penguin Random House LLC
1745 Broadway
New York, NY 10019
crownpublishing.com
penguinrandomhouse.com

Library of Congress Cataloging-in-Publication Data is on file with the publisher.

Hardcover ISBN 978-0-593-23980-3
Ebook ISBN 978-0-593-23981-0

Editor: Kevin Doughten
Editorial assistant: Jessica Jean Scott
Production editor: Craig Adams
Text designer: Andrea Lau
Production: Heather Williamson
Copy editor: Lawrence Krauser
Proofreaders: Pam Rehm, Chuck Thompson, Janet Biehl
Indexer: J S Editorial, LLC
Publicist: Penny Simon
Marketer: Chantelle Walker

Manufactured in the United States of America

1st Printing

First Edition

The authorized representative in the EU for product safety and compliance is Penguin Random House Ireland, Morrison Chambers, 32 Nassau Street, Dublin D02 YH68, Ireland, https://eu-contact.penguin.ie.

For Mom, my inspiration

"In my end is my beginning."

—T. S. Eliot, *East Coker*

CONTENTS

AMERICA, U.S.A.

Before each chapter I have placed bars of original music written for this book by the award-winning classical composer Joel Thompson. Together, the notations make one complete composition. The music captures the haunting beauty of the nation. It opens with a deconstructed blues sonority, where the major and minor third are present in the same chord. The sound captures the core idea of the book and sets the stage for the elegy that mourns the country we thought we knew. The middle part explodes the motif with sounds of conflict and violence as the upper and lower registers of the piano assert themselves. This is the lived experience of the country shorn of the comfort of a storybook version of America and its promise. That part then gives way to the hope of a prayer—that somehow and in some way this country can be better. But then the blues sonority returns. Hope shadowed by ambivalence at the crossroads. America, U.S.A.

Disillusioned; weary ♩ = 64
ppp
8

INTRODUCTION

BITTERNESS AT THE BOTTOM OF THE CUP

I do not love America, and never have, especially now. It seems to me misplaced or dangerous to love something so abstract and so morally dubious. Love is most often felt and experienced close to the ground—in the life lived in a particular place and time, and in memories that take up residence in the heart. I suspect "love of country" is shorthand for the heartfelt relationships and experiences that make us who we are—things that happen in the place we call home, no matter how complicated that place may be. James Baldwin was right: "Whoever is part of whatever civilization helplessly loves some aspects of it, and some of the people in it." And I suppose that is why, in part, we are willing to risk our lives in defense of this place, and of what it might become.

But in America, those feelings and experiences have always been stained by the ugliness of what white people believe about color—that somehow, or in some inscrutable way, the color of one's skin determines your value. You end up spending much of your life trying to prove to others and to yourself—not because you are obsessed with white people but because you want to live—that you are not a "nigger." Some Americans may believe that this view is a relic of a past that we have long left behind. *After all,* they might say, *we elected a Black president and vice president. Look how far we have come. Stop complaining,* I hear them say.

You teach at Princeton University. You are not *a victim.* But I speak from the experience of a life lived in this country, and I trust what I know, what I have seen, and what now sits in the pit of my stomach.

Each one of us must face the battle with this place to live fully, and to try to beat back the bitterness that threatens to consume us. It's enough to drive you to madness. I can still feel the sting of my neighbor's dad screaming at his son to stop playing with "that *nigger,*" wondering then what was wrong with him and asking myself what was wrong with me. An adolescent version of a familiar cry arose: *Why did God make me a stranger in my own house?* Would I resign myself to such a world, or slip into what W. E. B. Du Bois described as a "silent hatred of the pale world . . . and mocking distrust of everything white"? Either way, a wound deposited by a calloused heart made it difficult, if not impossible, to love the country that hurt me. I had to learn, instead, how to survive it.

Bitterness settles in the heart of a child and innocence is lost, because the world announces in stark terms that you, no matter how young you may be, do not belong here. This happens in every corner of the country. The hurt I felt all those years ago wasn't an isolated incident or something unique to Mississippi or the South. *America* believed what that man said about me, and that *word*—that belief—did not die with the civil rights legislation of the 1960s or the election of Barack Obama. Its sentiments and sensibilities have not been relegated to the dustbin of history. Too many lives have been lost since then to believe that. Instead, these ideas about race and about Black people have lurked beneath the surface of American life like a Leviathan. Today, the monster is in full view, eating the souls of the damned.

I saw it with the election of Donald Trump in 2024 as millions of white Americans, and a smattering of others, declared that the country belongs to them. I can hear it in the summary judgments about diversity, equity, and inclusion (DEI): that, by definition, diversity (and the word always seems to refer to Black people) involves the compromise of standards; that Black people in leadership positions, or students who are admitted to Ivy League schools and elite state colleges, or professors like me really did not earn their place—that any attempt to address racism in this country amounts to reverse discrimination. I see the monster in masked ICE agents snatching people out of their homes, at courthouses, in front of schools as parents wait for their children—people the American government has determined do not belong here. Those who still believe themselves to be the "true" Americans repeat an old, insidious idea about white people that requires a certain view of Black and Brown people. The "true" Americans desperately need, and still want, their "niggers."

No. I do not love America. I only wish that the country could be better, more decent and just, and in wishing that, I confess that I love deeply those who have borne and must bear the brunt of the country's madness. Even if most Americans don't see it, that love includes us all.

—

I have set out in this book to assert a certain view of this country, one that I hope will help us make sense of our current malaise as we celebrate 250 years since the founding. America is at once a nation of laws that reflect, ideally, the equal standing of each individual *and* a white Republic. Freedom animates our way of life *and* it is the possession of white people to give to others and to take away. These values are irreconcilable and show that a paradox rests at the heart of the nation. When the tension between these two features of the country becomes unbearably felt and known, white America risks everything, including the well-being of the country, to resolve it. The Civil War is just one deadly example of an unsettling truth. Donald Trump's ascendance is another: some white people would rather destroy the country than face the doubleness that makes it what it is.

I mean by this doubleness something akin to what W. E. B. Du Bois wrote about in his 1903 classic, *The Souls of Black Folk,* when he declared that the problem of the twentieth century was the problem of the color line. It remains our problem, too. Du Bois used the metaphor of the veil to describe the separation between the worlds of Black and white folk, and he detailed the effects of that duality on the way Black people saw themselves:

> It is a peculiar sensation, this double consciousness, this sense of always looking at one's self through the eyes of others, of measuring one's soul by the tape of a world that looks on in amused contempt and pity. One ever feels his twoness—an American, a Negro, two souls, two thoughts, two unreconciled strivings, two warring souls in one dark body, whose dogged strength alone keeps it from being torn asunder.

But, to my mind, this peculiar sensation of "twoness" is not limited to Black folk alone. It is the condition, truly the inheritance, of all Americans. Its beginnings are found in America itself.

American double consciousness is the consequence of a nation that defines itself with the foundational principle of the equality of men and, yet, holds others as chattel or resigns them to second-class status. The principle and the practice cannot coexist without contradictions, and to hold them together, as if they can, is a form of madness. American double consciousness is the outcome of a nation that represents itself as "the shining city on the hill" and, yet, sees itself darkly through the eyes of those who have borne the whip's lash, who look upon the nation with contempt and pity, who inevitably judge and find the country wanting—a ruthless mirror that lives and breathes. It is the split that comes with the American promise and contempt for that promise—warring ideals, from the beginning, that have threatened and continue to threaten to tear the nation apart.

America can never fully banish this sense of twoness—and, at times, it cannot bear the gaze that looks back at it in a haunting reminder. Desperately afraid of being exposed, particularly to themselves, most white Americans have been led by that fear, and continue to be led, into a kind of delirium that erupts, repeatedly, in unimaginable violence and draconian policies. They lash out. They destroy or render entire populations invisible, lock them away in prisons, push them to the edges of our communities, or deport them in order to keep the country, or their idea of the country, from being torn asunder.

If the problem of the twentieth century, as Du Bois announced, was the problem of the color line, and the color line was a consequence of American double consciousness, and that doubleness persists even today, then the problem of the twenty-first century is the problem of America's desperate avoidance of self-awareness—its refusal to know itself fully, and the deadly consequences for people and the world that follow from that refusal. Ours is a time of shattered mirrors.

We are experiencing a continuation of the betrayal that began with Donald Trump's first term in office. His election in 2016 was, as many have noted, a response to Barack Obama's presidency and the Black Lives Matter movement. Trump served as an expression of the panic around demographic shifts (the so-called browning of America), an avatar for white grievance, and a vehicle for the mainstreaming of white nationalism. After the horrors of George Floyd's murder, and the protests that forced the nation to see its own ugly underbelly, and Trump's defeat in 2020, many people believed that the country had turned a corner, that the fever dream had finally broken. But, even with Biden's presidency, Americans remained in the storm of the after times, caught between a dying world with its splintering ideologies and a frightening emergent order that comes in glimpses and starts where even the pretenses of liberalism no longer matter.

Trump's reelection in 2024 signaled that a large swath of white America was unwilling to struggle any longer over race matters. Instead, he reasserted the fantasy of a white Republic. With stunning efficiency and clarity, his administration set out to destroy the basic governmental infrastructure of civil rights. He attacked DEI in the public and private sectors; instructed federal agencies to stop enforcing key civil rights protections; engaged in an all-out assault on American education, using diversity initiatives as examples of reverse discrimination; gutted the civil rights division of the Justice Department; ended consent decrees with police departments around the country; attempted to upend over a hundred years of jurisprudence with his effort to end birthright citizenship; and implemented cruel immigration policies. It feels as if Trump and his supporters pine not only for a time before Ferguson and Minneapolis, but for the days before the civil rights movement—the days of segregation. They also seem to yearn for an understanding of the nation's past that made segregation necessary and a fact of life. Black people and white people knew their place then. White people were at the center of everything, innocently inhabiting a nation of unblemished virtue and seamless progress. Black people were on the margins, quietly playing bit parts in the great nation's history. This, they believe, is the true American story—storybook democracy.

—

July 4, 2026, marks the 250th anniversary of the founding of the nation. Anniversaries of this magnitude occasion opportunities to tell the American story, to look back and reaffirm the basic ideals of the country, and to reflect on the present challenges the nation may face as Americans look toward the future. Declarations of "love of country" abound. But not all of what is celebrated has to be true. American anniversaries are often moments to turn a blind eye to the evils of the past and the present—to suppress the fact of America's divided soul. Stories of America's greatness are told to affirm the belief that ours was and remains the greatest country on earth. In these accounts, American patriotism (love of country) lacks the ugliness of traditional forms of nationalism, because a democratic idea animates our past and present, not a commitment to blood and soil—the kind that resulted in declarations of the superiority of the white Anglo-Saxon, in the brutal Holocaust of Europe, and in the wars that left the world in tatters. Our love of country is different, we tell ourselves, because of the idea of America expressed in the Declaration of Independence and made real with the U.S. Constitution.

But, like the centennial, sesquicentennial, and bicentennial events commemorating the founding, the semiquincentennial exposes the maddening split at the heart of the country. Today, Americans remain bitterly divided, and those divisions are rooted, in part, in the irresolvable ideas that America is a beacon of freedom and that it must remain a white Republic. Distrust has seeped into every facet of our political lives and festers in those intimate spaces where hatred grows unchecked. As John Dos Passos, the author of the 1938 classic *U.S.A.*, wrote, "We are two nations." But the duality goes beyond the standard divide between the wealthy and the working class, or red and blue states. The demands of Black Lives Matter around policing and Confederate statues, claims about white privilege and anti-racism, and attempts to remedy long-standing racial inequality offered a mirror to the country. Charitable gestures were not enough for those who demanded racial justice and who called for a more honest public history of America. The protests insisted, as have protests many times before, on a reckoning with the contradiction in the nation's soul.

The backlash has been swift and harsh.

In what felt like a blink of an eye, questions about race and history were cast aside. The country, or at least a large portion of the country, retreated into the safety of its fantasies, reached for a politics (and politicians) that shamelessly denied the reality of racism, embraced white nationalist rhetoric like the so-called Great Replacement, and sought redemption in the demonization of anything associated with Black Lives Matter. In an exchange on X, Christopher Rufo, the right-wing activist leading the assault on DEI in American higher education, accused me of being unable to "accept that BLM divided the country, destroyed institutions, gutted entire neighborhoods, and increased the homicide rate in black communities." He declared that "the BLM era is over"—just five years after the public murder of George Floyd.

Mirrors shattered, people who claimed to be allies now worried about the overreach of "wokeness," and the celebration of 250 years since the founding hides the broken glass beneath our feet.

Like the celebrations before it, the semiquincentennial reaches back to a storybook America that requires either the banishment of Black people from view or the reduction of our role in the country's history, so as to affirm America's ongoing quest to be a more perfect union. These ritual moments in the nation's life offer telescoped instances of the doubleness that has haunted the country since its beginning. They often traffic in myth and celebrate American exceptionalism, ignoring the realities that call both into question—realities like the compromises in the Constitution to protect slavery, or the maddening decision by the participants in the Constitutional Convention to refuse to abolish the transatlantic slave trade until 1808, twenty years after ratification. (Even then, the trade in Black people did not effectively end until the Civil War.) Or how they counted those in bondage as three-fifths of a person for purposes of apportionment, giving the slaveholding states outsized power and influence on the direction of the fledgling nation. The Constitution, with its Fugitive Slave Clause, made the country a nation of slaves and slavecatchers. Every individual, every community was conscripted in the effort to return an escaped slave. America, split in two, became a nation, as Frederick Douglass said, full of "wild beasts." The celebrations—and the 250th is no different—ignore the undeniable fact that the founders made a tragic choice that corrupted the American soul, and Americans have been bound by it ever since.

Each of these celebrations arrived at a fraught juncture in the history of the country—marked by backlash and racial violence. All insisted on the uniqueness of the American idea based in the sacred documents of the Declaration of Independence and the Constitution. That uniqueness was also expressed in the deeply felt belief that this country belongs to white people. Two unreconciled strivings in one national body.

In each chapter I return to an anniversary year and look closely at events that reveal this argument. In 1876, we see the consequences of American double consciousness with the violent collapse of Reconstruction and in the barbaric assaults on Black people necessary for reconciliation and reunion. In the aftermath of the calamity of the Civil War, in a moment when the nation could have freed itself from the contradiction institutionalized by the founders, the centennial celebration offered a vision of the country rooted in its original sin, which required the banishment of Black people from any significant role in the history or future of a country built for and by "the white American."

The 1926 celebration expanded this view as it struggled with the implication of European immigration to the United States after the First World War. America's racial hierarchy and the idea of the white American evolved as European ethnics joined the fold, though not without resistance. The 1920s were, in a way, the decade of the Ku Klux Klan, and the organization's view of European immigrants was, to put it mildly, hostile. Black people were still made to play minor parts in the history of the country—flat background characters to be disciplined with violence if they dared step out of place. One can get a sense of the two warring souls of the nation in 1926 as the Klan petitioned to have its Klonvocation on the fairgrounds for the nation's 150th anniversary celebration in Philadelphia, a request that was initially approved.

The 1976 celebration represented an attempt to tell a somewhat different story. In the shadow of the social revolutions of the 1960s, it aimed to lift up the ethnic diversity of the nation, and to absorb the story of Black America into the American story of the ongoing quest for a more perfect union. But we can also see the contradictions distilled in the 1976 Stanley Forman photograph *The Soiling of Old Glory,* which shows a white teenager attacking a Black man with the American flag during an anti-busing protest in downtown Boston, as the betrayal of the civil rights movement gained momentum. And here we are in 2026, with authoritarian forces swept into office on a wave of white grievance and hatred reaching back to 1876 and 1926 in powerful and disturbing ways. It feels as if the nation is about to burst apart at the seams, because some believe that *their* country has been hijacked by radical "others." The country has carried the sins of its founding forward.

—

America, U.S.A. explores America's double consciousness as a way we might account for those sins. The title of the book riffs on Dos Passos's *U.S.A.* trilogy—three books, originally published separately over six years and bound together as one in 1938, that sought to offer a description of the roiling chaos of the country in the run-up to the economic crash of 1929. There is no particular protagonist or coherent plot; we see social forces moving interrelated characters about. Greed and self-interest rule, and working people (or "midway people in somewhat ambiguous positions") find themselves trapped in a world where the pursuit of money defines life, with no visible exit. Even the liberatory aims of radical labor movements may be corrupt (revealing Dos Passos's indifference to rigid ideological talk of class struggle). Lionel Trilling put it this way:

> Dos Passos is primarily concerned with morality, with personal morality. The national, collective, social elements of his trilogy should be seen not as a bid for completeness but rather as a great

> setting, brilliantly delineated, for his moral interest. In his novels, as in actual life, "conditions" supply the opportunity for personal moral action. But if Dos Passos is a social historian, as he is so frequently said to be, he is that in order to be a more complete moralist. It is of the greatest significance for him that the barometer of social breakdown is not suffering through economic deprivation but always *moral degeneration through moral choice* [emphasis added].

It is not what the characters do in Dos Passos's novel, but how they act and who they become as they act. What we see over and over again are decent people betraying their commitments. They are not who they say they are. As Trilling wrote, Dos Passos's "people are those who sin against themselves and for him the wages of sin is death—of the spirit." Those who try to live their ideals end up broken, as if selling one's soul for a mess of pottage would have been a better road to take.

But for as much as Dos Passos rendered the importance of moral choice, I have always found that this concern in the novel is shadowed by a glaring absence. *U.S.A.* has little to nothing to say about race and how it shapes the country and the moral choices repeatedly made by "the midway people" in the novel. Black voices, when heard, are in a dialect more akin to the white actors on the radio show *Amos 'n' Andy.* In fact, the way Dos Passos reaches for America's past, "to locate freedom . . . , to suggest that at one time Americans were truly free," requires a willful blindness to the presence of unfreedom that made American freedom possible in the first place. "We stand on quicksand," Dos Passos wrote, until we are able to "ponder the course of history and what leverage might pry the owners loose from power and bring back (I too Walt Whitman) our *storybook democracy*" [emphasis added]. A romance with America's past lurks beneath the surface, and this is its tragic flaw.

Dos Passos eventually voted for Barry Goldwater, who resisted the civil rights revolution in the 1960s, and, in many ways, has become the godfather of our current moment. He also became a favorite of the likes of the ultra-conservative William Buckley. What we find in his other works on American history is a refusal to grapple with the doubleness of his protagonists: that Thomas Jefferson could be, at once, a defender of freedom and a slaveholder. Dos Passos detested "double-minded" temperaments or "split personalities." I am sure he refused to see the same in the country as a whole. Instead, for him, the founding fathers set the path that defined the future of the country. We must take in "the clean words our fathers spoke," he wrote in *U.S.A.* No more revolutions were needed. No concern about the moral choices made back then.

But what might it mean to access the American past without the crutch of romance, a storybook version of the country's history—to take in the totality of the chaos that is the U.S.A. and find there a doubleness that confounds and reveals the source of our ongoing misery?

This country, with its ideas and ghosts, remains a bundle of contradictions: a place of freedom, a place of unfreedom; a land of unimaginable wealth and unbearable poverty, where the equality of men and women guides our way and white people stand above it all; where God saturates everything but repeatedly comes up missing in how we live together; where liberty is cherished and selfishness is freedom. America, U.S.A., is a country of longing and restlessness, a place of titillating happiness and paralyzing melancholy; where we confidently know what we are and have little patience with who we *really* are; where politicians exploit fear and hatred, and where ordinary people, if they decide, can change the course of history. America, U.S.A., is haunted by the madness at its heart, and the reality of race resides there, coiled tight. That fact, and the fear of the doubleness unraveling this fragile experiment, plagues this nation. That fear is the wheel within a wheel.

—

History isn't fate. It is not the arresting of hope because the past is impossible to put right. Instead, history and memory are repositories of funded experience—a toolbag full of successes and failures, horrors and joys—that allow us to act today with more than luck. To ignore the past, to make of it a fairy tale, or to deny it altogether will seal our fate. The philosopher George Santayana was right: "Those who cannot remember the past are condemned to repeat it." Remembering is not alone sufficient to secure a better future. What and how we remember—and what and who we exclude from our stories—matter, because those memories and stories shape how we act today and how we fight for our future. I turn to these American anniversary celebrations not simply as a chronicle of the wrongs of our past, but as a resource (as revelation!) to help us imagine a way forward out of this madness—to see that the American problem of history is the problem of lacking conscious awareness of who we are, which so many in America so desperately avoid.

To develop this point, I use historical vignettes within the form of the essay. Toggling between past and present amid assertions of American greatness and the racism that drives our days. Along the way, I remember T. S. Eliot's words in *Four Quartets:* "The backward look behind the assurance / Of recorded history," and "the backward half-look / Over the shoulder, towards the primitive terror." The vignettes work like discarded patches of cloth with a specific story told on each; I stitch a quilt of meanings about the journey of the country over the last 250 years. Out of the bits and pieces of tattered fabric, a particular story of America emerges that signals a way forward for the nation—like the quilts that offered a message to slaves who were preparing to steal their freedom. The image of the quilt is not meant to offer a unified account of the past or an unfolding of history toward some redemptive end. Rather, the patchwork of bits and pieces reveals the workings of hardened hands weaving a story about particular moments, significant events, a collage of colors that, taken together, capture immediate experiences, beauty, and aspiration. My approach is more than to repeat overheard stories and fragments of talk that one cannot comprehend. Instead, the stitching of this quilt aims to render the usefulness of the past, however ugly, in the context of our present battle for this nation.

—

In 2020, I ended my book *Begin Again* by saying that Trumpism presented Americans with a choice: we could either continue to lie to ourselves about the superiority of white people and choose that lie's illusion of safety, or we could finally do the hard work of ridding ourselves of the assumptions of race that have stained this nation since its founding. I held on to the belief that we could be better and that we could work tirelessly for a third American founding, a New Jerusalem. But the country made a different moral choice. A sizable portion of white America had a powerful allergic reaction to self-examination, doubled down on its illusions, and elected Donald Trump again. They turned their backs on the so-called racial reckoning and retreated into the comforts of categories that cut off the humanity of others from their own. *We have gone too far,* they said. Transgender athletes became an avatar for fears and rage. *Identity politics blocks the way to what really matters,* both political parties declared. Inflation was the excuse. Hatred, greed, and grievance were the motivation. The shift was so breathtakingly fast that one could only conclude that people had lied after the murder of George Floyd—that the outpouring of concern for racial justice was mere sentimentality and performance. Whatever happens next, I wrote, will be up to us. I believed that we could choose a different path—that we could, God willing, confront the terrors and panic that have driven generations to lose their souls. I suppose that is still true.

But now—as it was then, when I reached for James Baldwin to find resources to beat back despair—I struggle with a rage that threatens to consume that faith. After 250 years, and after all that has been done and said, Black people still face the consequences of a country that insists it must remain white. By now, and given our history, one would hope that we would have honestly confronted the split. The soil of this place has been soaked with blood because of it. Many Americans throughout our history have lost their sense of morality, or lost their minds, because they either believed the country must be white or had to bear the brunt of that belief's implications. We should know better.

But America, U.S.A., did it again. Over seventy-seven million Americans voted for Donald Trump in 2024, and many of them have retreated into a familiar ugliness. They ignored the chaos of his first term, turned a blind eye to his felony convictions, and wrung their hands over "the crisis at the border" and the so-called unfairness of diversity, equity, and inclusion. As if Donald Trump gave them license to ignore the rule of law, to cast aside an idea of America rooted in the principles of the Declaration—

that all men and women are created equal—and allowed them to be unabashedly white—to claim, without anxiety and guilt, that the country was theirs. He spoke to their anxieties and hatreds. And now, during the semiquincentennial of the nation, Donald Trump sits behind the Resolute Desk, again.

Panic sits at the root of it all. There is a sense that somehow the country that belonged to them has been lost, and the darker souls of this nation are exacting their revenge by using the power of government to discriminate against white people, denying their children admission to elite universities and colleges, filling their rightful seats with unqualified Black people, and forcing them to feel guilty about the past and responsible for racism. Revenge is an old paranoia. And many in white America have simply tired of the demand for racial justice. That is old, too. In their minds, as it has always been, racial justice is a philanthropic enterprise, a sentimental, charitable gesture to extend to us. And when the admission of past wrongs is not enough and demands are still made, the question is asked, with exasperation, "What else do you want?" Rage soon follows. A cycle born of America's double consciousness.

Ralph Ellison wrote in 1970 that "whenever the nation grows weary of the struggle toward the ideal of American democratic equality," it reaches for the illusion of secession—*the fantasy of a lily-white America.* He explained,

> I refer to the exasperation and bemusement of the white American with the black, the black American's ceaseless (and swiftly accelerating) struggle to escape the misconceptions of whites, and the continual confusing of the black American's racial background with his individual culture. Most of all, I refer to the recurring fantasy of solving one basic problem of American democracy by "getting shut" of the blacks through various wishful schemes that would banish them from the nation's bloodstream, from its social structure, and from its conscience and historical consciousness.

We have seen this throughout the history of the country—from schemes during the antebellum period to send free Black people to Liberia; to

President Lincoln's insistence that free Blacks accept colonization because white people "suffer from your presence"; to the lies of the Lost Cause; to American immigration laws like the Immigration Act of 1924, which insisted that ours must remain a white nation; to the horrors of ICE and the clamoring around the border today and the bitter fights about what to teach our children in schools. In each instance, the nation seeks to "get shut" of us. And, for Ellison, this is "a fantasy born not merely of racism but of petulance, exasperation and moral fatigue. It is like a boil bursting forth from the impurities in the bloodstream of democracy."

The fantasy of a lily-white America offers comfort and justification for the betrayal of democratic ideals. It has been, and continues to be, a way to deal with the duality at the country's heart. Americans find themselves in this continuous battle, recognizing freedom and justice as central to the country's self-conception only to reject both, with startling brutality, in the name of white racial superiority. Shifting between sentimentality and rage. And those of us who have to bear the burden of it all must find the resources to keep from succumbing to an intolerable bitterness of spirit, because, no matter what they do or what they believe about us, we still have the responsibility of raising our babies.

Lonnie Bunch, the secretary of the Smithsonian, once told me that America is much more than an idea. It is an argument about who we take ourselves to be—an argument between the dueling sides of this nation. The formulation is a bit startling in that it forces a reconsideration of the standard view of America as a beacon of freedom, and the feeling that, in times of crisis, we need only invoke its meaning and our purpose as Americans becomes clear. The question of who we are as Americans has already been settled in the founding ideas, according to the standard view, which is a stark choice: we either choose to embrace it or refuse its promise. Consensus is the power of its incantation.

But the invocation of consensus hides and conceals something much more chaotic and fundamental: the divided soul of the nation. Secretary Bunch's words point us to the ongoing battles that shape our understanding of America. Struggles over its meaning as a nation and over the contradictions that make up our history. Divided over the issue of race and culture, we have waged war, both physically and figuratively, with ourselves to figure out, or to avoid figuring out, exactly who we are. The country eventually left three-quarters of a million soldiers and sailors dead because of it. And we are still fighting battles. This is our tragic inheritance.

Celebrations of the Fourth of July aim to settle any uncertainty about our national identity by affirming the greatness of the American experiment and telling a story of our virtuous beginnings and our ongoing effort to build a more perfect union. The ritual, like a capping stack, sets out to shut down messes. The battles waged over our national identity are buried or obscured by expressions of patriotism and adoration for those who founded the country, a reaffirmation of the ideals that set us apart from other nations, and a renewed embrace of the promise of freedom that makes America a shining city on the hill—as if the path and victory of the country was secured in its beginnings by enlightened slaveholders. No need for a new revelation: all subsequent ages become retrospective, building sepulchres of the fathers. Beyond the fireworks and barbecues, the day off and family get-togethers, the Fourth stands (or stood) as a critical day in the ongoing effort to think of the country as something more than a political entity.

But what is that something more, and why is it to be discovered in the founders? In the throes of the social revolutions of the mid-1960s, the sociologist Robert Bellah maintained that American political culture reflected commonly shared religious beliefs, which informed and shaped political debate and dissent. He referred to this as America's civil religion. This religious dimension of American political life, although informed by the Judeo-Christian tradition, was not reducible to that tradition. Instead, civil religion involved "a set of beliefs, symbols, and rituals" that fortified a particular idea of the country with ethical principles that transcended it. Those principles aligned the mission of America with the task of carrying out the will of God on earth. As Bellah put it in his 1967 essay "Civil Religion in America," "Civil religion at its best is a general apprehension of universal and transcendent religious reality as seen in or . . . as revealed through the experience of the American people."

The religious underpinnings of American civic and political culture offered resources for the ongoing reform and renewal of the American idea—they offered the terms with which to judge the nation. But Bellah was clear that civil religion could be used to justify nefarious ends or "as a cloak for petty interests and ugly passions," like the greed of corporations or the hatreds of racists. When those interests and passions undermined the nation's ideals—whether in its treatment of Native peoples, slavery and Jim Crow, subordination of women, exploitation of workers, child labor, or exercise of military power around the globe—the country failed to live up to its covenant. In that sense, Americans were backsliding, and invocations of those ethical principles amounted to calls to repent, setting the stage for reform. Even when Americans argued about slavery or the equal rights of women, those arguments assumed the ideals of the country (e.g., ideals of liberty and the equality of men rooted in Anglo-Protestant Christianity) and, as such, reinforced the stated values of the nation even if the actual practices of its people contradicted them. Our goodness remained unquestioned. Americans were a chosen people and the country, the New Jerusalem.

America's civil religion presupposed that we know who we are and that we jointly share this vision. This religious scaffolding provided the basis for a background consensus that could hold off the chaos, which resulted from the doubleness that rested at the nation's heart. When understood in this way, America's civil religion ironically short-circuits the kind of self-examination required to resolve the split, because the nation's virtue is secured in the belief system that makes it possible in the first place. The transcendent faith in the American idea expressed within the nation's rites and rituals confirmed the special status of the American project and the American people: *We are a divinely ordained nation with a redemptive role in the world, no matter what we do.* With its founding fathers and yearly celebrations (the Fourth of July, Memorial Day, etc.), with its invocation of the sacred documents of the Declaration of Independence and the Constitution, with its story of the unbounded freedom of its people—with this faith, as Dr. Martin Luther King Jr. said in 1963, "the jangling discord of our nation" could be transformed "into a beautiful symphony of brotherhood."

But, the truth is that many Americans do not believe in the ideas of liberty and equality, especially when it comes to those who are not white.

Even the founding fathers, those paragons of virtue, did not truly believe in those ideas, which makes appeals to them all the more perilous. We need only think of the moral exceptions to the "sacred" documents that they created or the slave auction block next to the church house. Appeals to a transcendent faith in America are often revelations about fears of division and fragmentation—fears that the nation is coming apart hidden behind an evangelical faith in the idea of America itself. This book seeks to bring into view the hypocrisy and melancholy underneath our fervent national declarations. I know, and most Americans know but refuse to admit, that we are not who we say we are. We cleave to illusions to keep the truth at bay.

The French writer who gave us in 1835 and 1840 our best description of American democracy also noted the ominous clouds that trailed the exuberant promise of our fragile experiment. Alexis de Tocqueville wrote in *Democracy in America:*

> Among democratic nations, men easily attain a certain equality of condition, but they can never attain as much as they desire. . . . At every moment they think they are about to grasp it; it escapes at every moment from their hold. They are near enough to see its charms, but too far off to enjoy them; and before they have fully tasted its delights, they die.
>
> That is the reason for the strange melancholy that haunts inhabitants of democratic countries in the midst of abundance.

I do not want to deny the power of envy and the relentless pursuit of money as the source of the strange melancholy that Tocqueville describes here. He understood quite clearly that "the incomplete joys of this world will never satisfy [the human] heart." That becomes all the more unbearable in a country of extraordinary means and wealth—a nation where the promise of happiness and the success of freedom are constitutive of its identity, and where the experience of failure is an everyday occurrence. What does it mean to be unhappy in the Promised Land? To fail here? Perhaps Tocqueville saw something that helps explain the epidemic of loneliness that suffocates this country today: the sense of social isolation, the shattering of communal bonds, the overall social anomie that has left Americans feeling unmoored.

But Tocqueville failed to see the double consciousness that defined the young nation and continues to shape it today. That the white people who talked incessantly about equality and freedom lived amid abundant cruelty. Many of them engaged in it. Imagine those people they held as slaves who bore the brunt of it all, and who lived in the shadows of America's dream: they knew intimately what could not be attained, of the illusiveness of a certain equality of condition, of the ways these so-called freedom-loving people moved about them, even sold them and their children. The life those particular white people lived, with all its charm within arm's reach, in a nation supposedly chosen by God, ironically depended upon these darker souls. From that double life, Du Bois wrote, the "life every American Negro must live, as a Negro and as an American, as swept on by the current of the nineteenth century while yet struggling in the eddies of the fifteenth century—from this must arise a painful self-consciousness, an almost morbid sense of personality."

That morbid sense was not theirs alone. Those who said they were committed to freedom, who declared they were the New Israelites and that the bounty of America was a divine idea, they knew and lived the lie. The strange melancholy that haunted white America was in fact a blue note deposited in the soul of the nation, which made the cries for a transcendent faith in the country all the more intense, like a sudden shout in a Pentecostal church on a Sunday morning or a frantic dance because the spirit has taken over. Haunted by a theological terror that God's judgment awaits because of the evil that white men and women do, these so-called New Israelites clung to a power not subject to the whirlwind of the world—to enduring and unchanging principles, a source of hope and guaranteed possibility.

No wonder James Baldwin described America, U.S.A., as a loveless place:

> I have always been struck, in America, by an emotional poverty so bottomless, and a terror of human life, of human touch so deep, that virtually no American appears able to achieve any viable,

organic connection between his public stance and his private life. This is what makes them so baffling, so moving, so exasperating, and so untrustworthy.

The degeneration from the moral choices of the nation menaced those Americans who claimed the country belonged only to them. Ironically, American civil religion guides our eyes to this aspect of American life. Not to consensus but to what *the desire* for consensus conceals: we keep turning away from the madness of our refusal to resolve the split that makes us, tragically, who we are.

—

Not everything in America, U.S.A., is about race; yet so much, if not everything, is. I have in my head an image that helps explain why race matters so much in this country. Imagine the parchment upon which the Declaration of Independence and the Constitution were written. Think of the inkwell used to sign those documents and imagine it spilling all over the pages. Black ink everywhere, spreading across the parchment out of control. A mess. Chaos and confusion. Like spilled oil racing across the face of the water of the Gulf of Mexico (or is it the Gulf of America?). Everything is touched; nothing escapes contamination. You would have to hold the paper up to the light of a candle to see the written words hidden underneath the stains. That's how race works in this country. The spilled ink represents the idea of "the white American" that stains our stated principles and covers every aspect of our lives. Wherever he or she shows up, not as an individual human being, but as an idea of white racial superiority, we are forced to reckon with the calamity.

Norman Mailer insisted that "history is interior." We carry the contradictions and the longing within us. Our task then is to confront that history or, better, to confront ourselves and how we have come to see the world, and to reckon with what has been done in our name for 250 years. We must inhabit the stories, not to wash away our sins or to ignore the stains or the bitterness that lurks, but to imagine ourselves anew and to make of this place something worthy of life. I have to admit, though, I am finding it hard to imagine that any of this is possible, especially now, but we must if we are to be saved.

This book wrestles with the story about the nation's beginnings and its hubris, because I love the people here. But I see and feel what I see and feel, and our current days are not promising. I am a descendant of those "improbable aristocrats" who dared to live fully amid "the wild beasts" and who offered generations a grand inheritance. That fact, more than anything I can imagine, makes this country *my* possession. No matter what is said about us as the fever dream spikes again, we are not interlopers who need to prove ourselves repeatedly. Our loves close to the ground and in the ground make this place something worth fighting for.

Disillusioned; weary ♩ = 64
ppp
pp
8
p

CHAPTER ONE

FREEDOM IS THE WHITE MAN'S GIFT

On the back of his copy of the manumission papers for Moses Gordon, issued in 1776, John Parrish, a Quaker abolitionist in Philadelphia, scribbled a sentence about Gordon's death two decades later. Gordon chose, Parrish wrote, to "drown himself rather than being Sold from his connections." An offhand note. A reminder of the all-too-human stakes of the fight against slavery.

Moses had been captured as a fugitive under the terms of the Fugitive Slave Act of 1793. For a little over ten years, he had lived in Philadelphia as a free man, attended church (perhaps at the African Episcopal Church of St. Thomas on the corner of what was then Fifth and Adelphi Streets, pastored by Absalom Jones, the first African American to be ordained an Episcopalian priest), met and married the love of his life, and, with her, raised four children. He worked hard to secure his family's needs and found himself a part of a vibrant community of Black people, some of whom, like himself, had escaped slavery.

His life in Philadelphia, of course, was haunted by the specter of the peculiar institution. Not only by the fact of slavery in the South—that some Black people suffered as the property of others—but by the hard reality that even if you *escaped* slavery, even if you managed to build a life uniquely your own, you would be forever condemned to look over your shoulder for the four horsemen who wanted to drag you back to hell. This was by design. The Constitution made it so that people like Moses Gordon could not feel secure in their freedom, even in a so-called free state. Forty-eight years after Moses was captured, Frederick Douglass described that world in his 1845 autobiography:

> Let him be a fugitive in a strange land—a land given up to be the hunting-ground for slaveholders—whose inhabitants are legalized kidnappers—where he is every moment subjected to the terrible liability of being seized upon by his fellow men. . . . I say, let him place himself in my situation . . . among fellow men, yet feeling in the midst of wild beasts.

In Philadelphia, no matter the life he lived, Moses remained stolen property. He was a thief in "the contorted sense" that he had stolen himself. He could be made free only by white men, and his life proved that just as easily as white men can make you free, they can take it away. Article IV, Section 2, Clause 3 of the Constitution guaranteed to slave owners the right to reclaim escaped slaves, and the Fugitive Slave Act of 1793 gave license to the hunt.

Moses's life in Philadelphia was not his first experience of freedom. Caleb Trueblood, a slaveholding North Carolina Quaker, had come to believe that slavery was a sin against God, and in November 1776, just three months after the signing of the Declaration of Independence, he released Moses from bondage. It was a radical act. Colonial North Carolina had passed a law that strictly forbade "masters from liberating their slaves . . . except for meritorious service." The law was necessary, some argued, because Quakers like Trueblood threatened the foundations of the institution; increasing the size of the free Black population unsettled the assumptions underlying slavery itself. What is a Black slave to think when she sees free Black people living among her? Slaveholders, no matter how hard they tried, could not escape the paranoia that came with holding others in bondage, even as they argued that slaves were loyal and content with their status. The existence of fugitives and the free suggested otherwise. Both sounded a note of dread in the hearts of slaveholders.

Four months after Caleb Trueblood freed Moses Gordon, the North Carolina legislature passed another law. The preamble to the statute made clear the crime manumission represented: "Divers evil-minded persons, intending to disturb the peace, did liberate and set free their slaves." No matter the ardor surrounding the ideas of liberty and freedom so central to the American Revolution, North Carolina legislators—and they were not alone—continued to defend and expand slavery. The law ordered those manumitted illegally to be captured and "sold to the highest bidder." Moses had been free for two and half years when he was arrested by the sheriff and sold in July 1779 to William Skinner, a brigadier general in the North Carolina militia. Skinner served as a judge until 1789 and owned forty-seven people. Imagine the broken heart and the rage that accompanied Moses as he was placed in chains and handed over to another white man. To taste freedom and to lose it, against the backdrop of declarations of liberty and freedom, must have been a bitter pill to swallow.

For the next six years Moses Gordon harbored freedom dreams. He eventually escaped Skinner's grasp under the cover of morning darkness in October 1785. Soon he was hundreds of miles away. But Skinner never relented. Moses had stolen *his* property. Skinner offered a reward for Moses's return.

Ten Silver Dollars Reward

> Will be paid for apprehending and delivering to me, my negro man, named Moses, who, after being detected of some villainy, ran away this morning about four o'clock; or, I will give five times the sum to any person that make due proof of his being killed, and never ask a question to know by whom it was done.

Wanted dead or alive, ultimately, for the villainy of wanting to be free. Skinner's reward had no expiration date. It announced, no matter what needed to be done or how long it took, that Moses Gordon belonged to him.

Moses was captured finally and jailed in 1797, over ten years after his escape, and many years after having created a new life with a family and in a beloved community. When faced with the prospect of living once again as a slave, he chose death by his own hand.

Skinner had the power of the law behind him. The Fugitive Slave Clause in the Constitution and the Fugitive Slave Act of 1793 empowered slave owners to seek "rendition of [their] property in federal or state court. The law also imposed a fine on anyone who 'knowingly and willingly' obstructed the return of a runaway." These were the results of the maddening compromises that paved the way for the founding of the nation. Just five years after the ratification of the Constitution, lawmakers felt no need to end slavery or the slave trade; instead they decided to secure the rights of those who owned slaves. As the historian Ira Berlin puts it, "The Declaration of Independence made equality normative, leaving only one logical rationale for denying freedom to any people: namely, that they were not human." That lie made it possible for Black people who dared to steal their freedom to be hunted down like dogs.

The "resolution" of the problem of believing in equality and holding people as slaves, if one can call it that, required holding in the balance two contradictory positions: that ours was a country committed to both freedom and unfreedom—that slavery could sit, however uneasily, alongside the developing myth of America as a city on a hill or as the "Redeemer Nation." Everyone touched by the peculiar institution was complicit. This was America, U.S.A. The fact that Black people were held in bondage or relegated to second-class status mattered little in the nation's redemptive mission of spreading freedom and democracy around the world. The American future was, and would be, unburdened by its failures. America, slaveholding or not, was a divinely sanctioned project, and that consensus myth secured our national virtue despite the divisions that threatened to crack the country wide open.

The divided soul of the country was not simply a failure to live up to stated ideals, nor was it an abstraction—it had concrete effects, felt in the lives of those who bore the brunt of it. America, U.S.A., was split between its commitments to liberty and equality and to the idea of white superiority. In one moment, the country could embrace the idea of liberty and freedom for all—that *could* include Black people, and it did, for some and for a brief time during the Revolution. And then, as quickly as storm clouds can hide the sun, the mood darkened and that freedom could be snatched away. The act was especially cruel—a repetition of the evil and hubris at the heart of slavery and the slave trade itself: these traffickers of human beings would arrogate to themselves, as if they were gods, who could be free or not, and could easily change their minds. Black people were swept up as profit and prejudice collided with justice and virtue. People like Moses Gordon knew this intimately. What might freedom mean here, in this place, where so many languished in chains and so many claimed freedom as their possession? What might it mean for the nation when the measure of freedom is found in white men?

—

Both the Constitution and the Fugitive Slave Act were born in Philadelphia, the nation's capital until 1800 and in many ways still the beating heart of the American story. Not for nothing were all major anniversary celebrations held there until well into the twentieth century, and, of course, the city also holds some of the most sacred sites and objects in the American story. In all my years of visiting, I've rarely spent much time in the city's historic district, even when I lived there as a graduate student. Perhaps it's my temperament, or perhaps it is my ambivalence about declarations of "love of country," but that part of Philadelphia never interested me; I preferred the jazz scene, especially Ortlieb's Jazzhaus on North Third Street, or the bustling pace of South Street on a Saturday afternoon, with its throngs of people gathered inside and outside Tower Records.

As such, the way the city tells its story, and the country's story, felt fresh to me when I encountered it later. I first saw the Liberty Bell just a few years ago when my in-laws, Jamaican immigrants who fled political violence in 1980, wanted to take in the city's historical sites. This was the birthplace of their adopted country, and so it held some meaning to them. I reluctantly tagged along, feeling an awkward sense of possession and dispossession. Yes, this was the place where the United States of America was founded. My country. But patriotism, for me, was off-limits, or at least complicated. The idea of America as the birthplace of freedom carried the stench of hypocrisy. My in-laws understood this, but theirs was a different experience—they *chose* to come here. I was a descendant of slaves. James Baldwin had given me language for what I felt:

> To be an Afro-American, or an American black, is to be in the situation, intolerably exaggerated, of all those who have ever found themselves part of a civilization which they could in no wise honorably defend—which they were compelled, indeed, endlessly to attack and condemn—and who yet spoke out of the most passionate love, hoping to make the kingdom new, to make it honorable and worthy of life.

This was Baldwin in 1972. So much has changed and so much has stayed the same.

As I walked from site to historical site with my in-laws, the reality of the country's politics shaded everything. We were soaking in a particular story of America's beginnings—the place where the Declaration of Independence was signed and the site where the Constitution was ratified—in a pitched moment of the nation's continued struggle with the contradictions that have always threatened to unravel American democracy. An assault on voting rights. Police killings of Black people. Recent events had added new chapters to Philadelphia's American story—large protests erupted here in 2020 after the murder of George Floyd. Part of Center City burned, the Pennsylvania National Guard was called in, and a curfew was put in effect. In response to the protests, the city was forced to engage with its own history of racism. Leaders decided to remove a statue of the notoriously racist mayor and former police commissioner, Frank Rizzo. "The statue is a deplorable monument," then mayor Jim Kenney said, "to racism, bigotry and police brutality for members of the Black community, the LGBTQ community and many others." The city exploded again just a few months later when police shot and killed Walter Wallace Jr., a twenty-seven-year-old Black man in the middle of a mental health crisis armed with a knife. His parents had called for an ambulance. The police showed up instead. Walter was shot fourteen times.

These contradictions stayed with me, and so I decided to revisit Independence Square in July 2024. I was working on this book in the run-up to the 250th anniversary of the nation, and had grown interested in the early "Negro petitions" around the immorality of the slave trade and the Fugitive Slave Law, submitted to Congress in Philadelphia in 1797 and 1800. These were the first formal political efforts by free Black people in the newly formed country to invoke their constitutional rights and the role and responsibility of Congress in protecting them. They insisted that the freedom the country had espoused in its own fight for independence, and enshrined in the Constitution, also belonged to them. That freedom, they maintained, could not be seized or taken away by others who claimed possession of them. I decided to see Congress Hall, the seat of the nation from December 1790 to May 1800, and to get a sense of the place where the debates happened. I kept thinking: *What would have been the fate of America had the members of Congress made a different moral and political choice about freedom, about Black people, and about themselves? Would the country still be saddled with the race problem? How would the story of the nation be told differently?*

Philadelphia today is a city of contrasts. Beautiful skyscrapers, powerful centers of education, with a richly diverse population. Museums and cultural sites give the historic city a sense of vibrancy. Yet it remains one of the most residentially segregated cities in the country, second only to Chicago. As I walked toward the security screening area at Fifth and Chestnut Streets, amid the sounds of cars blaring music and blowing horns and people talking, I noticed a huge Israeli flag on the side of the Weitzman National Museum of American Jewish History. It declared that THE WEITZMAN STANDS WITH ISRAEL, a welcome sign of sorts to Independence Square and a reminder of the horrors in Gaza and of the world outside. I made my way through security to Independence Hall and the Liberty Bell Center, and something felt strange. The neatness of Independence Square felt a bit off to me, not Disneyland fake but still somehow contrived. Nostalgia was everywhere, not as a sentiment of loss or as a lament that the virtuous days of the country's founding were no longer available to us, but as a romance with fantasy. These were monuments to storybook democracy.

People from all around the world come here to experience American history—to get a sense of the American story of freedom. When I visited in 2024, the city's Visitor Center Corporation had decided to be more deliberate in its efforts "to build an authentic connection with diverse audiences." With its "In Pursuit of a More Perfect Union" marketing campaign, the board connected "its work to current events to give it more resonance and immediacy . . . [to celebrate] the respective cultures of diverse audiences [and to] promote local artists, businesses and ongoing dialogue." As I waited in line for the tour of Congress Hall, I heard different languages. Slavic, Spanish, English with Philly and South Asian accents, a Southern drawl. These were America's multitudes—the vast diversity of the country ready to take in a particular story of the nation's beginnings. I listened to our tour guide talk about séances while a dad desperately tried to manage his daughter, who pulled on his hand. His other daughter played in the dirt and gathered leaves and twigs into a neat pile. Her hands and fingernails showed her labor. Neither girl expressed much interest in the pending tour. The tour guide, who was a park ranger, was a short white man with a marine-like crew cut and demeanor, and he had a MASTER RANGER CORPS badge sewed on his taupe shirt. Another park ranger, with two Pride/trans flags stuck in her, or perhaps their, backpack, walked briskly. Another ranger, with a long black beard with hints of gray and hair that refused discipline, ran to catch up. In line, the people in front of me described the horrible traffic on the Ben Franklin Bridge. They chatted as if they were old friends, while the noise of the city hummed around us. Another talked about how her flight was canceled, and how excited she was to have the opportunity to "take in the history of Independence Square." She added, "I love this kind of stuff."

We finally entered Congress Hall; a bust of Benjamin Franklin hung above the doors to the House of Representatives. The tour guide began to weave his story.

As he spoke, I thought about the debates over the petitions. In January 1797, four Black men, residents of Philadelphia and formerly enslaved in North Carolina, petitioned Congress for a remedy to the ongoing effort by their former owners to re-enslave them. North Carolina had passed legislation that allowed "the capture and sale of any former slave freed without the court's consent." Given that many of the country's founders were slave owners and faced the problem of runaway slaves, the U.S. Constitution included a similar provision:

> No Person held to Service or Labour in one State, under the Laws thereof, escaping into another, shall, in Consequence of any Law or Regulation therein, be discharged from such Service or Labour, but shall be delivered up on Claim of the Party to whom such Service or Labour may be due.

This came to be known as the Fugitive Slave Clause.

The four Black men who petitioned Congress sought relief from its burden. Each of them had been freed by their Quaker owners, but the law took that freedom away, which made it necessary for them to escape. "We were reduced to the necessity of separating from some of our nearest and most tender connnexions, and of seeking refuge in such parts of the Union where more regard is paid to the public declaration in favor of liberty and the common right of man." The consequence of the law meant that they would be "hunted day and night, like beasts of the forest, by armed men with dogs, and made a prey of as free and lawful plunder."

The men's petition would be followed by another in December 1799 and debated in 1800 when seventy-one free Black men from Philadelphia asked Congress to end the slave trade and to reconsider the Fugitive Slave Act of 1793, because "the solemn compact, the Constitution, was stained and violated by the trade of kidnapping."

As the tour continued to unfold, I looked around the room in Congress Hall in which we stood. Here was where the body of Congress had received these petitions and heard the arguments brought before them. In this room, white men decided who were the true possessors of freedom in the country. I noticed the seats and the well, and thought of the words of the men who rejected both African American petitions. "These people have been talked to; they have been tampered with," one congressmen said. He meant that the men could not possibly have arranged for these petitions themselves; instead he assumed that radical Quakers, who wanted to end slavery once and for all, were really behind the appeals. I kept turning the phrase over in my head. *Tampered with.* Isn't that what Toni Morrison's grandmother had said about her? This congressman couldn't believe that Black people wanted to live freely; nor that we would petition Congress on our own for that freedom. And, in a way, it didn't matter. For him, whether the issue involved Quakers or slave owners, freedom was the white man's gift to give or to take away.

As I tried to envision this debate, the ranger giving the tour was deep in a tale of storybook democracy. He described the peaceful transfer of power when President Washington stepped aside for John Adams. Even King George III of England, he noted, expressed his admiration for the president's decision. "If he does that," King George III said, "he will be the greatest man in the world." The ranger paused confidently and smiled proudly as he let the story sink in. I thought of Trump and January 6.

The ranger then told the rapt audience that the seating arrangement in the chamber had not been divided by party, and that the primary challenge among them involved navigating the remarkably different cultures between the North and the South. My ears perked up. I leaned in. This was so much the story of both the founding and the Fugitive Slave Act—the struggle among the Northern and Southern colonies to secure a union in the face of their vast difference over slavery. Finally, here was the moment in which we would get into it. It was, I figured, impossible to talk about this period in American history without talking about slavery—about the Three-Fifths Compromise, about the Fugitive Slave Clause, about how slavery collided with the ideals of the Revolution. Instead, the park ranger with the marine crew cut and the voice of a drill sergeant talked about the different ways men from each region greeted each other. One with a handshake, the other with a bow.

As the park ranger walked us to the Senate, I noticed the peeled paint on the walls of the House chamber, the cheap replica furniture with worn armrests. It seemed appropriate, especially today. America is no longer a place where the appeal to innocence, that sense of divine mission and inherent goodness, matters outside of the storybook version of the country. Weathered by tragic choices and the cruel consequences of white racial superiority over generations, the reality is that American innocence has long been lost.

In my head, the congressmen's words in those early days of the Republic bounced off the walls. America's double consciousness was in full view. James Jones of Georgia could not imagine that the rights delineated in the Constitution applied to those Black people, to people like me. He spoke to his fellow white men: "I would ask gentlemen whether, with all their philanthropy, they would wish to see those people deliberating in the councils of the nation?" The word "philanthropy" churned in my head. The matter of justice didn't concern him. As we left the chamber, I looked back and saw white ghosts still arguing in those cheap, tattered chairs, and I thought of Moses Gordon and the note scribbled on the back of his manumission papers. He chose a different kind of freedom.

—

With every anniversary of the nation's founding, the divided soul of America—this idea of the country as a beacon of freedom and a white Republic—is experienced in the convulsions around race that threaten to tear the country apart. As Americans celebrate 250 years of existence, we are faced with a resurgence in white nationalism. Panic has grabbed hold of millions of Americans as they fret about the so-called Great Replacement, among other things, and that panic has led many to believe that the primary purpose of Donald Trump's administration is to take back the country *for them.* Trumpism, among the many things that it is and aspires to be, is a restorative project: it aims to reclaim an American past where white people were at the center—the standard-bearers, the measure for what is truly American. In this vision, the diversity of the nation is an ancillary feature of the American story, Ellis Island a minor subplot.

The dramatic expansion of ICE aims to ensure that this vision of the country is made real. In the "One Big Beautiful Bill," the Republican-led Congress allocated $170 billion for immigration and border security, and $75 billion in extra funding for ICE to aid in the agency's arrest and deportation efforts, and for the immigration detention system. ICE is now the highest-funded law enforcement agency in the federal government—larger than the FBI. And its purpose extends beyond the law. It is charged to help make America white again. Whatever view of America, U.S.A., emerged during the 1960s social revolutions, whatever gains around race the nation has made since that period—whether it was the Civil Rights Act of 1964, or the Immigration and Nationality Act of 1965, or the election of the first African American president—these Americans want to snatch them away. They want to rip apart the infrastructure put in place to remedy, however piecemeal, historical harms. They want to do away with the tensions that come with the exposure of America's double consciousness. These Americans want to turn back the clock to ensure a future for the country that looks like what they desire.

Sentimentality and rage rest at the heart of this lurching back and forth between attempts to address racial injustice and the denials that racial injustice exists at all. Consciences pricked by the realization of cruelty in our midst often spur attempts to repent for the country's national sins. Americans engage in the mortification of the flesh. Images of dogs sicced on children marching in Birmingham, the video of George Floyd crying out for his mother as he lay dying with a police officer's knee on his neck, or children crying as moms are arrested by ICE officers outside of their school—these are all behaviors and practices that fail to align with storybook America. In the face of public outrage and protests, the country tries to repent and reassert its inherent goodness. "This isn't who we are," politicians and pundits declare. White America sees its complicity in the cruelty and seeks absolution in its admission rather than in remedying the cruelty. When that absolution is not given and Black people continue to demand justice, resentment boils over. Cries of *Enough!* are heard. Shouts for the rule of law ring out, and all hell breaks loose.

We see examples of this cycle of sentimentality and rage across American history. Think about the aims of Reconstruction and the ugliness of Redemption; or the moral power of the Black freedom movement of the mid-twentieth century and the backlash that culminated in the election of Ronald Reagan; or the response to George Floyd's murder and today's assault on all things DEI. An admission of guilt has been made; an acknowledgment of racism has been given. And that, a segment of white America believes, should be enough. But Black people pushed too hard and, like a spring coiled too tight, white America snapped.

The motivation to repent for racism, more often than not, has little to do with Black people—with those who have endured, and continue to endure, the cruelty of racism or some particular policy—or even with the broader question of justice. Rather, white America seems to desire freedom from the judgment that says, with contempt and pity, *You are not who you say you are.* For how can the country be a beacon of freedom *and* a white Republic? How can both be true? A desperate desire for the absolution of sin is needed, a confession that wipes the ledger clean and allows for a healthy-minded American innocence.

Sentimentality buries the harsh reality underneath what the poet Wallace Stevens called "a failure of feeling." In matters regarding race, it distorts the moral sense insofar as it misrepresents Black people and the reasons for their suffering in order to indulge white America's feelings. Through the sentimental eye, we become these flat, uncomplicated characters who needlessly suffer and cry out for white America's sympathies and charity. Living, breathing Black people lost in blurry, wet eyes crying crocodile tears for their condition; rarely, if ever, are we actual human beings whose complex humanity must be confronted. Instead white Americans ask, "What can we do *for* them; how might we change their conditions?" Harriet Beecher Stowe's character Uncle Tom stands in for the actual slaves in her midst. Urged on by Stowe's sentimental moral appeal, those who decried the evil of slavery were then horrified by the idea that these people, freed from bondage, might want to vote and take on the burdens of American citizenship. Or, later in the early twentieth century, wealthy white patrons wept at the performance of Negro spirituals, what Du Bois called the "sorrow songs," on stage in a Jim Crow theater for white people only. White self-indulgence characterizes the sentiment. Black people can be easily forgotten or rendered invisible in the blink of an eye. No wonder Oscar Wilde, in *De Profundis,* thought of the sentimentalist as "one who desires to have the luxury of an emotion without paying for it." White America cries its tears and leaves the world exactly as it is.

Sentimentality also terribly simplifies the moral situation. In some ways, we saw this in the discussions of Robin DiAngelo and white privilege, and Ibram Kendi's ideas about anti-racism. "The only remedy to racist discrimination," Kendi asserted, "is antiracist discrimination." Let's leave aside the fact that justice talk, to my mind, should not be rendered as a form of discrimination. In these prescriptions, white Americans were urged to turn inward and to search within themselves for traces of racist commitments—to engage in ongoing self-flagellation, as if that would be enough to bring about a racially just society. What an ironic indulgence of their feelings! But this sentimentality would shape larger approaches to the "problem." Corporations announced massive investments in diversity, inclusion, and equity, but through programs of dubious effectiveness. In an obvious lament about it all, David Bromwich wrote in *Harper's* magazine that "the manner of these declarations [of commitment to diversity and social justice] was . . . unusual. Pledges of solidarity commonly took the form of confessions. . . . The point was not to explain conditions." And when the demands for critical self-examination did not result in absolution, when all this self-flagellation on the part of white Americans did not bring forgiveness, only more demands, the whiplash was harsh and intense.

Sentimentality is intimately connected with the rage that often comes with its failure. No wonder Baldwin understood it as "the mark of dishonesty, the inability to feel . . . ; and it is always, therefore, the signal of secret and violent inhumanity, the mask of cruelty." You see it in the way the country has turned so vicious following the outpouring of sentiment after George Floyd's murder—how people have become so mean-spirited as they express their hatreds and grievances, how DEI, once considered a remedy to racial harms, is now seen as a curse and the weapon of a radical cabal hell-bent on destroying America. Behind the tears and cries that *we can be better* was a devious smirk, which revealed that all of this was just a lie.

When sentimentality fails, as it inevitably does, the turn to rage is seamless, because the oppressed Black victim that cries out for sympathy is bound to the radical Black person who refuses subjugation. First, we are the blameless and caricatured victim. Then, when we continue to press our case, we become the raging radical who is the object of intense hatred—Black people constantly demanding justice threatens chaos. Both the victim and the radical are caricatures. A monstrous Nat Turner is the flip side of the pious Uncle Tom. This is the source of what the historian Carol Anderson calls "white rage": that allergic reaction to the demand for Black freedom and the ongoing resistance to white domination—rage directed toward that figure who refuses either to submit or to forgive.

If storybook America is to hold, then one way or another the nation's sins must be wiped clean, either by confession or by violence, both real and symbolic. White rage justifies the undoing of any effort to resolve the warring souls of America and to live genuinely the American promise. Here, in the hands of those who cry sentimental tears, freedom remains white America's possession to give. And when white America tires of the effort, they work, with passion and rage, at "getting shut" of the problem by any means necessary.

What matters here, what has always mattered in America, U.S.A., is that the country simultaneously remains a beacon of freedom and a white nation. But since the beginning, the presence of Black people (and Native peoples) has unmasked the lies that hide the doubleness. That deceit became the source of our national suffering, because white Americans had to lie to themselves and to the world about their commitment to liberty and equality for all.

—

Too many Americans have been willing to toss their democratic commitments into the trash bin in defense of lies and on behalf of an insidious idea that the color of one's skin determines one's value. In this formulation, Black people, among others, become less than human—this was part of the argument for slavery. We are lazy and criminal—they used lies like these as reasons to deny us full citizenship. Immigrants, both today and a century ago, threaten to pollute American society—another lie, a justification, no matter the story of Ellis Island, for cruelty at the border and at home. When people are made less than human, one is given license to treat them accordingly. You can separate families, snatch them from their loved ones, sell them on auction blocks—even their babies—or round them up, separate them from their children, and send them wherever you like. American history soaked in a sentimental dishonesty offers cover for it all. In the storybook, America must always ultimately stand for good, an idea supposedly rooted in Judeo-Christian principles that undergird the nation's founding and give the country its unique mission in the world. Civil religion has been conscripted to protect America's national innocence. No matter what the country does, no matter how cruel the policies, we are always, as the Philadelphia Visitor Center Corporation proclaimed, on the road to a more perfect union.

But that version of the American story runs up against the rage that reveals something darker and more sinister. White rage can take many forms, but its intent is always to secure storybook America. Today, that effort involves banning books and passing legislation that forbids teaching subjects that make our students feel uncomfortable. DEI has become the latest cudgel used to beat us all into submission. All with the aim of making real the fantasy of a lily-white America. The lies take root in the habits of our daily living; they color how we see the world and how we live, or fail to live, our values. Above all, the lies absolve the nation of any responsibility for what has been done or is being done in our name, so Americans can tell themselves that innocence remains. Moses Gordon's ghost screams otherwise.

—

Every generation, we find ourselves grappling, in one way or another, with the fact of racism and racial inequality in this country. But something deeper is revealed in the repetition: race splits America's national consciousness in two, and the country has twisted and contorted itself to hide and conceal the monstrous consequences of the doubleness that sits at its heart, and that has kept so many white Americans from discovering who they really are as Americans. Ralph Ellison described it this way:

> Since the beginning of the nation, white Americans have suffered from a deep uncertainty as to who they really are. One of the ways that has been used to simplify the answer has been to seize upon the presence of black Americans and use them as a marker, a symbol of limits, a metaphor for the "outsider." . . . Perhaps this

> is why one of the first epithets that many European immigrants learned when they got off the boat was the term "nigger"; it made them feel instantly American.

But this is "tricky magic"—illusions and sleights of hand that lead some to believe that this is a white Republic, even as the sounds and bustle of American living suggest something much more soulful. As Ellison suggested, what is really troubling for some is that, deep down in the cracks and crevices of this country, America "is also somehow black"—a reality our commemorations, and especially this 250th anniversary, desperately try to deny.

We see the strain of it all in the debates around 1619 and 1776 and the story of the founding in relation to slavery. The 1619 Project sought "to place the contributions of black Americans at the very center of our national narrative." These descendants of the slaves who first stepped on the shores of North America in 1619 turn out to be "the nation's true founding fathers," because of their ongoing battle for freedom. The project sought to hold up a mirror to the country in order for it to see itself differently.

The 1776 Commission, an advisory committee established by President Trump in his first term, countered the 1619 Project by insisting on the importance of what it called a "patriotic education." Its members aimed to produce a story of America's founding "by truthfully recounting the aspirations and actions of the men and women who sought to build America as a shining 'city on a hill'—an exemplary nation, one that protects the safety and promotes the happiness of its people." The contradictions and failings of the country, especially regarding slavery and Black people, must be understood, the commission argued, within the overall sacred project that is the United States. Slavery, by this argument, doesn't condemn America. In fact, the ideals of the Republic "planted the seeds of the death of slavery in America."

One does not have to argue either position to see that the question of American national identity in the early days of the Republic involved coming to terms with the fact that this was a land where people owned other people. That fact, along with the profits it generated and the laws used to justify it, deposited a profound panic in the heart of American life, exemplified in the ever-present fear that slaves could rebel and seek a horrible revenge. Jefferson himself trembled for the country at the thought that God was just and that He would punish the nation for the sin of slavery. The question of American national identity would always be menaced by what was sacrificed to become a nation. Nine decades after the founding, emancipation and the Fifteenth Amendment did not settle matters. "The discussion of emancipation—even the smallest suggestion of emancipation," the historian Ira Berlin wrote, "elevated the significance of race, ratcheting up both the volume and level of debate over freedom's meaning."

> As the struggle for universal freedom gained in intensity, *the gulf grew between those who embraced the Declaration's literal meaning in order to create an interracial democracy and those who divided humanity into white and black, and parsed the attributes of freedom along racial lines* [emphasis added].

No matter the distinctions, from the vantage point of the country, freedom remained the white man's possession.

Whether one begins with 1619 or 1776, both origin stories orient us to the past in a particular way for specific purposes. The former washes America in its sins; the latter absolves them in the promise that is America. Neither confronts the split and the bitterness that come with the repetition of the tragic choice—the decision, at every juncture, to be a white nation. For those who cling to the storybook version of the founding, the aim is to make of us, as Ralph Waldo Emerson wrote, "idolaters of the old," where "we linger in the ruins of the old tent, where once we had bread and shelter and organs, nor believe that the spirit can feed, cover, and nerve us again. . . . We walk ever with reverted eyes, like monsters who look backwards."

I am not so much interested in origin stories. These often aim to take us outside of the messiness of history, away from the complexity of what human beings have done and suffered, away from the choices they've made and the consequences that follow. Origin stories find comfort or assurance in a linear narrative, where the origin dominates everything that comes afterward. An inheritance that binds the feet. The evil of slavery in 1619 colors all that follows. The so-called genius of 1776 dictates how we tell the story of the country, warts and all.

I am more interested in "beginnings," in whom we choose to include, and what we choose to exclude. "The voice of the Almighty saith, 'Up and onward for evermore!'" Emerson wrote. "We cannot stay amid the ruins." *We* are doing work here. *We* matter. Not as mere chroniclers of the past, but as weavers of stories that are relevant to how we live our lives today, actively choosing some details and deliberately leaving others to the side. Where and how we begin our stories about the past remains relevant in the ongoing work of discovering who we are as a nation *and* in the confrontation, in this 250th year of our national existence, with the problems that threaten to rip the country apart.

—

While Moses Gordon waited in jail to be returned to William Skinner, the four Black men who had been manumitted by Quakers in North Carolina, and who fled to Philadelphia to escape re-enslavement, petitioned the House of Representatives in January 1797. They invoked Moses, a "fellow-black now confined in the jail of this city." And they passionately appealed to Congress to recognize the evil of the law that made some people fugitives, and others the kidnappers of men, women, and children:

> If, notwithstanding all that has been publicly avowed as essential principles respecting the extent of human right to freedom; notwithstanding we have had that right restored to us . . . we trust we may address you as fellow-men, who, under God, the sovereign Ruler of the Universe, are intrusted with the distribution of justice, for the terror of evil-doers, the encouragement and protection of the innocent, not doubting that you are men of liberal

> minds . . . who can admit that black people (servile as their condition generally is throughout this Continent) have natural affections, social and domestic attachments and sensibilities.

The petitioners dared to assert their humanity in the face of the dehumanizing practices of slavery, and to call out what that institution demanded of others to maintain it, even those who did not own slaves and who loathed the practice. The Fugitive Slave Clause and the laws supporting it left untouched neither the soul of the nation nor anyone in it.

The petition before Congress offered a chance to chart a new course. But Congress declined the request. Slavery and emancipation were matters for the states, they maintained. The Constitution deemed it so. The nation's soul be damned.

Three years later, seventy-one Black Philadelphians, including Absalom Jones and Richard Allen, the founder of the African Methodist Episcopal (AME) Church, petitioned Congress again. Not only did they challenge the morality of the Fugitive Slave Act; they petitioned for their rights as "a class of Citizens":

> We are incited by a sense of Social duty, and humbly conceive ourselves authorized to address and petition you in their behalf, believing them to be objects of representation in your public Councils, in common with ourselves and every other class of Citizens within the Jurisdiction of the United States, according to the declared design of the present Constitution, formed by the General Convention and ratified by the different States, as set forth in the preamble thereto in the following words—viz—"We the People of the United States in order to form a more perfect union, establish Justice, insure domestick tranquility, provide for the Common Defense, and to secure the blessings of Liberty to ourselves and to posterity do ordain etc. . . ."

The slave trade violated this compact, they argued. The Fugitive Slave Clause extended the evil by transforming men into "men-stealers," a grossly immoral practice. With the invocation of the preamble, these men claimed the rights guaranteed by the Constitution, and they claimed the right of representation. In the end, the petitioners called on Congress to "prepare the way for the oppressed to go free, that every yoke may be broken."

From the beginning, slaveholding interests demanded that the petition be tabled. John Rutledge of South Carolina was vehement in his opposition. He believed the Quakers to be behind this persistent effort, just as they were behind it in 1797. These Black men, again, had been *tampered with.* "When the Congress sat at New York, they spent much time and attention on the subject," said Rutledge,

> but no sooner had it been decided that nothing could be done, than the same scenes were acted over again by repeatedly petitioning. These gentlemen who used to come forward, to be sure, had not avowedly come forward again, but had now put it into the hands of the black *gentlemen.* They now tell the House these people are in slavery—I thank God they are! If they were not, dreadful would be the consequence.

Rutledge was clear: no matter the philosophy behind the Revolution—what he referred to as "this new-fangled French philosophy of liberty and equality"—the issue of slavery remained off-limits if the country was to survive. As he put it, "Some of the States would never have adopted the federal form of Government if it had not been secured to them that Congress would never legislate on the subject of slavery."

Others defended the right of the Black men to bring forth the petition even as they questioned whether Congress had the authority to take up their concerns. Mr. H. Lee of Virginia reminded his colleagues as they debated the issue that they were sent to Congress "to protect the rights of the people and the rights of property." And the property of the people of the Southern states consisted of slaves. Mr. Dana of Connecticut (illustrating that the North had its investments in the profits of the slave trade) went as far as to claim that the petition "contained nothing but a farrago of the French metaphysics of liberty and equality," which, if treated seriously, would "likely produce some of the dread scenes of the

St. Domingo." The Haitian Revolution and the real fear of "Black revenge" shadowed the debates. The men in Congress Hall were clear: the American Revolution did not include the liberty of those who were the property of men.

George Thatcher of Massachusetts was the lone dissenter. Thatcher "was willing, for the sake of argument to admit that slavery did exist and was sanctioned by laws and the constitution of the United States." But even so, he argued, "surely, it would be desirable that this great evil be done away without injury, nay, with advantage, to the possessors." He was willing to pay slaveowners for their loss. And, in response to his colleagues' rejection of that "new-fangled French philosophy," Thatcher declared that what France had done "was admirable . . . , and well executed, to liberate their slaves. So far we ought not to be behindhand with their *philanthropic* conduct" [emphasis added].

In the end, John Rutledge responded to George Thatcher's desire "that this great evil should be destroyed" with a warning that foreshadowed the carnage of the Civil War:

> I recollect that gentlemen in France used arguments like the gentleman from Massachusetts: "We can indemnify the proprietors." But how did they do it, or how can it be done?—Not at all. Farther, we were told these things would take place, we need not be alarmed; it was inevitable; that it was reasonable, and unavoidable. Sir, it will never take place. There is one alternative which will save us from it, but that alternative I depreciate very much; that is, that we are able to take care of ourselves, and if driven to it, we will take care of ourselves.

The threat of succession quieted even those amenable to taking up the moral issue of the slave trade and the Fugitive Slave Clause.

United States representatives read and debated for two days on January 2 and 3, 1800, only in the end to reject the petition by a vote of 85 to 1. They concluded that Black people, free or slave, stood outside the protection of the Constitution—the tragic choice.

As the historian Andrew Delbanco powerfully writes, "Runaway slaves and those who pursued them . . . found themselves in a borderland between *two nations pretending to be one*" [emphasis added], a pretense predicated on a choice at the calamitous annunciation.

—

In 1804, four years after Congress rejected the petition and in the year of Haiti's formal independence, several hundred young Black men gathered in the Southwark district of Philadelphia not too far from what is now Independence Square. They organized themselves in military formation with swords and other weapons, commemorated the Fourth of July by marching through the streets of the city for two days, and threatened the white people they encountered. At one point, it was reported, the men were heard "damning the whites and saying they would shew them [like in] St. Domingo." Theirs was a different kind of celebration of the Fourth of July, one in which they would strike the blow for their own freedom—a freedom they claimed and possessed.

Moses Gordon, however, choose freedom in death. Freedom-snatchers forced the choice upon him. What might his life teach us today? How might his particular journey, and the rejection of those early petitions, expose the beating heart of America, U.S.A., and how might the cruel repetition he endured chasten our celebration of American freedom after 250 years? What was revealed then, and what we know now, is that too many in this country believe that freedom is the white man's gift to give and to take away. The "morbid sense" about which Du Bois wrote—and which the melancholy Tocqueville noted so long ago—still covers the land.

I am reminded of the enslaved men of the Sweet Home plantation in Toni Morrison's classic novel *Beloved.* Their owner, Mr. Garner, gave them wide latitude. They were men insofar as Mr. Garner believed he himself was a man; their freedom was an extension of his own. But with his death, and the arrival of Schoolteacher, the brutal brother of the dead slave master, the men were treated as nothing but slaves and subject to the cruelty that came with being one. The character Paul D, now free but struggling with the memories of his days enslaved at Sweet Home, tells of his experience wearing the iron bit, a cruel instrument used by slave masters, to bridle a slave's tongue; and of an old rooster, called Mister. It is a story about freedom-snatching—of the harrowing implication of white men having the power to offer freedom and to take it away. Paul D describes sitting bound, with his hands behind his back and a bit in his mouth, only to see a rooster that he had helped break out of his shell standing above him—free and fully his mean self. That sight drove him to the brink of madness.

> "Yeah, he was hateful all right. Bloody too, and evil. Crooked feet flapping. Comb as big as my hand and some kind of red. He sat right there on the tub looking at me. I swear he smiled. . . . I wasn't even thinking about the bit. Just Halle and before him Sixo, but when I saw Mister I knew it was me too. . . . One crazy, one sold, one missing, one burnt, and me licking iron with my hands crossed behind me. The last of the Sweet Home men.
>
> "Mister, he looked so . . . free. Better than me. Stronger, tougher. Son a bitch couldn't even get out of the shell by hisself but he was still king and I was . . ." Paul D stopped and squeezed his left hand with his right. . . .
>
> "Mister was allowed to be and stay what he was. But I wasn't allowed to be and stay what I was. Even if you cooked him, you'd be cooking a rooster named Mister. But wasn't no way I'd ever be Paul D again, living or dead. Schoolteacher changed me. I was something else and that something else was less than a chicken sitting in the sun on a tub."

Broken, Paul D was forced to contend with what that experience deposited in his soul. Freedom belonged to them—even to a damn rooster he'd helped save. With this scene, Morrison takes us to the heart of the moral calamity that follows from the hubris that someone, because of the color of their skin, can claim freedom as their possession. This is a novel, but it is no fiction.

Still today we are forced to contend with the whirlwind of sentimentality and rage, as many in white America claim freedom and the country as their own. Amid this racist clamoring, I am left with the sinking feeling that, despite all the talk of ours being the greatest nation on earth, we have become ghostlike, standing on the edge of the final catastrophe, clinging to hope, not haunted by the past alone, but stricken by a future that has come and gone. Here the redemptive promise of America—that sacred future inaugurated on July 4, 1776, which has allowed the country to look beyond its vice and failures—feels empty. Relics and ruins remain. Storybook appeals amount to sticking one's head in the sand. What America can be—what it *could* be—seems lost, as the present, with its cruelty and loneliness, and with Donald Trump in the White House again, chokes on the past that the country refuses to remember. I keep asking myself, and perhaps this is the bitterness in me, what happens to the American idea, what happens to the meaning of the Fourth of July, when the future is no longer available to it? When we may not have another chance to make it all right—to make good on the American promise—because too many white Americans are too damn committed to being valued above everyone else?

ppp
p
pp

CHAPTER TWO

WHAT IS THE FOURTH OF JULY TO US?

"The past is all that makes the present coherent," James Baldwin wrote, "and . . . the past will remain horrible for exactly as long as we refuse to assess it honestly." Celebrations of the Fourth of July tend to gum up earnest attempts to examine the country's history. We get caught up in the storybook notion of America's greatness and in the power of the American idea. Fireworks, good barbecue, and the day off matter most. National sins are of little concern. But what happens when the Fourth of July is not seen as a moment of celebration, but is exposed as a repository of buried anguish and lies that allow our national sense of identity to cohere?

The image of Black men marching and brandishing weapons in Philadelphia on the Fourth of July, in the shadow of the Haitian Revolution, disturbs easy patriotism. The image, for some, makes Black people in this country questionable patriots—who harbor, beneath a scowl or smile, a keen disloyalty rooted in experience that justifies it. How many Moses Gordons could we number? How many could justifiably doubt the country's moral resolve to address the problem of freedom and slavery?

Frederick Douglass would count among that number. He was a fugitive who stole and fought for his freedom, and he lived long enough to witness America's freedom-snatching as the country turned its back on the promises of emancipation. In a sense, he was the grand expositor of America's madness for much of the nineteenth century. Drawing on his dreams for the nation and his accumulated disappointments helps me express what I see and feel on this 250th anniversary of America, U.S.A.

On July 5, 1852, in the heat of the battles around slavery and the Fugitive Slave Act of 1850, Douglass delivered his famous speech, "What to the Slave Is the Fourth of July?" He exposed the lie of a nation's celebration and revealed the duality at its heart. "The Fourth is yours, not mine," he declared. With this speech, Douglass made explicit a standing practice in Black America as the country began to commemorate its founding—a resounding dissent to the nation's public self-imagining, a running commentary that refused the lie of America as a beacon of freedom. Black folk were not simply objects of the whims of white men and their twists and turnabouts regarding freedom. They fought and argued over the Fourth of July's meaning *for themselves* and for the country.

Douglass's question stands today, but in a slightly different register: "What is the Fourth of July to us?" It is directed not only to the descendants of the enslaved, but to the nation as a whole. Since the social revolutions of the mid-twentieth century, Americans like to believe that they have settled, for the most part, the serious questions around race and racial inequality. With the reelection of Donald Trump in 2024, they decided it didn't even matter if the questions were settled. Our current days reveal that many desire to "get shut" of the problem of Black people and others. Many still believe this place is a white Republic. What will be our running commentary in the face of what we see today?

—

In all of this, history matters. It even haunts. History isn't a fixed basket of facts that escape our comprehension. It is more than a chronicle of events and people. What we bring to it, and for what purposes, matters. Our memories of America's past can be sources of power or the iron shackles that bind our feet. That is, the mistakes and failures of the country can inform how we address the problems of today, or we can resign ourselves to the idea that the past is in the past, irreversible. Our orientation to the past, then, can be more than remembering it or submitting to it. Instead, we look to the past for resources, not to affirm our goodness or to illustrate our sins, but to grasp more clearly the problems in the present that confound us.

Confronting the past is different than remembering or submitting to it. I might remember a childhood wound. I could describe its details, give you the date it happened and how it happened. But to remember the details is not to confront what that event means for me today, or how the wound shapes the way I deal with relationships, or how I desperately try to hide my sensitivity and vulnerability because of it. Those childhood tears still matter. Santayana got it partly right. Remembering is necessary—but not sufficient to guarantee that I won't repeat the same thing with my own child. Something more is required: an understanding of that moment of wounding that can be found only in confrontation—an acceptance of the wound in all its ugliness, and of responsibility for its effects—that could orient me to my role as a parent in a more loving and thoughtful way. The same holds for the nation. It is not enough to remember the details of slavery, or of the past more generally, but to confront its meanings for who we are as a nation today. In that sense, history comes to us in the ongoing work to make ourselves better people and a better nation.

We ought not listen to those who demand our submission to the past as if the American Revolution were all that is needed, and all that is required of us now is to take in "the clean words" of the founders. It would seal our fate to do such a thing, or hurl us into the naïve illusion that we can somehow escape history. Instead, we must orient ourselves honestly to the past to better understand the present—especially if we believe that we can change the direction of the country. Tell better stories, draw on the lessons of our failures, and use the experience, what the philosopher John Dewey called "funded experience," to better address the problems we face today, and set the stage for imagining and making a better future. T. S. Eliot returns:

Time present and time past
Are both perhaps present in time future,
And time future contained in time past.

Confronting history is especially critical in a time where Trumpian forces retreat into the safety and comfort of older prejudices that have long simmered beneath our way of life and now boil over again. America has never resolved the question Frederick Douglass asked about the meaning of freedom here—the answer to which, he believed, involved the central role and place of Black people in this Republic. Whenever it comes close to answering the question, the country lurches back to an old and settled idea about white America, turning its back on the very Declaration that brought it into existence.

Confronting the past, in this sense, insists that Americans face the whip of the whirlwind that has shaped the country for 250 years. This is why I reach today for Douglass's July 5 address. His words reveal the ongoing dissent that happens within the context of celebration—the refusal, in the tumultuous decade before the nation turned on itself, to accept the lie that hides the split. Reading him, we see that America's past is rife with contradiction and abject failure as well as with promise and hope. Herman Melville was right: "I know a wind in purpose strong—It spins against the way it drives." No easy appeals to a more perfect union. No claims to innocence. Only the recognition that the country sometimes eats its own entrails and lies about it.

Coming to terms with the past involves scouring the archive and our memories in the hope that we can account for the present that has us all by the nape of the neck. It requires an incantation of sorts: not to stand passively and report as Dos Passos claims, because we refuse to confront what has happened to us and be haunted. Instead, we must do what the writer Imani Perry calls us to do, and that is, with words and deeds, to flip the script. "See through time in order to see today. . . . Haunt the past to change the present and claim the future."

July Fourth has always carried in tow the day after, July 5. We can speak back. We have always spoken back. And, in doing so, Black people have claimed an understanding of freedom that seeks to release the country from the debilitating effects of the sense of twoness that drives us all mad. Douglass did so in his speech not by rejecting the entire American project, but by leaning into the principles voiced in the Declaration of Independence—the same principles invoked by those Black men who petitioned Congress to end the transatlantic slave trade and to abolish the Fugitive Slave Act, and who claimed the rights of the Constitution for themselves and for other Black people. Decades passed between their efforts and Douglass's speech, and more than a century between his speech and our time. We are still claiming freedom as our own, and we still endure the whip of the whirlwind.

—

At the intersection of Corinthian and State Streets in Rochester, New York, nestled between nondescript office buildings and a parking lot, stands a statue of Frederick Douglass with its huge hands opened wide. It faces the First National Bank of Rochester–Old Monroe County Savings Bank, a building erected in 1924, with four Greek columns reminiscent of the old Corinthian Hall designed by the architect Henry Searle and built in 1849. Douglass seems to beckon and, from a certain angle, suggests a confidence in the power of the spoken word. He stands like he knows he is right.

The statue is a near-replica of the original Stanley Edwards sculpture unveiled in 1899, when Douglass became the first Black person to be memorialized with a statue in the United States. The replica, part of Rochester's 2018 celebration of Douglass's 200th birthday, is one of thirteen sculpted by Olivia Kim and placed in significant locations around the city to mark Douglass's incredible life and activism. Douglass's youngest son, Charles, modeled for the Edwards sculpture; Kim cast the hands of her statue from those of one of Douglass's modern descendants, Ken Morris Jr.

Of all the statues around the city, however, this one at the intersection of Corinthian and State drew my attention. It sits at the site where Douglass asked his exacting question, "What to the slave is the Fourth of July?" as racial violence swelled around the country. "The existence of slavery in this country brands your republicanism as a sham," he shouted to the rapt audience in Corinthian Hall. "Your humanity as a base pretense, and your Christianity as a lie. It destroys your moral power abroad; it corrupts your politicians at home. . . . It makes your name a hissing, and bye-word to a mocking earth."

Corinthian Hall had stood at the center of social and political life in Rochester since its opening in 1849. Douglass moved to the city of fifty thousand two years before with the intention of launching his career as an independent journalist. Rochester was an important city in the abolitionist movement, and with reform movements more broadly. Susan B. Anthony made Rochester her home base during this period. The region also gave birth to new religious groups such as Spiritualists, Mormons, and Millerites, and it was home to an active local Black community that included the Black abolitionist Austin Steward, a former slave. In Rochester, even though Douglass experienced "the vulgar prejudice of color, so common to Americans," he found a community supportive of his paper and his abolitionist ambition. He had named his new newspaper *The North Star,* rented an office in the Talman Building at 25 Buffalo Street, and boarded with Charles Joiner, a local Black business owner, until he was able to bring his family to Rochester a year later.

Douglass would find himself in Corinthian Hall repeatedly throughout his years in Rochester. Originally called the Athenaeum, the building eventually took its name from the four distinctive Corinthian columns that adorned the wall behind the stage. With its high ceilings and elegant chandeliers, it was the primary venue for concerts, fairs, and lectures in the city. Susan B. Anthony described Corinthian Hall as "the most magnificent auditorium west of the Hudson." The likes of Anthony, Henry Ward Beecher, and Ralph Waldo Emerson spoke from its podium.

So much swirled around at the time. The nation convulsed over the issue of slavery. Douglass wondered if the country was redeemable and, eventually, whether the evil of slavery could be ended only with violence, a thought that later led him to meet with the radical John Brown. In 1851, Douglass had openly broken with the white abolitionist William Lloyd Garrison, who believed that the Constitution was a slaveholding document and thought that engaging in politics within the current system only reinforced the immorality of the state.

In his speech, Douglass offered an anti-slavery interpretation of the Constitution, where the radical equality expressed in the Declaration of Independence framed the preamble. Black people were not banished to the shadows, but stood as rights-bearing Americans. The promise of the Declaration and the protection of the Constitution belong to all who claim this place as home. For him this was not simply a moral claim. Politics mattered in forcing the nation to understand itself apart from the ideas of white racial superiority that distorted its principles a politics that involved a forceful rereading of the country's sacred documents, all of which were on full display as he asked his hard question and offered what some took to be his rude answer.

The date was significant, too. Organizers had moved the program to Monday, July 5, because the Fourth had fallen on the Sabbath. But July 5 had a historical importance all its own, one Douglass understood. In a way, the date was appropriate to his message.

—

By the early 1800s the fervor of the Revolutionary Age was waning. Americans groped for some sense of national cohesiveness or consensus as most expressed their loyalties within the confines of their states or local communities. The Fourth of July aspired to be the day to rekindle the patriotism of the Revolution and to tell the story of America's commitment to freedom. Our national history, it was believed by some, was in fact the story of freedom. But this story fragmented along the lines of varied and often local interests. Celebrations were organized by partisan and reform groups with different agendas, exposing the weakness of the idea of a *national* political community. In fact, most were not clear on who exactly were *the people* who made up such a national community. Local attachments mattered more.

From the beginning, celebrations of the Fourth were fraught with irony as groups like the Federalists—who believed in a strong federal government, to the detriment of the states—and their opponents, as well as reform movements that ranged from anti-slavery, to suffrage, to temperance, all used the occasion to promote their agendas. In these early days, the Fourth of July was not "an occasion for consensus" but rather an indication of the diversity that characterizes a fledgling nation. In the slaveholding South, for example, slave auctions were often held on July Fourth. Throughout the Northeast, the American Colonization Society—founded in 1816 on the premise that free Black people could not fully integrate into American society and should thus be repatriated to Africa—used the day to raise funds to expedite their emigration schemes. It was clear, for some, that the land of the free was also the land of slaves and second-class citizens. No wonder that as the Fourth became uniformly the day to express patriotic zeal (the U.S. Congress made July Fourth a federal holiday in 1870, five years after the Civil War), free Black people were not allowed to participate in most celebrations. In fact, during this early period of the Republic, the Fourth of July became one of the more menacing days of the year for free Blacks in the North.

As Douglass prepared his address for Corinthian Hall, he had to have heard stories about the "July Days" of 1834 in New York City, when a mob attacked an integrated July Fourth gathering at Chatham Street Church. Rumors had circulated that the church condoned amalgamation, and on July 7 that year—the mob had forced the postponement of the gathering from July 4—violence erupted and the building was burned to the ground. The mob then turned its attention to St. Philip's African Episcopal Church on Center Street, where its pastor, Reverend Peter Williams, was accused of officiating an interracial marriage. One reporter from the *New-York Commercial Advertiser* wrote, as he saw the mob tear up the hand-carved pews and pull down the altar, "We have just returned from one of the most disgraceful scenes we have ever witnessed!"

The violence spilled into the streets, and in an odd allusion to Passover, the mob "demanded that white families illuminate their windows so that their race might be identified, and their homes be passed over; the mob would attack homes with darkened windows only."

In some ways, the violence of these angels of death, which lasted almost ten days, made sense. The mere presence of Black people at the

Fourth of July celebrations, acting as if freedom belonged to them, exposed the lie at the heart of this ritual of remembrance by the nation: ours was not a nation committed to liberty and equality. That exposure triggered white rage, which aimed to banish from view the evidence of the lie. Black people had refused to submit to the terms of their existence in this country. The cost of that refusal was unbridled violence. The rage of the mob sought to exorcise any hint of the sins that might dispel their fantasies about the country. And that rage would be expressed repeatedly across generations: from these July Days to the mob violence post-Reconstruction, to the destruction in Tulsa and the "Red Summer" of 1919, to the horror of Buffalo in 2022.

Amid the frenzy, not just in New York but around the country, Black people spoke back to America and claimed freedom as their own. We celebrated the days of liberation that gave voice to what freedom *might* look like in this country, where the color line took on symbolic significance in the practice of signifying the hypocrisy of American freedom. These alternative commemorations embraced an idea of freedom consistent with the Declaration of Independence and exposed the fact that white Americans were not who they said they were. In these ritual gatherings, the celebrants held that the only remedy for the country's sins was to be found, not in violent acts of expiation like the July Days in New York, but in full emancipation. If America was to be free, Black folk had to be free, which meant that white people would have to give up the idea that their race made them superior. Twenty or so years later, white people tried to destroy the country rather than give up the idea of their racial superiority and exclusive right to freedom. Even after the Civil War, that idea would rise from the ashes of the dead and take hold as a national ideology, irrespective of region, that has endured. And today their descendants might destroy the country again.

The earliest example of these freedom celebrations centered around January 1, 1808, and the end of the transatlantic slave trade. Another was in response to the abolition of slavery in the British West Indies on August 1, 1834; and, of course, Juneteenth was a celebration of June 19, 1865, and the final recognition of the Emancipation Proclamation in Galveston, Texas.

But the date that came to have symbolic significance in both its relation to the Declaration and its sense of Black people's desire for freedom was July 5.

Since the end of slavery in New York on July 4, 1827, African Americans across more than five states celebrated what was called New York's Abolition Day on July 5. It was an ironic commentary on the hypocrisy of Independence Day. The day after July Fourth offered something between a celebration, memorial, and critique. Decrying the nation's hypocrisy, the Black community gathered to celebrate an idea of freedom that the nation refused to embrace. Black people came together in churches and drew on church liturgies as they commemorated the day. Black preachers typically delivered the keynote address. On July 5, 1827, for example, Nathaniel Paul, pastor of the African Baptist Church in Albany, New York, offered a vision of the future for Black people rife with religious meaning:

> The God of Nature has endowed our children with intellectual powers surpassed by none; nor is there anything wanting but their careful cultivation in order to fit them for stations the most honorable, sacred, or useful. And may we not, without becoming vain in our imaginations, indulge the pleasing anticipation that within the little circle of those connected with our families there may hereafter be found the scholar, the statesman, or the herald of the cross of Christ. Is it too much to say that among that little number there shall yet be one founded like the wise legislator to Israel, who shall take his brethren by the hand and lead them forth from worse than Egyptian bondage to the happy Canaan of civil and religious liberty?

In Paul's hands, Black people were the New Israelites and white America was worse than Egyptland.

July 5 commemorations often involved picnics, gun salutes, and processions. They were elaborate affairs, and the public displays had political and symbolic meaning that directly and indirectly opposed the collective memory and forgetfulness—the disremembering—of the nation. As African Americans publicly celebrated the end of slavery in New York, they placed in stark relief the contradiction between the ideals celebrated on the Fourth of July and the way Americans actually lived their lives among the enslaved, throughout the South and the North (New Jersey would not formally end slavery until 1866), with racial restrictions that clearly signaled white lives were more valuable than others. On July 5, Black people remembered the moral costs of slavery and exposed the divided soul of the nation. The celebrations struck a discordant note amid ritual calls for national consensus.

New York's Abolition Day was one of these important moments on the other side of the color line, a precursor of Juneteenth, when Black people in the United States cultivated freedom dreams and called attention to our tragic inheritance. In all of these moments, America's civil religion—that effort to provide a religious scaffolding for the country to generate consensus—was turned on its head. Austin Steward delivered a July 5 address in Rochester, New York, in 1827. He gave thanks to God and remembered the afflictions of the past. He offered a sophisticated reading of America's democratic principles and turned to the Exodus story to foreground the sorrows that framed the joy of deliverance:

> Like the people of God in Egypt, you have been afflicted; but like them too, you have been redeemed. You are henceforth free as the mountain winds. Why should we, on this day of congratulation and joy, turn our view upon the origin of slavery? Why should we harrow up our minds by dwelling on the deceit, the forcible fraud and treachery that have been so long practiced on your hospitable and unsuspecting countrymen? . . . Why should we remember, in joy and exuberance, the thousands of our countrymen who are today, in this boasted land of civil and religious liberty, writhing under the lash and groaning beneath the grinding weight of Slavery's chain? . . . But away with such as these; we will rejoice, though sobs interrupt the songs of our rejoicing, and tears mingle in the cup we pledge to Freedom.

In this moment, Steward likened the plight of those darker souls to the people of God in Egypt, and he called attention to the blight that covered the country's ideals of freedom and equality. These darker souls, in his hands, refused the idea of America as the Redeemer Nation. Instead, Steward on this Abolition Day placed slaves and former slaves, with "tears mingled in the cup of freedom," at the forefront in the retrieval of the true meanings of democracy. America was Egypt, the seat of Pharaoh resided in Washington, D.C., and Black people were the chosen people of God.

—

Twenty-five years to the day after Steward's speech in Rochester, Douglass walked to the podium in Corinthian Hall. With nearly six hundred people packed into the auditorium, for a moment the color line blurred, and the worlds of white and Black folk could be seen and felt at once—not as stereotype or as mystery, but as a country split in two by the barbarous practice of slavery and the racial ideas that gave it life. A kind of double exposure. What resided in the shadows among the darker souls of this nation was now available for all to see, in the full light of a summer day in Corinthian Hall. Douglass spoke like the prophets of old, and the audience, whether they understood the symbolic meanings or not, found themselves commemorating July 5 and, by extension, participating in a ritual to reimagine the country—an aspirational America free from its chains.

Much has been written about Douglass's July 5 oration. David Blight, in his Pulitzer Prize–winning biography of Douglass, describes the speech as a symphony in three movements. The first movement honors the genius of the founding fathers; the second details the hypocrisy of slavery and racism in the country; and the third offers the nation resources to imagine itself differently and to think of the Constitution as an antislavery document with an ethical mandate. Douglass ends, according to Blight, with "visions of hope" for an immature nation. He freedom-dreams *for* the country.

But, for me, especially given what we currently face in America,

U.S.A., the speech does something more. Douglass lays bare the tragic split that compromised the foundation of American democracy. This split is more than mere hypocrisy; it cuts to the heart of the nation's self-conception. The answer to the country's moral crises, then, is not that all Americans need only live up to our principles (something akin to Gunnar Myrdal's answer to the American dilemma). No: what Douglass demanded, and what the country requires, is a confrontation with that aspect of itself that clings to the idea that it is a white Republic and that freedom belongs only to white people. This view doesn't present the belief in white racial superiority as some kind of false consciousness on the part of the nation; nor does it suggest that the country requires a more truthful understanding of itself. Instead, the idea of a white Republic is a constitutive part of who and what America is. This is the acceptance necessary for the confrontation with the past. Honest self-awareness of that fact, and accepting responsibility for it, constitutes the beginning of the remedy—not just an admission of hypocrisy, although that admission is an important first step.

Even as Douglass acknowledged the importance of the day (he refers to July Fourth as America's Passover), as a Black person in the United States, where slavery condemned so many to a life of toil and servitude, he claimed no possession of the significance of the Fourth. How could he claim the day as his own? He was once a fugitive who stole his own freedom, and many others still languished unfree and in chains. "It is the birthday of *your* national independence, and of *your* political freedom," he told the crowd. "This, to you, is what Passover was to the emancipated people of God. It carries *your* minds back to the clay, and to the act of *your* great deliverance; and to the signs, and to the wonders, associated with that day." Even as Douglass celebrated the wisdom of the founders, he was clear about the meaning of the day for him and his kin:

> I am not included within the pale of this glorious anniversary! Your high independence only reveals the immeasurable distance between us. The blessings in which you, this day, rejoice, are not enjoyed in common. The rich inheritance of justice, liberty, prosperity and independence bequeathed by your fathers, is shared by

> you, not by me. The sunlight that brought life and healing to you, has brought stripes and death to me. This Fourth July is yours, not mine. You may rejoice, I must mourn.

Freedom, as white America celebrated it, belonged only to white America. The cruelty of slavery called into question the moral claims of the nation about that freedom. And, in Douglass's hands, that cruelty was not some abstract reference, or an account aimed to produce tears. Instead, he forced the audience to confront the "crack . . . sound of the slave whip" and the moral implications of those "human flesh-jobbers," who profited in the snatching of people. With each word, the audience was implicated in the horror and terror of slavery. With each sentence, Douglass made clear why he could claim no possession of the Fourth, and why the audience should feel the same. He held up a mirror that revealed the soul of the nation.

Douglass announced that "America is false to the past, false to the present, and solemnly binds herself to be false to the future." The country tells itself a story that secures its virtue. The cruelty of slavery is banished from view so that the rich inheritance of freedom and justice can be celebrated without contradiction.

This cycle persists today. Just think about the assault on American history when conservatives claim that so-called wokeness distorts the American past and aims to make white students believe they are inherently racist. States like Florida passed into law the "Stop WOKE Act," which restricts teaching issues related to racism, sexism, and homophobia. The goal has been, and continues to be, to redact any account that calls into question the storybook version of American democracy. In Douglass's era and in our own, the country seeks to escape its sins by escaping time itself—by snatching the idea of America out of the messiness of history and securing it in a fantasy that could give less than a damn about reality.

Douglass insisted that America confront its choices in the lived experiences of all its people—not above the fray and outside of what men and women actually do, or with nostalgia, or in the haze of national mythology, but in the fitful encounter with the ugliness of who Americans are, as evidenced in the cruelty of slavery. For Douglass and many in the anti-slavery movement, the idea that led some to believe they could hold another human being in bondage—and others to profit from it or turn a blind eye to it—indelibly compromised the soul of the nation. And yet that conclusion did not necessarily mean that white abolitionists accepted the social and political equality of Black people. For many, the institution of slavery malformed the Republic but this belief did not require rejecting the idea that white men were superior and the rightful possessors of freedom. For a Black man to make the claim about slavery and freedom, then, took on added significance. Douglass did not come to this conclusion as an object of philanthropy or charity, but as someone who asserted his right to claim that freedom as his own.

What, then, might this supposed day of freedom mean to those who bore the brunt of the country's refusal to live up to its promise?

> What, to the American slave, is your 4th of July? I answer: a day that reveals to him, more than all other days in the year, the gross injustice and cruelty to which he is the constant victim. To him, your celebration is a sham; your boasted liberty, an unholy license; your national greatness, swelling vanity; your sounds of rejoicing are empty and heartless; your denunciations of tyrants, brass fronted impudence; your shouts of liberty and equality, hollow mockery.

For the darker souls of this nation, the Fourth of July amounted to a cruel gesture, a lie told by people who snatch away promises, who are desperate to believe they are righteous when the evidence suggests something more sinister.

For Douglass, this desperation was particularly evident among those who professed to be Christian and who defended slavery. Such people conscripted God to justify their evil. Pro-slavery churches supported the Fugitive Slave Act. The Church was "not only indifferent to the wrongs of the slave," Douglass maintained, "it actually takes sides with the oppressors. It has made itself the bulwark of American slavery, and the shield of American slave-hunters." One can imagine the discomfort of those who sat in the seats of Corinthian Hall.

Douglass echoed his scathing criticism of the hypocrisy of American Christianity in his 1845 autobiography, *Narrative of the Life of Frederick Douglass: An American Slave:*

> We see the thief preaching against theft, and the adulterer against adultery. We have men sold to build churches, women sold to support the gospel, and babes sold to purchase Bibles for *the poor heathen! All for the glory of God and the good of souls!* The slave auctioneer's bell and the church-going bell chime in with each other, and the bitter cries of the heart-broken slave are drowned in the religious shouts of his pious master.

Far too many Christians, Douglass suggested, could not disentangle their faith from the evil of "tyrants, man-stealers, and thugs." These were white Christians who would distort the Gospel, the ancestors of those who have today seized the state and would condemn most to the gallows—those who would even claim that empathy is a sin. Douglass spoke directly to them. Invoking the book of Isaiah, he bellowed from the podium, "YOUR HANDS ARE FULL OF BLOOD."

Even Douglass's hopeful vision for the nation at the end of his speech remained blues-soaked. He wrapped his huge hands around the strange melancholy that gripped the nation. The fate of the young Republic rested with our ability to confront who we really were as a precondition for who we might become. Lies about the past and the present bound the country to a future where white Americans, and a few others, would continue to live by lies. Douglass urged white Americans to deal with what was happening to them on the inside, to acknowledge that the two warring souls of this nation threatened to undo everything. No amount of sentimental tears or expression of white rage will end our national torment. Ours is a country of tortured souls repeatedly trying to rip out its heart. I am reminded of the cries in Dante's eighth circle of hell: "Why do you split me?"

I hear Douglass's words echoing down to our own times:

> Fellow citizens! . . . [The existence of slavery] is the antagonistic force in your government, the only thing that seriously disturbs and endangers your Union. It fetters your progress; it is the enemy of improvement, the deadly foe of education; it fosters pride; it breeds insolence; it promotes vice; it shelters crime; it is a curse to the earth that supports it; and yet, you cling to it, as if it were the sheet anchor of all your hopes. Oh! Be warned! Be warned! *A horrible reptile is coiled up in your nation's bosom; the venomous creature is nursing at the tender breast of your youthful Republic; for the love of God, tear it away, and fling from you the hideous monster, and let the weight of twenty millions crush and destroy it forever* [emphasis added].

The promise of America is conditioned on its willingness to rid itself of the serpent that eats its entrails. Douglass's "vision of hope" at the speech's end was qualified by the choices Americans must make and their rejection of the idea that justified slavery: that God had made white people to rule instead of making all men and women equal in His sight.

—

As I stood in front of the statue in Rochester, I could not help but think of the choices made over the 170-plus years since Douglass spoke those words, of the monstrous reptile still in the bosom of the nation, and the tragic realization, as the country celebrates another anniversary, of the lies of the past shadowing the lies of the present and confounding the future. Trump and MAGA Republicans are clear that they want to Make America White Again. They are attacking any effort or aspiration for a genuinely multicultural and multiracial democracy. Stephen Miller is just one example of those who claim that white people are the real victims. Miller and those who agree with him feed the horrible reptile.

But they are not alone. History corroborates their effort. Each time

America has had the opportunity to break free from the ghosts of the past, the majority of white Americans have chosen, again and again, the security and comfort of the storybook version of the American idea that conceals what is happening to us. The Sixth Congress did it when its members rejected the petitions of those free Black men; the Congress did it again when it failed to live up to the promises of Radical Reconstruction and allowed the redemption of the South; the nativists in the second decade of the twentieth century did it when they passed draconian immigration laws and offered a model for Hitler and the Third Reich; and the country did it when white America turned its back on the '60s revolutions and embraced the so-called forgotten Americans. They all fed the reptile, too.

Charles Long, a scholar of religion, put it this way: "At each of these junctures the American revolution is aborted and the clever priests skillful in the ways of ritual purity and manipulation come upon the scene to ensure the repetition of the American ritual." In those moments of crises and potential change, all that is needed to secure the country's identity is a reassertion of the inherent goodness of America—an affirmation of the unchanging principles of faith that undergird the divine project that is this nation. And if we do make change—abolish slavery, for example, or allow women to vote—that transformation becomes a further affirmation, reflecting the ongoing effort to become a more perfect union. Because at its core, the clerics declare, America has always been good. Their prescribed task in moments of upheaval is to return to the great principles that brought the country into existence and reaffirm them in the way Americans live their lives. Raise the flag—especially on July Fourth—and remember that, for all of the country's faults and failures, America, U.S.A., remains the greatest country on earth. Melville's *White Jacket,* published in the same year as the Fugitive Slave Act of 1850, reminds us of the hubris at the heart of the ritual of consensus:

> We Americans are the peculiar, chosen people—the Israel of our time; we bear the ark of the Liberties of the world. Seventy years ago, we escaped from thrall, and besides our first birth-right—embracing one continent of earth—God has given to us, for a future inheritance, the broad domains of the political pagans,

> that shall yet come and lie down under the shade of our ark, without bloody hands being lifted.

Native peoples and those still in chains would decry the lie that the country's hands were not bloodied. In fact, Black people shouted, these were not the chosen people at all.

Douglass lived to see Abraham Lincoln issue the Emancipation Proclamation, the ratification of the Thirteenth Amendment, *and* the passage of the first Jim Crow laws. Betrayal and serpents. Regarding the Emancipation Proclamation, he declared with tremendous excitement at the Cooper Institute in New York on February 6, 1863, "We are all liberated by this proclamation. Everybody is liberated. The white man is liberated, the Black man is liberated, the brave men now fighting the battles of the country against rebels and traitors are now liberated." Freedom dreams realized. That unbridled optimism would be swallowed whole in just a few years.

Even after the brutal war and the abolition of slavery, there would be those, like Walt Whitman and many others involved in the anti-slavery movement, who rejected the idea of black citizenship. In 1874, just three years after the publication of his masterpiece *Democratic Vistas,* Whitman wrote in "A Hint to Preachers and Authors": "As if we had not strained the voting and digestive caliber of American Democracy to the utmost for the last fifty years with the millions of ignorant foreigners, we have now infused a powerful percentage of blacks, with about as much intellect and caliber (in the mass) as so many baboons." Slavery ended, and yet freedom remained in the hands of white people (it was theirs to give). The violence unleashed when Black people insisted that they were free soaked the land in the blood of former slaves.

That violence and blood has been a consistent feature of the so-called Redeemer Nation every time Black people have dared to challenge America, U.S.A. The Black men who marched in the Southwark district of Philadelphia on July 4, 1804, shouting about their freedom and threatening white Philadelphians with swords and other weapons, knew of the limitations of petitioning government for freedom, and of the violence that came with being Black in this country. White people could turn on a dime, and Black folk could lose the people they loved. Their march through the streets of the Old City offered a warning: that they would be willing to strike the blow for their own freedom, just as they had in Haiti. That sentiment didn't disappear, because the violence of white rage did not wane.

—

About seventy-three miles east of Rochester lies the city of Buffalo. In 1843, a National Convention of Colored Citizens was held in the city and Reverend Henry Highland Garnet delivered his famous "Address to the Slaves of the United States." Garnet had lost faith in the country—perhaps like the men who marched through Philadelphia some forty years earlier. In the decades since the Revolution, the newly created Supreme Court had upheld the 1793 Fugitive Slave Act in *Prigg v. Pennsylvania;* Congressman Joshua Giddings of Ohio had been censured in the House of Representatives in 1842 because of his anti-slavery stance; white and Black abolitionists had split over political tactics; and Black people in the North could not claim freedom for themselves because they were bound to those held in bondage in the South. The racial climate of the country was arid and hostile, and Garnet had had enough. He called for slaves to strike the blow for their own freedom.

> You had far better all die—die immediately, than live as slaves, and entail your wretchedness upon your posterity. If you would be free in this generation here is your only hope. However much you and all of us may desire it, there is not much hope of redemption without the shedding of blood. If you must bleed, let it all come at once, rather die freemen, than live to be slaves. It is impossible, like the children of Israel, to make a grand exodus from the land of bondage. The Pharaohs are on both sides of the blood-red waters! . . .
>
> Let your motto be RESISTANCE! RESISTANCE! RESISTANCE!

Opposition came immediately from within the convention. Delegates complained that Garnet's speech advocated excessive violence and, strategically and tactically, such action would be fatal to free Black people in slave and border states. In a passionate speech, Frederick Douglass urged the convention to try "the moral means a little longer," and by one vote (19 to 18) the convention agreed with him. He believed then that the country must be transformed by moral means. But the violence in the years after his famous speech in Rochester would shake his resolve, as the vile brutality of the post-Reconstruction years revealed the callousness of America's heart. Pharaoh was indeed on both sides of the blood-red waters. Perhaps Douglass was wrong. The horrible serpent cannot simply be tossed aside. It shares the heartbeat of the nation

Well over a century after Douglass delivered his speech in Corinthian Hall and Garnet announced in Buffalo that pharaohs were on both sides of the Red Sea, Payton Gendron, an eighteen-year-old white male from Conklin, New York, drove over two hundred miles to east Buffalo, exited his car with a semiautomatic rifle with the word NIGGER scrawled on its barrel, and opened fire at the Tops Friendly Market. He was dressed in tactical gear and live-streamed his killing spree on Twitch.

Gendron purposefully chose this area because of its high concentration of Black residents. Buffalo is the sixth most segregated city in the country and the third poorest city in the nation. Thirty-five percent of African Americans and 40 percent of Black children in Buffalo live below the poverty line. In 2021, African American unemployment in the city stood at 11 percent. Masten Park on the East Side, where the Tops grocery store is located, is like most Black neighborhoods in poor cities teeming with Black people trying to make ends meet. Severe residential segregation has drawn a hard line between Black and white residents in the city. One reporter likened Main Street to the Berlin Wall, a divide, like railroad tracks in small Southern towns, that separates Black and white neighborhoods.

Before the horror on May 14, Black people lived in a city that fundamentally devalued and disregarded them, no matter which political party governed. They lived and died by a thousand daily cuts in "the city of good neighbors." Professor Keeanga-Yamahtta Taylor noted,

> For decades, Black life has been seen as disposable. Buffalo is one of the poorest cities in the nation, and the poverty is concentrated

> in the neighborhoods with the largest Black populations. Racism there comes not only in the form of a teenage white supremacist murdering Black people at a grocery store, it is also evident in the policies that encourage disinvestment from public schools attended by Black students, in the annual failure to develop affordable housing policies, and in the continued use of fees and fines that disproportionately impact Black residents.

Freedom remains the possession of white people. Gendron stepped into this opportunity desert, one among many in this country, and killed ten people and injured three others.

Among the dead was Celestine Chaney, a sixty-five-year-old grandmother. She had survived breast cancer and three brain aneurysms but lost her life because a young white man thought she threatened the extinction of the white race. Ruth Whitfield was the oldest among the dead. She was eighty-six, the mother of the former Buffalo fire commissioner Garnell Whitfield Jr. She had just visited her husband in a nursing home and stopped by the market to buy a few groceries. "My mom went every day to take care of my father," Mr. Whitfield said. "Clipping his nails, shaving, taking his clothes home to wash and iron . . . , making sure he was dressed. She was ever present in his life and the only reason he is alive today is because of her."

Garnell Whitfield Jr. would later testify before a Senate Judiciary hearing. "Mrs. Ruth Whitfield was my mother," he said to those in the room, "the heart and rock of our family and my father's soulmate of 68 years."

> She was the person who held us together . . . probably just like your mother did for your family. . . . Our lives are forever changed . . . forever damaged by an act of profound hate and evil. Nothing will ever take away the hurt, the pain or the hole in our hearts. For her to be ripped from us by someone so full of hate, is impossible to understand and even harder to live with. But we are more than hurt . . . we are angry!

Mr. Whitfield demanded action from the senators. "Is there nothing that you personally are willing to do to stop the cancer of white supremacy and the domestic terrorism it inspires?" he pleaded. He had lived a reality that Black people have had to endure since the beginning of the country, one in which they can lose their lives or loved ones when white people decide they have had enough.

The political theater of the hearings only made him angrier. "It was very difficult," he told me, struggling to keep himself together. It had been five months since the murder of his mother, and no matter the speeches and his travels around the country, he was still struggling. Guilt ate at him as his pain subsided a bit with each passing day; he wanted to hold on to his grief. He told me about the many people who, when he was Buffalo's fire chief, took their last breath in his arms, and of the countless times he'd had to console families who had lost loved ones. But now he felt as though he could not take care of his own family. "You're gonna have to forgive me, 'cause I'm a crier." He sniffed as he spoke. "I'm not gonna pretend. I miss my mom, man. Every day."

The Senate hearings angered him, "because across the room, what you didn't see was the lack of people. And then Ted Cruz came in when it was time for him to spew his vitriol. He said his piece, and then he got up and left. You know what I'm saying? It was very disrespectful. It was offensive. . . . It was inhumane." Senator Cruz spoke for about eight minutes, delivering partisan talking points badly disguised as empathy:

> I wish we had a hearing focused on how to stop violent crime. I wish we had a hearing focused on the skyrocketing murder rates in this country that we're seeing right now. I wish we had a hearing focused on the skyrocketing carjacking rates that we're seeing in this country right now. I wish we had a hearing focused on policies advocated by congressional Democrats of abolishing the police and defunding the police that caused the crime to skyrocket. I wish we had a hearing on Soros' [district attorneys] that were elected with millions of dollars from Democrat donors who get into office and refuse to prosecute violent criminals, release

> violent criminals onto the street and then allow those violent criminals to commit, yes, yet more murders. That would be a hearing with some urgency.

No real concern about the dead. No acknowledgment of the racist ideology that motivated Payton Gendron. When Cruz finished, he got up and left the chamber. In the end, Mr. Whitfield's question about whether the Senate had the will to stop white supremacy and domestic terrorism bounced off the walls of a half-empty room. A failure that echoed what happened in Congress Hall in 1797 and 1800.

At the hearings, the spectacle mattered more than the lives of those lost in Buffalo or the reasons why Ruth Whitfield was dead. "The lights came, they're chasing me around, want to see us cry, want us to show our pain, but they weren't here to really find out what was going on," Mr. Whitfield said with suppressed fury. Sentimentality motivated the cameras—they wanted only an outpouring of feeling. "I understand that I have been used." He knew the cameras and reporters that blanketed Buffalo would eventually leave the city. "They were chasing a story, sensationalizing it. They're trying to get ratings, basically, that's what they do." Sentimentality masks cruelty, still.

Mr. Whitfield talked about the history of Buffalo, how racist the city is, and how May 14 made matters worse. He insisted that the country confront the fact that "the American dream is a nightmare for those who don't have access to it," and that more is required of us than simply acknowledging white privilege or declaring ourselves anti-racist. We must tap the root of our sorrows. "I don't know how you expect us to sit here and keep living this lie," he told me.

> America is built on violence, is built on racism, at its core, its root. You know the thing about therapy, I found in my life, is that people avoid it, because when you go to therapy, you got to put everything on the line. And the very thing that you're trying to protect by going to therapy is the thing that you find is making you sick, you know? So people don't go. It's no different in America, as far as I am concerned.

As I listened to Mr. Whitfield, plainspoken and direct, wrapped in his grief, I thought of Douglass's words on July 5, begging the country to "fling from you the hideous monster." I thought of Baldwin's observation, in *Notes of a Native Son,* "that people cling to their hates . . . because, once hate is gone, . . . they will be forced to deal with pain." Americans, tortured souls, do not want to deal with what makes them sick.

Payton Gendron wanted to "spread awareness to my fellow whites about the real problems the West is facing" and to "encourage further attacks that will eventually start the war that will save the Western world." For Mr. Whitfield, what's at the heart of the paranoia about the "Great Replacement" among people like Gendron is fear. "They are not concerned about us replacing them," he said. "Their concern is that they will have to replace *us.* They know they're not better than us. They know that." So they lie. Fear *and* panic are at the root of it all. We saw that fear during the July Days in 1834, and Frederick Douglass exposed it in the way the country celebrated its founding on July Fourth—the nation had to make Black people invisible. As it has always done, the exposure of fear and panic triggers white rage, and Mr. Whitfield lost his mother because of it.

—

What happens to a country that must believe a lie because of a deep-seated fear that the truth will rip it apart? Opposing strivings, unreconciled, come with a cost. Trapped in madness for 250 years. Douglass knew this in 1852 in Rochester; Garnell Whitfield Jr. knows it today. We see it in the horrors of then and in the horrors of now. Americans cling to their storybook in order to avoid confronting that madness. Dr. Martin Luther King Jr. put it this way in *Where Do We Go from Here: Chaos or Community?,* his last book:

> Ever since the birth of our nation, white America has had a schizophrenic personality on the question of race. She has been torn between selves—a self in which she proudly professed the great principles of democracy and a self in which she sadly

> practiced the antithesis of democracy. . . . No one surveying the moral landscape of our nation can overlook the hideous wreckage of commitment twisted and turned to a thousand shapes under the stress of prejudice and irrationality.

No matter how many mirrors the country shatters, how many lives it destroys, most in white America refuse to relinquish the idea that freedom belongs only to them—that this country is theirs. America's national identity has been disfigured, because of it. Some white Americans are willfully blind, having plucked out their eyes so that they might remain white. In their blindness, can they even feel Garnell Whitfield's grief for his mother? The words of Senator Cruz suggest not.

In the end, American history stains us all—even those who believe that this past of chains, rope, and fire has nothing to do with them—with a willful blindness to escape the pangs of guilt and responsibility. It is not enough, then, to remember Douglass's speech in 1852. It is not enough to recall the tumultuous decade in the run-up to the Civil War, or the violence that attends Black people's demands to be free. We must confront that past, accept it, and take the responsibility to grab hold of its lessons so that we might understand more fully the darkness out of which a Patrick Gendron comes, and glimpse what it will take for us to be better people.

We are often told that the struggle within the American story is one between better and lesser angels. This is a fight, at least for the Christian, that each of us must experience because of the debacle in the Garden of Eden. To be sure, original sin stains American madness—but it does not exhaust it. The true battle grows out of our repeated refusals to discover who we can be, to prefer illusion and fantasy over acceptance and responsibility. Whether we admit it or not during the celebrations of the 250th anniversary of the nation, race rests at the center of the strange melancholy that haunts America, U.S.A. Douglass gestured to this when he asked the hard question, "What to the Slave Is the Fourth of July?" We know this strange melancholy intimately as we ask the question today, "What is the Fourth of July to us?" The horrible reptile still nurses at the breast of an aging Republic.

poco string.
pp
poco allarg.

CHAPTER THREE

1876: CENTENNIAL

On the 100th anniversary of the nation, Americans groped for a sense of themselves against the backdrop of a searing drama that involved white people and the "Negroes" they created. What kind of country would emerge from the ashes of war? In *Democratic Vistas,* Walt Whitman lamented that America had become a nation bustling with the energy of commerce, "endowed with a vast and more and more appointed body, [but] with little or no soul." And then there was the burning moral question about the humanity of Black people and what to do with them. The question was set aside, or at least framed by lies about who Black people were and, by extension, lies about who white Americans imagined themselves to be. The centennial celebration reached for a unified vision of the nation even as the embers of sectional strife burned hot, and that vision required the erasure of Black people.

In Vicksburg, then the largest city in Mississippi, a group of Black Republicans gathered to celebrate the Fourth of July, 1874. They had come together to commemorate not "Independence Day" but the fall of Vicksburg eleven years ago to the day, when, after a bloody forty-seven-day siege, General John C. Pemberton surrendered to General Ulysses S. Grant. For those gathered to celebrate, not only did the Fourth of July mark the defeat of Confederate troops in Vicksburg and the beginning of the end of the Civil War, it was also a day of jubilee, ostensibly a day representing the beginning of the end of the scourge of slavery.

For many whites in Vicksburg, this Fourth of July gathering was an obvious provocation. Not only had Black people forgotten their place with the public display of their so-called freedom; they were now threatening "Negro rule" as some sought public office.

Throughout the South, white Democrats had begun to reassert their dominance in the political arena, and they did so with stunning violence. On Easter Sunday, 1873, in Colfax, Louisiana, Christopher Columbus Nash, a white Democrat and former sheriff of Grant Parish, led a violent coup. Several hundred white men armed with rifles and a small cannon opened fire on the courthouse where Black Republicans had claimed their governing authority after being duly elected. The courthouse caught fire, and even as the Black men showed the white flag of surrender, they were butchered by the mob. Colonel James Longstreet, the former Confederate general who was now the commander of the Metropolitan Police in New Orleans, dispatched Colonel T. W. DeKlyne to Colfax to restore order. He "found heaps of dead black bodies scavenged by dogs and buzzards."

> We were unable to find the body of a single white. . . . Many blacks were shot in the back at the head and neck; one man still lay with his hands clasped in supplication; the face of another was completely flattened by blows from a gun, the broken stock of a double barreled shotgun being on the ground near him; another had been cut across the stomach with a knife after being shot; and almost all had from three to a dozen wounds. Many of them had their brains literally blown out.

One hundred and fifty Black people had been killed. About a week after the carnage, Captain Jacob Smith of the U.S. Army, with a hundred men under his command, arrived in Colfax and arrested eight of the perpetrators, all of whom would be charged under the Enforcement Acts of 1870 and 1871, laws designed to protect the rights of African Americans from the extralegal violence of groups like the Ku Klux Klan.

But the national environment had changed dramatically in the year between the Colfax massacre and the Fourth of July celebration in Vicksburg. The Panic of 1873 sent the country spiraling as speculation and the nation's railroad companies faltered, leaving the U.S. economy in tatters. The impact of the depression, which consisted of sixty-five months of economic contraction, shattered the older ideal that all labor should be respected equally and the Victorian fantasy of inevitable progress. Cutthroat capitalism devastated workers as widespread unemployment overran hopes and dreams among everyday people. Deep class divisions emerged as business interests rallied against labor—going as far as to characterize labor leaders as "enemies of society." The pride in free labor, invoked to challenge chattel slavery just a decade earlier, now lay in ruins.

The midterm elections in autumn of 1874 resulted in a landslide for Democrats. The party picked up ninety-three seats, which gave them, for the first time since the eve of the Civil War, the majority in the House of Representatives. It was their version of a "red wave." To be sure, the state of the economy—with crop and land prices collapsing, the stock market crash, and the panic surrounding the credit system, government corruption, workers out of jobs, and labor unrest—affected the election outcomes, but the escalation of racial violence in the South and "white fatigue" throughout the country also helped sweep the Republicans out of office. Just nine years after the surrender at Appomattox, the nation had grown weary of the aims of Reconstruction. Half of the House committee chairmanships were now in the hands of Southerners. It seemed that Black people's demands for freedom and full citizenship had gone on too long and the political costs were too high.

Figures like Horace Greeley, the founder of the *New-York Tribune* and once a radical Republican, clamored for bridging the divide between Southern and Northern political factions by embracing a more "moderate" position regarding the equal rights of African Americans. With the ratification of the Fifteenth Amendment in 1870, which gave Black men the vote, many who identified as anti-slavery advocates now thought their task done. *The New York Herald* would declare, in October 1874, upon the death of Gerrit Smith, the famed abolitionist who supported John Brown, that the "era of moral politics" had come to an end. With Colfax and Vicksburg, sentimentality had given way to brutal rage.

Those whom Frederick Douglass called the "apostles of forgetfulness" weaved a story of the nation that affirmed its unique mission in the world as white Southerners killed Black people indiscriminately. Lies would become "a kind of superior truth" that served as a ballast for America, U.S.A. Black people demanding full equality could not intrude or interrupt the fantasy. Neither could their slaughter. To do so was to threaten a sense of national identity as fragile as a butterfly's wing.

As men, women, and children gathered in Vicksburg to celebrate the Fourth of July in 1874, a group of white men on horseback attacked the crowd. As they began shooting, people scattered, screaming in panic. Imagine the horror in the children's eyes as mothers and fathers fell dead right in front of them. Whites rampaged as if the sight of blood intensified their frenzy. The county sheriff, Peter Crosby, a Black man, was helpless in the face of the escalating violence. He sent a letter to Lieutenant Governor A. K. Davis, who wrote to President Grant. "Armed bodies of men are parading the streets both night and day, the city authorities are utterly unable to protect the lives and property of the citizens," Davis wrote. "Regretting the necessity—I am constrained to ask that two companies of United States troops be at once ordered to Vicksburg to ensure the citizens against the domestic violence which is imminent. Please answer it at once."

President Grant refused. Accused of using the weight of federal power to determine the electoral outcomes in a state, he had taken a political beating for his intervention in the Colfax, Louisiana, massacre. He was hesitant to make a similar call now. The violence in Vicksburg soon took an even darker turn. Mississippi governor Adelbert Ames worried about the consequences of Grant's decision in a letter to his wife: "I have tried to get troops, but the President refuses. It is thought he wants the support of the Southern Democrats for a third term. Most true it is that they are generally for him in this state. And they in Vicksburg who are rioting, who are ready for murder and frauds, laud him to the skies." Political expediency fueled the carnage.

Municipal elections in Vicksburg were scheduled for August, and Republicans put forward a ticket that consisted of white and Black men. This angered many local whites, some of whom believed the false rumor that Blacks were preparing "to slaughter whites on the August election day." The fear of revenge intensified the political scene. The city was on a knife's edge, with many whites on the verge of a violent uprising—a response to the insult of Black people's freedom. One observer noted that for weeks armed whites patrolled the streets by day and by night. They stood with their weapons as citizens registered to vote. They aimed to instill fear and to terrorize those who dared support Black voters and the Republican Party. In every way, white Vicksburg prepared for more violence. Democracy itself would soon be its victim, along with the 350 or so Black people murdered throughout the state by the fall of 1874.

By December 5, armed members of the Taxpayers' League—who criticized what they believed to be the excessive taxation and corruption used to fund Reconstruction policies (fiscal conservativism was a ruse to hide their disdain of Black enfranchisement)—had seized the Warren County courthouse and taken control of local government. Black militias and white militias clashed. As Blacks began to retreat, the violence intensified. The idea that these former slaves dared to defend themselves and their freedom sent the mob into a mindless rage. White Mississippians murdered indiscriminately. That day, at least twenty-one Black people were killed and two wounded. The violence continued into the next year, as white vigilante mobs attacked Black voters in key counties throughout the state. Democrats with their "Mississippi Plan"—the use of violence and intimidation to suppress Black voters—effectively overthrew the government as Governor Ames resigned and left the state. By 1876, white Democrats in Mississippi controlled every branch of state government.

President Grant's decision not to send troops in response to the Fourth of July assault had given white Vicksburg the license to kill and the freedom to engage in a coup. Grant put the point blithely: "The whole public are tired out with these annual autumnal outbreaks in the South, and . . . are ready now to condemn any interference on the part of the Government."

The continued racial violence in the South, even though it was directed mainly at Black citizens, soured many white Northerners on the idea of Black civil rights. Not only did Walt Whitman in 1874 balk at Black people voting, likening them to baboons, but many whites in the

North expressed their disdain for the federal government's continued effort to address the condition of former slaves. Some saw it as a misuse of federal power and an infringement on the civil rights of *all* Americans. E. L. Godkin, the editor of *The Nation,* loathed what he took to be the constitutional overreach of Pennsylvania Representative Thaddeus Stevens, chair of the Ways and Means Committee in the House, and that of Radical Reconstruction. Godkin embraced "classical financial liberalism: laissez-faire government, free trade, and the gold standard as moral principles." The matter of the status of Black people would be left to the states. Godkin joined with a chorus of other "liberal Republicans," writing, "Reconstruction seems to be morally a more disastrous process than rebellion" in that its aims would trample upon the individual rights of white Americans and upend the basic freedoms of liberalism itself. For these men, Radical Reconstruction had pushed too far. Others held the view that Black people lacked the intelligence to bear the responsibility of citizenship. Their prejudices were captured by books like James Shepherd Pike's *The Prostrate State: South Carolina Under Negro Government.* "Sambo takes naturally to stealing," wrote Pike. "Seven years ago these men were raising corn and cotton under the whip of the overseer. Today they are raising points of order and questions of privilege."

Pike was a journalist who, like Whitman, had railed against slavery and yet held noxious views about Black people. Reporting for the *New-York Tribune,* he detailed in a series of articles what he took to be massive political corruption in South Carolina under the control of Black legislators. These men, he believed, betrayed an innate inferiority and lacked the capacity not only to govern but to accept the burdens and responsibilities of citizenship. South Carolina, he wrote, using language similar to Whitman's, suffered under the rule of "a mass of black barbarism . . . the most ignorant democracy that mankind ever saw." Pike's conclusion would be echoed in the pages of *The Atlantic Monthly* and *Harper's,* where writers claimed that genuine transformation in the South could not happen until the failed policies of Reconstruction were tossed in the trash bin and Black people relegated to their proper place.

President Grant understood the danger of the waning support for Reconstruction as he read letters pleading for help from across the South.

The region was emboldened by those who insisted "that there . . . be no further interference on the part of the general government to protect citizens within a state where the state authorities fail to give protection." Such a retreat, Grant warned, meant the practical re-enslavement of Black people in the defeated Confederacy. "Under existing conditions," he wrote in a draft of his annual message in December 1874, as whites in Vicksburg rampaged, "the Negro votes the republican ticket because he knows his friends are of that party. Many a good citizen votes the opposite, not because [he] agrees with the great principles of state which separate party, but because, generally, he is opposed to Negro rule. This is a most delusive cry. Treat the negro as a citizen and a voter—as he is, and must remain—and soon parties will be divided, *not on the color-line,* but on principle" [emphasis added]. But Grant's warning fell on deaf ears.

No matter the desperate pleas from Black people across the South subject to the resurgent violence of vengeful whites, the country wanted to put the issue of slavery *and* Black people behind them. *The Nation*'s Godkin had declared as early as March 1872, "Reconstruction and slavery we have done with." Too much white blood had been spilled in war over this issue. Given that reality, as Frederick Douglass declared, the substance of Black people's freedom was cast aside from "the hour that the loyal North . . . began to shake hands over the bloody chasm." This would be a blood-drenched peace.

Southern congressmen, now in the majority, blocked the Justice Department's enforcement of laws aimed to protect American citizens from extralegal violence. The Supreme Court prepared itself to shut the door on the promises of Reconstruction. The Court's 1876 decision in *United States v. Cruikshank,* for example, gave license to the racial violence in the former Confederacy, setting free the men convicted in the brutal Colfax massacre; and the *Slaughter-House Cases* in 1873, which ruled that private violence was not the government's responsibility to litigate, effectively narrowed the scope of the Fourteenth Amendment. In addition, the cultural assumptions about Black people's character and capacities, revealed in the words of Pike and others, were fast becoming a justification for their violent subordination. Stereotypes and prejudices blinded white America to the horrors and cruelty of its racism, and of what was happening in places like Colfax and Vicksburg. Black folk were lazy, unintelligent, morally suspect, and prone to violence. While for some the rebellious South remained a concern, the problem was not the country. *Black people were the problem.* And with this shift in emphasis, America's goodness remained intact and its innocence assured as white America retracted its gift of freedom. Willful ignorance and lies made it so.

—

As violence choked the life out of Reconstruction, America, U.S.A., readied itself for its centennial celebration in 1876. Freedom belonged to white America, still. The country reconciled the ideals of democracy with its insistence on the superiority of white people. In spite of the blood spilled on many battlefields, the double consciousness remained. No matter the region of your birth, if you were white, the centennial celebration declared, the country and its promise belonged to you.

Some twenty years later, in his Harvard dissertation, "The Suppression of the African Slave-Trade," W. E. B. Du Bois captured the central problem that haunted this moment and its troubling implication for our own. "Each generation sought to shift its load upon the next," he wrote,

> and the burden rolled on, until a generation came which was both too weak and too strong to bear it longer. One cannot, to be sure, demand of whole nations exceptional moral foresight and heroism; but a certain hard common-sense in facing the complicated phenomena of political life must be expected in every progressive people. In some respects we as a nation seem to lack this; we have the somewhat inchoate idea that we are not destined to be harassed with great social questions, and that even if we are, and fail to answer them, the fault is with the question and not with us. *Consequently we often congratulate ourselves more on getting rid of a problem than on solving it* [emphasis added].

This delusion of ridding ourselves of the problem is the beating heart of American exceptionalism. After the catastrophe of the Civil War, some twelve years of effort to rebuild the Union, and unfulfilled attempts to address the role and place of the formerly enslaved, the country decided to engage in one of the most remarkable moments of disremembering in its history. It would use the 100th anniversary of its founding as the occasion to do so. Slavery would be put aside. Black people—the problem people—were ignored or brutally discarded, and the greatness of the American project was celebrated in the full light of its material successes. Evidence of the bounty of God's promise could be seen throughout the land, while the nation convulsed with unimaginable racial violence.

Black people still demanded full freedom, and they fought to hold on to the modicum of gains acquired during Reconstruction. That effort forced America to imagine itself apart from the split that had thrown the country into a brutal war. But as ever it does, sentimentality gave way to white rage. And that rage, as evidenced in the Mississippi Plan, sought to rid the region, and the nation, of the problem by putting Black people in their proper place, whether six feet underground or dangling from a white oak tree. Du Bois noted the country's refusal to grapple honestly with the divisions that splintered its self-understanding. He called out the readiness of Americans to pat themselves on the back after tinkering around the edges of the race problem, and the country's unwillingness, no matter the consequences, to relinquish the idea that white people mattered more simply because they were white. In this moment of Reconstruction's death, mirrors shattered. America, U.S.A., loathed to see the image of its monstrous ways unchanged. So the country raged until the storybook version of itself took hold once again—that efficient means of forgetting, secured by words about American greatness "mostly used to cover the sleeper, not to wake him."

Frederick Douglass had warned of this in 1870, complaining that the American people were "destitute of political memory," urging the nation not to forget the meaning of the war. His was a desperate plea as the violence swelled and Black bodies piled up. Some believed that the problem of the ex-slave had been resolved with the passage of the Fifteenth Amendment. Nothing further was necessary. But Du Bois was right as he reflected on the legacy of Reconstruction in *The Souls of Black Folk:* not a single Southern legislature was prepared to recognize the citizenship rights of Black people. "There was scarcely a white man in the South who did not honestly regard Emancipation as a crime, and its practical nullification as a duty." Even President Grant told his cabinet that the Fifteenth Amendment "had done the Negro no good." The Civil War may have ended with Black male suffrage, but that end—and history corroborates the claim—marked the intensification of a race feud.

The Nation celebrated the death of Reconstruction and declared that the "negro will disappear from the field of national politics. Henceforth, the nation as a nation, will have nothing more to do with him." Black people would be banished, made invisible. They would not be imagined as Americans but, rather, as problems that America had to address: either wards, victims, or mindless creatures destined to toil.

I am not suggesting here that the Jim Crow South emerged fully grown immediately after the collapse of Reconstruction like Athena out of Zeus's head. But what was present, from the founding of the country, was the idea of "the white American," this sense of white racial superiority and hierarchy, that became the basis for reunion and redemption; and that idea required the subordination of its "niggers." In the country's centennial year, Black people would be erased from any central role in the story of the nation. Even though Black people stood as the fundamental contrast that consolidated the very idea of the white American like the gold that gave money its meaning. Black folk were at the bottom of the well, far beneath white people—the measure of how far not to fall.

To be seen as a problem, to be approached as an object of charity, and to be managed by the state—this made of Black people empty vessels to be filled with the musings and terrors of those who lived among them but who did not really see or know them. And when the actual lives of Black people intruded upon the fantasies of white America—when the demands to be treated as human beings exposed the lies at the heart of the nation—the response, again, shifted from sentimentality to rage, one easily becoming the other. The whip of the whirlwind.

—

In the summer of 1875, Frederick Douglass delivered a Fourth of July address to a large gathering of Black people in the Hillsdale section of Anacostia in Washington, D.C. It was, appropriately, July 5, and given the racial violence engulfing the nation, America's celebration of freedom and independence rang hollow. Just as they did in Vicksburg, a crowd of Black men, women, and children gathered outside to enjoy family, eat good food, and listen to speeches. A twenty-five-member children's choir performed patriotic songs. John Mercer Langston, an educator and founding dean of Howard University Law School, offered words of encouragement as he urged those in attendance to close ranks and to understand the power and purpose of Black institutions. It was an important message given the heavily Democratic election results of 1874 and the violence rampaging throughout the South.

Douglass recognized the darkness of the days. He had experienced the cruelty of slavery, thought seriously about joining John Brown at Harpers Ferry, and witnessed the joy of jubilee as the Civil War ended slavery and as Reconstruction promised to build a multiracial democracy. Yet the excitement of his words at Cooper Institute in 1863 in response to the Emancipation Proclamation—that "we are all liberated"—tasted bitter on his tongue just a decade later. He knew of the horrors in Colfax and Vicksburg, of the brutal murders in Sumter County, Alabama, and the "perfect reign of terror" in Barbour County. He saw how so many white Americans in the North turned their heads away from it all. Now, as the nation prepared to celebrate its centennial, he would speak to a long-suffering people whose hopes for freedom were being snatched away.

One wonders what went through Douglass's mind as he put pen to pad. Depression. Sadness. Anger. He was struggling in his personal life. As his biographer David Blight notes, by 1875, Douglass felt adrift and angry. Resources had dried up. Without a job, or his newspaper to edit and comment in on the state of the nation, he "observed with fear the unraveling of Reconstruction from under the feet of his people." Douglass's life mirrored the lurching back and forth of America, U.S.A. He bore the brunt of the nation's hubris: the belief that somehow this place was a beacon of freedom even as it wallowed in the sins of slavery and racism.

His words that day called attention to the tragic implication of that contradiction, and its consequences: the repeated failures and betrayals, the empty gestures, and the insistence that Black people know their place. Burnt flesh and bodies riddled with bullets reminded him of who and what this country was, no matter what he imagined it could be. By 1875, the reality of dashed hopes shadowed Douglass's speeches. He was trapped, like we all are, in America's tragic choice.

With the centennial a year off, Douglass watched as the country engaged in that distinctive American ritual by which its people relieved themselves of accountability for past and present deeds. An open-ended future, they proclaimed. Unbounded possibility evidenced in what Whitman called the "magician's serpent" of moneymaking. This was the Gilded Age that Mark Twain skewered. The bounty of the frontier and the genius of our technological advance. Native peoples were savages to be tamed or eradicated. The past mattered little here.

Douglass listened as those he considered friends, now exhausted by their charity, asked the familiar question, "What else might the Negro want?" William Lloyd Garrison resigned as president of the American Anti-Slavery Society after the ratification of the Thirteenth Amendment. Harriet Beecher Stowe sidestepped the question of Black voting rights. Susan B. Anthony declared that white women were more deserving of voting rights than Black men. The New England Freedmen's Aid Society disbanded in the same year that Vicksburg erupted. The American Missionary Association (AMA), the first freedmen's aid society, founded in 1846, went as far as "pronouncing black suffrage a failure and the freedmen ungrateful for the organization's many efforts on their behalf." The problem of Black people, or what the AMA described as "the alienation between the North and the South, growing out of slavery," now represented for AMA's leadership the greatest danger to America.

As those who had rebelled and lost used violence to regain control of the South, many of Douglass's so-called white liberal friends now sought some kind of reconciliation. Disremembering justified their capitulation to the violence. The purposeful forgetting of the reasons for the war and the need for Reconstruction allowed them to blot out what the past revealed. Douglass understood that this disremembering made space for reunion between Americans from the North and South struggling with a sense of national identity in the aftermath of a war that had baptized the country in blood. But in the disremembering, Black people were cast aside and made the repositories of our national fears of the dark. Such a partition allowed for white Americans a retreat into the comfort of illusions—the storybook that affirmed the goodness of the country despite the evils right under our noses.

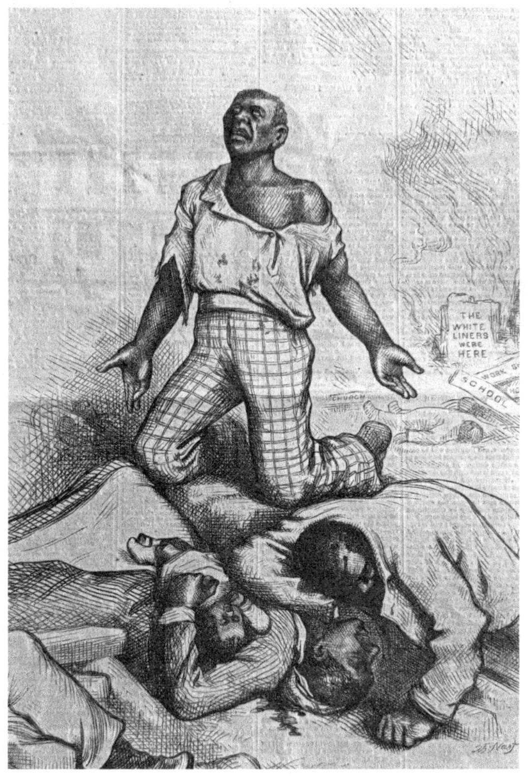

As Douglass spoke on that July day in 1875, he bore witness, again, to the country's refusal to live up to its creed. He confronted, again, the hard reality of America, U.S.A. And, as the preeminent leader of Black America, he offered words, again, to keep his people from succumbing to a bitterness that would make it easier to give up altogether.

I suspect he had to temper his rage. His people were victims of freedom-snatching. And in this moment, after all he had seen and experienced, white people still believed that freedom was their gift to give and to take away. I cannot help but think of Moses Gordon, manumitted by Quakers in North Carolina and re-enslaved. He stole his freedom and built a life in Philadelphia, only to be pursued, imprisoned, and enslaved again. Douglass was speaking some eighty years later. Slavery was no more. The Civil War amendments had been ratified. That much was true. But the fever dream had spiked again, and Black people were subject to unimaginable violence as the nation turned its back and prepared to celebrate its freedom. Douglass had to refute and refuse the illusion.

He reached for words to encourage a different kind of refusal than the one Moses Gordon chose. We could not abdicate our responsibility to one another, no matter how much white Americans in the South raged or how passively others stood by and let them do it. He reached for the Revolution of 1776, not to celebrate or glorify its heroes, but to call out an analog to what Black people now faced as the country prepared a centennial celebration that would cast aside any pretense to racial justice:

> The fathers of this Republic, as I have said, had their trial ninety-nine years ago. The colored citizens of this Republic are about to have their trial now. How we shall stand that trial, how we shall pass through it, how we shall come out of it, is to me a matter of great solemnity. The men of the Revolution went through the furnace, and came out pure gold. Shall we, the colored people, present a similar example?

The answer required an honest and unflinching account of how Black people and the country arrived at this crossroads where the devil lay in wait. On this July 5, Douglass was concerned about the fate of Black people in the face of white America's violent betrayal.

He told the crowd that their freedom had been, in many ways, the result of a quarrel between white men. That fortune had smiled upon them and "favored us with a liberal hand." Matters could have easily been otherwise had the South won. "We are the creatures of a conflict of social elements which we did but little to create," he said. "The white people of this country quarreled and came to blows, and it was our lot to be on the side of the victorious party." But in 1875 the winds had shifted, and those who once fought so violently against one another now sought reconciliation. "Men cannot, ought not and will not quarrel and fight forever," said Douglass.

> . . . So sure as the stars shine in the heavens, and the rivers run to the sea, so sure will the white people North and South abandon their quarrel and become friends. The whole American horizon is already fringed with the portents of this coming union. Boston, Lexington and Bunker Hill have already sent forth their silvery notes of peace and unity to the whole nation, and next year Philadelphia, the birthplace of the Declaration of Independence, will lift to the sky its million voices in one grand Centennial hosannah of peace and good will to all the white race of this country.

He understood what was happening: the centennial celebrations would tell a story of the nation that rejoiced in reunion, and that reunion required the erasure of Black people. The event would be a national affair in which the "silvery notes of peace and unity" from sacred places in our national history would render the true cause of the Civil War invisible in a national ritual of disremembering. The country would revel in its technological advancements, as capitalists celebrated America's economic resolve despite the Panic of 1873, and as white people reasserted the superiority of white Anglo-Saxon blood. An idea of America, alabaster white, would rise from the ashes of war and Reconstruction.

To foretell this national consensus was not to deny the stark divisions that continued to confound a robust sense of American national identity. Regional differences continued to cast a dark shadow over the country's politics. Bitterness between Republicans and Democrats remained. With over 600,000 dead, how could it be otherwise? Any idea of American identity was refracted through regional experiences and culture, and carried with it the uncertainty of national belonging and obligation. Despite the success of the Democrats in the 1874 elections, South Carolina, Florida, and Louisiana were still occupied by federal troops in 1876. Deep suspicions remained. There were even serious doubts among some Americans about the wisdom of efforts to organize the centennial celebration.

Massive unemployment, government corruption, and the unbridled greed of business interests led some to believe that Americans had little use for "an overgrown and spread-eagle Fourth of July."

Profound contradictions threatened American democracy during this period. As William James put it, that "bitch-goddess Success" overwhelmed all other values. This obsession with prosperity resulted in what James described as a kind of "moral flabbiness," a condition that seems rampant today. But when it came to matters of white men, as Douglas knew, race stained everything. What emerged from the Gilded Age, even with its labor unrest and class divisions, was an idea of the white American that helped bridge the bloody divide between North and South. This idea shaped how the country would face the rest of the world, and how many Americans would come to understand themselves.

The white American was the inheritor of the grandness of the West—the most democratic expression of white civilization—and was, as such, the possessor of freedom. One can see the implication of this view at work in the violent subordination of Black people throughout the South and in the relative silence among those in the North who witnessed it. Most white Americans agreed, despite the horrors of war, that their race was superior and that white Americans expressed that superiority in the most compelling of ways. Their men were naturally disposed to be the leaders of this country, only to find themselves penned in by the "niggers" in their midst—turned against each other because of them. The Scottish intellectual Thomas Carlyle described the predicament from across the Atlantic in *Shooting Niagara: And After?*

> To me individually the Nigger's case was not the most pressing in the world, but among the least so! America, however, had got into *Swarmery* upon it . . . and felt that in the Heavens or the Earth there was nothing so godlike, or incomparably pressing to be done. . . . Half a million . . . of excellent White men, full of gifts and faculty, have torn and slashed one another into horrid death, in a temporary humour, which will leave centuries of remembrance fierce enough: and three million absurd Blacks, men and brothers (of a sort), are completely "emancipated"; launched into

> the career of improvement—likely to be "improved off the face of the earth" in a generation or two!

The emerging consensus among white Americans to which Douglass referred was not based on an idea of justice and equality but arose "out of the relation of slavery, a peace that may be seen and felt in a prison . . . a peace where the heels of one class are on the necks of another." The process of reconciliation between the North and South meant that America, U.S.A., no matter the lingering wounds and divisions, had to be decidedly white. That agreed-upon racial hierarchy, with white people as the superior race, would be the great equalizer, overcoming the particular differences of region, religion, and culture—especially in relation to the "absurd Blacks" who had brought them to the brink of destruction.

As such, Douglass maintained, the political reality of Black life had changed and was continuing to change. White America, especially in the South, had made its choice, and Black people now faced the storm. "When this mighty quarrel has ceased," he told the crowd,

> when all the asperities and resentments have gone as they are sure to go, when all the clouds that a few years ago lowered about our national house, shall be in the deep bosom of the ocean buried, when this great white race has renewed its patriotism and flowed back into its accustomed channels, the question for us is: in what position will this stupendous reconciliation leave the colored people? What tendencies will spring out of it, and how will they affect us? If war among whites brought peace and liberty to the blacks, *what will peace among the whites bring?* . . . These questions, my friends, make me thoughtful. The signs of the times are not all in our favor. There are, even in the Republican party, indications to get rid of us [emphasis added].

Douglass was clear: "Peace among the whites" meant horrors *for us.* Politically, culturally, and existentially. This was not an abstract conclusion. The violence in the South, the active indifference to that violence in the North, and the dead bodies left in the wake made it real.

Black people would have to stake their claim on this country, if they so chose, by claiming possession of the very documents that brought the country into existence. The Constitution and the Declaration of Independence did not declare that freedom belonged to white people, but to *the* people. But that claim of possession by Black people would not be naïve, as if the founders' racism weren't clear. It would happen in the full light of the history of the country and an awful state of affairs where "a disposition is seen to shake off the negro and accept the old master's class."

On the 99th anniversary of the nation, Douglass cried out for Black people to trust themselves, to build institutions that would sustain their interests, and to free themselves from the charity of others. White people might rage, but Black people were still responsible for their own freedom. They must claim it for themselves. Justice was not a charitable enterprise, he insisted. Black people ought not be reduced to objects of philanthropy and expected to show gratitude for something that should be naturally theirs. Instead, with a bold riff on the opening paragraphs of the Declaration of Independence, Douglass once again used the occasion of July 5—the day that historically called attention to America's double consciousness—to declare Black independence from "the swarm of white beggars that sweep the country in the name of the colored race." He could no longer tolerate the hypocrisy of white liberals and of those who filled their pockets or assuaged their consciences on the backs of Black people.

Douglass was angry. Who could blame him? The so-called friends of Blacks now seemed to believe, like former slave masters, that Black people were not worth the cost. They preferred the price of their ticket, and that meant being white without the burden of guilt. Or they simply made money in the name of justice for all:

> In our judgment we have been injured more than benefited by the efforts of so-called benevolent societies. While they may have helped a few, they have injured the many. They originate with and are organized by some good men, but they invariably fall into the hands of a peculiar class of men—men who combine shrewdness with religious zeal, and who whether they sing, pray or preach,

> always "mean business." They are ever on the lookout for just such associations as special colonization societies, African civilization societies, African educational societies, Lincoln and Howard universities, and freedmen's banks. They follow these with a scent as keen as the shark's, which in old times followed the slave ship to eat the flesh of dead and dying negroes.

I can't help but think Douglass had in mind the American Missionary Association, which was actively accommodating itself to the white South. His call for Black self-reliance as Reconstruction collapsed acknowledged the sour smell of changing winds. He rejected the paternalism of white liberals, declaring that "we are no longer slaves, but freemen; no longer subjects, but citizens, and have a voice and vote with all other citizens. . . . We must not beg men to do for us what we ought to do for ourselves."

On this day of celebration, Douglass claimed possession of the opening lines of the Declaration of Independence not on behalf of the nation, but on behalf of the people who suffered from its failings. And, in doing so, perhaps he offered the country a different path forward as the nation barreled toward an idea of itself that would read FOR WHITES ONLY.

The July 5, 1875, speech drew a lot of attention from the press. Democrats grabbed hold of his idea of Black self-reliance and used it to criticize the remaining policies of Reconstruction, laughing over the prospect of "the colored people's desertion of the Republican party." Others believed that Douglass was urging Black people to reject the goodwill of so-called friends of the Negro. Douglass understood the rhetorical bind: to tell the truth about what was happening to us would only bring about more harm, because of what it revealed about them. Douglass rejected this restraint outright. He spoke the truth no matter what the press said, demanding justice rather than alms.

The nation still refused. Alms were offered instead. Violence policed it all. Reunion required affirming the superiority of white people, a ritual fantasy that would be handed down to future generations. The upcoming Centennial Exposition would be the first major occasion to posit a sense of national identity in the shadow of the war, and that identity required that Black America be hidden from view.

—

On May 10, 1876, the opening day of the Centennial Exposition in Fairmount Park in Philadelphia, just a few miles from the hall where white men denied the first Black petitions to Congress, a crowd of over 186,000 people gathered to hear President Grant speak. This was to be a celebration of American genius, of "our own and foreign skill and progress in manufactures, agriculture, art, science and civilization." Prefaced by Richard Wagner's "Centennial Inauguration March," President Grant spoke quietly about the grandeur of the American project. We were no longer the child in relation to the "older and more advanced nations" across the ocean. Americans had finally answered Ralph Waldo Emerson's call in "The American Scholar." "We have listened too long to the courtly muses of Europe," Emerson declared in 1837. "We will walk on our own feet; we will work with our own hands; we will speak with our own minds." The Centennial Exposition was an homage to the "Progress of the Age." New values were supplanting old ones. With the horrors of civil war behind them, Americans could now revel in unfettered possibility. At least, that's what the organizers hoped to convey.

Frederick Douglass sat among the dignitaries on the main platform as President Grant spoke. He almost didn't make it. As the crowd had gathered outside the gates before the exhibition opened, important guests passed through to the cheers and chants of those who recognized them. But the gray-haired Douglass found himself on the outside crushed among the throngs of people waiting to enter. The Philadelphia police refused to admit him. They did not believe that "a nigger" would be allowed among this august body for this special occasion. Douglass argued in vain, showing his ticket of admission to the platform dais. The police still refused. A *New York Herald* correspondent reported, "It was feared he might have gone out with the crushed and fainting, if Senator Conkling had not seen him, and vouching for his right to be present, enabled him to pass the line."

But Douglass's presence on the platform at the opening of the exposition was mere window dressing. The greatest orator in the nation was to be seen and not heard on this day. He sat silently as the nation celebrated its beginnings and its coming-of-age.

Over the next six months, nearly ten million Americans would visit the exposition. They marveled at new inventions like the telephone and typewriter. They stood amazed at the seven-hundred-ton Corliss steam engine, which signified the emerging power of America. It was clear, at least to the organizers of the exposition, that American ingenuity and technological prowess would usher in a new age of material prosperity for the young nation and situate the country as a leader among the nations of the world.

Of course, such boastfulness ignored the hard realities that gripped Americans. People were struggling in the country, and political corruption had diminished trust in government. Native peoples were imagined as harmless "primitives" in contrast to white civilization—even as word of the startling defeat of General Custer by Native Americans reached Philadelphia. Women were relegated to the margins as the hard work of machines contrasted with the genteel demands of the domestic sphere. And Black people were basically invisible or seen as servants.

When they were seen, they were not looked kindly upon. Reviewing the Centennial Exposition, William Dean Howells wrote in *The Atlantic Monthly* that "the bronze statue of Emancipation (I suppose), a most offensively Frenchy negro, who has broken his chain, and spreading both his arms and legs abroad is rioting in a declamation of something (I should say) from Victor Hugo; one longs to clap him back into hopeless bondage." He mentioned the exhibit of Cleopatra "fanned by a black slave." He described a civil and intelligent tour led by "another, black," of the Mississippi home, which was "wholly built of Mississippi woods." And he raved about the food in the Southern Restaurant "served by lustrous citizens of color." Howells made no mention of the collapse of Reconstruction or of what was happening throughout the South. He gave no consideration to the place of Black people in the very idea of America. Despite the glaring absence, or perhaps because of it, Howells declared that "no one can now see the fair without a thrill of patriotic pride."

In fact, the relative absence of Black participation in the 1876 Centennial celebration and the paucity of exhibits about Black life spoke volumes about how the organizers imagined the nation's past, present, and future. Many Black Americans had hoped the Centennial Exposition would occasion an opportunity to chart a different vision of the country. On the floor of the House of Representatives in May 1874, Black congressman Josiah T. Walls of Florida "argued that the Centennial would bring the nation together for the first time since the Civil War, and 'discourage and extinguish all feelings of sectionalism'" among white Americans. Walls stood among many in the Black community who believed that the Centennial also offered an opportunity to present to the nation the fullness of Black humanity. But the white organizers had a different vision.

Much of the effort on the part of Black communities throughout the country to contribute to the Centennial was ignored. Black Americans were forced, repeatedly, to confront racist views that placed them outside of the celebration. In April 1874, for example, Philadelphia police sponsored an event to help raise funds for the Centennial Exposition. Pusey A. Peer and his wife, a Black couple who lived in the city, purchased tickets, eager to support the exhibition, only to receive a devastating reply: "The policemen sponsoring the event insisted that they would not have the 'Centennial Benefit' stained by 'nigger money.'" This was one well-publicized insult among many. Black workers were actively rejected to help with the construction of the exhibits; nor were they hired to staff the celebration in any significant capacity. One Black person from Georgia who visited the exposition noted that "he could not discover among all that mass of people one single Negro in the discharge of any duty save as restaurant waiters and barbers in the hotels." Philadelphia journalist Colonel J. W. Forney called attention to the glaring absence and contradiction:

> that the great show of the American people's industry and independence will close with the one link in the chain of its complete history left out. Although the chains of slavery have been broken . . . , the prejudice against him . . . have prevented him from taking any part or having a prominent part of this marvelous un-

dertaking in celebration of one hundred years of American independence.

Pennsylvania judge William D. Kelley appealed to the exposition's commission to invite Frederick Douglass "to read the Emancipation Proclamation after the Declaration of Independence was read on the Fourth of July" and to deliver an address from the platform of Memorial Hall. Nothing came of his request. Instead, Douglass found himself called a nigger by a police officer who could not believe that a Black man would be invited to such an occasion.

—

Although the racial violence seizing the country asserted the superiority of the white American, it would take some time for the view of American national identity presented at the Centennial Exposition to become common sense. For those who aspired to be one nation, the wounds of the Civil War required constant tending. If they would not heal, the wounds would need to be at least forgotten or narrated in a broader story about reunion and redemption. This never quite happened. The war left a large amount of scar tissue in the American psyche. One region wallowed in defeat. Another thought of itself as virtuous in its victory. A president lay dead because of it all. Moreover, the effort to remedy the problem that started the war in the first place never truly materialized. Reconstruction was killed by those who rejected its aims, enabled by the moral cowardice of those who stood by as it happened. To be sure, after the war the federal government was more robust and its power more sweeping, but slavery and racism, to use the words of James W. C. Pennington, a former slave who wrote *The Fugitive Blacksmith,* "*mis*-created or *mal*-created" the men and women who survived the carnage. Slavery was no more—the Constitution now said that Black men could vote. But white America still believed themselves the sole possessors of freedom.

In the end, a terrible evasion sat at the heart of the nation's self-conception in its centennial year. All of which required—demanded, really—a willful blindness, a thinness of imagination, and a contrived innocence that made America, U.S.A., monstrous. By the count of South Carolina Congressman Robert Smalls, as the century came to a close and Jim Crow took hold of the South, 53,000 Black people had been killed because of reunion and redemption. The historian Eric Foner summarizes it this way:

> What remains certain is that Reconstruction failed, and that for blacks its failure was a disaster whose magnitude cannot be obscured by the genuine accomplishments that did endure. For the nation as a whole, the collapse of Reconstruction was a tragedy that deeply affected the course of its future development. If racism contributed to the undoing of Reconstruction, by the same token Reconstruction's demise and the emergence of blacks as a disenfranchised class of dependent laborers greatly facilitated racism's further spread, until *by the early twentieth century it had become more deeply embedded in the nation's culture and politics than at any time since the beginning of the antislavery crusade and perhaps in our entire history* [emphasis added].

On the 100th anniversary of the country, as Reconstruction struggled with its last breaths, a consolidated idea of white America, one that could overcome or at least quiet regional differences, emerged as one of the lasting features of "the second founding"—an idea of white racial superiority that would obliterate any pretense of living up to the power of the declaration that all people are created equal.

poco allarg.
f
Fatigued ♩ = 64
allarg.
pp
3
Tension; ice-cold ♩ = 80
p sub.

INTERLUDE

THE PLAGUE YEARS

The old man fell to his knees as his heart gave out. Frederick Douglass died in the front hallway of his Washington, D.C., home on February 20, 1895. From the moment Douglass stole his freedom, he never stopped working for the America he wanted, despite the broken promises of Reconstruction. As he took his last breath, a carriage was arriving to take him to a local Black church in Hillsdale, the neighborhood where he delivered his July 5 speech in 1875. Had he lived, Douglass was to offer another scathing critique of the country's betrayal—for the spirit of slavery, he believed, still defined America, U.S.A., all these years later. That spirit was evident in the Jim Crow laws sweeping across the redeemed South. One saw it in the horrific lynchings that left bodies dangling from Spanish red oaks and in the continued willingness of most white Americans, in the North and the South, to turn a blind eye. Douglass's heart quit. I imagine the country, and accumulated disappointment, broke it.

His final years, amid the dawning of Jim Crow, coincided with a harrowing and unsettling period for the nation, a time of death and birthing. Just a little over a year earlier, on January 9, 1894, at Metropolitan AME Church in Washington, D.C., Douglass had levied a biting criticism of the state of the country. His "faith in the nobility of the nation" had been shaken, and though he remained hopeful that "all will come out right in the end," he knew that "the immediate future look[ed] dark and troubled." Since the collapse of Reconstruction, violence, disenfranchisement, peonage, and a generalized disregard for the basic rights of Black people had become daily features of American life, all part of the sacrifice of "the negro" required for reunion and redemption. The historian Rayford Logan described this period in the late nineteenth and early twentieth centuries as "the nadir," the lowest point in African American history.

I have always been a bit uneasy about the use of that word. The lowest point is a matter of perspective and comparison. As the nineteenth century wound down, the horrors of slavery had not been forgotten, and Black folk, despite the nation's madness, built institutions, relentlessly pursued literacy and education, created a vibrant Black press and political organizations, and expressed creatively, with sound and word, the tragic beauty of their lives. They even created a national anthem for themselves. From this perspective, the period is hardly the lowest point in African American history.

To be sure, the hardening of the idea of "the white American," that peculiar inheritance from the second founding, unleashed unimaginable misery. Blood soaked the nation's soil. But the stench and the cries in the bowels of slave ships, those who jumped and were thrown overboard ("bone soldered by coral to bone"), the screams as babies were sold away, the last breaths taken without ever being free in a land that claimed freedom as its own—that cruelty remains the bedrock horizon. *That* was the nadir.

These, instead, were the plague years.

In 1894, as Douglass stepped to the pulpit in Metropolitan AME Church, Samuel Smith, accused of murder in Greenville, Florida, was lynched, one of 132 Black people lynched in the country that year. Douglass did not know what was happening to Smith, but the wave of terror engulfing Black communities could not be ignored. "I cannot shut my eyes to the ugly facts before me," Douglass said. Lynching had by then become a dramatic American ritual in which the bloodlust of the white mob asserted a particular idea of community and power that required the charred bones of Black victims.

The abomination shadowed Douglass's remarks. With his weakened heart and an unsteady hand, he railed against the idea that the country faced what some called "the negro problem." The phrase, Douglass argued, implied that the troubles of the nation rested with the inability of Black people to take on the burdens of citizenship. The "problem," from this point of view, was not the cruelty of slavery or white prejudice, but the consequence of innate deficiencies in Black people. A matter of blood.

Ten years earlier, Nathaniel Southgate Shaler, a professor of natural science at Harvard University who'd taught W. E. B. Du Bois, had published an essay in *The Atlantic Monthly* entitled "The Negro Problem." Shaler argued that the experiment of freeing Blacks had resulted "in even worse conditions than slavery brought them." Proximity to whites during slavery, he claimed, had improved the circumstances of Black people—they acquired certain habits of mind and the power of will lacking among "Negroes" generally. But emancipation had led only to a reversion back to what Shaler described as "their ancestral conditions"—an animal savagery. A close study by whites "into the nature of this race," he wrote, "will perceive that the *inner man* is really as singular, as different in motives from themselves, as his outward aspect indicates." Black people, in his estimation, bordered on being different *in kind* and, as such, presented a fundamental threat to the American way of life—"a danger to America greater and more insuperable than any of those that menaced the great civilized states of the world."

Shaler was not trying to justify arguments to return Black people to slavery or to incur the expense of colonizing them elsewhere. Rather, he took his project to be a *liberal* one: Black people were simply not ready to bear the responsibility of freedom. Future president Woodrow Wilson would echo the point in 1901. The emancipated were "excited by a freedom they did not understand," he argued, also in the pages of *The Atlantic Monthly*. They were "exalted by false hopes; bewildered and without leaders, and yet insolent and aggressive; sick of work, covetous of pleasure—a host of dusky children untimely put out of schools." Just as the paternalism of the slaveholding South offered this "childlike" race opportunities for improvement by way of proximity and contact with whites, it was up to white America to do the same now that these people were free, though their lives "flow in channels foreign to our own."

Shaler concluded that "if the negro is *thoughtfully cared for,* if his training in civilization, begun in slavery, is continued in his state of freedom, one may hope to find abundant room for him in our society."

Douglass vehemently disagreed with Shaler's framing. The "problem" of the Negro had little to do with us, he thundered from the pulpit in 1894. Rather, it was bound up with the deep-seated prejudices of white men and women and with their refusal to live up to the principles of the Declaration of Independence and the Constitution. In fact, if Black people dared to behave as if they were free—something the majority of white America refused to tolerate—they could be lynched. To refer to "the negro problem" was to say less about Black people but rather to assert the superiority of white Americans. *We* are not *them,* the argument went.

To call the crisis in the country "the negro problem," Douglass argued, was, in effect, to make "the negro responsible and not the nation." It set the stage for a philanthropic approach to Black people, ripe with sentimentality, where alms stood in for justice—the "negro" must be "*thoughtfully cared for.*" And, if that wasn't enough, the question of what else could be done for "the negro" led inevitably to "haven't we done enough," at which point sentimentality gave way to rage, saturated with the vindictiveness of the guilty that required ridding the nation of Black people once and for all.

Douglass was brutally honest. "The South [and, by extension, the nation] has always known how to have a dog hanged by giving him a bad name," he exclaimed.

> When it prefixed "negro" to the national problem, it knew that the device would awaken and increase a deep-seated prejudice at once, and that it would repel fair and candid investigation. As it stands, it implies that the negro is the cause of whatever trouble there is in the South. *In old slave times, when a little white child lost his temper, he was given a little whip and told to go and whip "Jim"*

> *or "Sal" and thus regained his temper. The same is true, today on a larger scale* [emphasis added].

As Douglass well knew, the problem here was not "Jim" or "Sal," but the storming adolescent—that "child" holding unfettered power over another human being. With a small detail about the cruelty of slavery, Douglass revealed the essence of a national ritual repeated across generations: Black people are made the scapegoat to calm an intemperate nation. Whenever the country feels like it is coming apart at the seams or that its diversity threatens to overwhelm everything, white America reaches for the whip.

This was 1894. With a bad heart and a lifetime of experiences with a storming, adolescent nation, Douglass seethed with righteous indignation. By the time he died in 1895, Mississippi had passed a law to disenfranchise Black people and make white supremacy legal. A year later, the Supreme Court made it the law of the land with its *Plessy v. Ferguson* decision. The effort at reunion between the North and the South after the Civil War, begun during the centennial in 1876, was now explicit. The nation had carried its sins forward. America, U.S.A., was by law a white nation.

The meaning of America as a white nation would evolve as the country grew. From the end of the nineteenth century into the first two decades of the twentieth, America, U.S.A., endured the disruption and challenges caused by demographic shifts as more than twenty million Europeans migrated to the United States. Some called this changing nation a melting pot. Others reached for hyphenated identities (e.g., German-American, Irish-American, etc.) as migrants strove to retain the traditions and customs of the Old World. Still others understood the "immigrant invasion" as a threat to America as an *Anglo-Saxon* nation. Theodore Roosevelt declared, even as he tried to hold off virulent nativism, that "there is no room for the hyphen in our citizenship," insisting that immigrants relinquish old traditions.

One thing was certain, however: Black people were at best second-class.

Law and mob violence ensured it. Academic "knowledge" justified it, as the hardening of racial divisions prompted new ideas of race masquerading as science, especially eugenics. These gave extant prejudices the authority of established fact, deepening the belief that the white race could be improved by leaving behind the more undesirable races. Popularized by books like Madison Grant's *The Passing of the Great Race: Or the Racial Basis of European History* (1916) and Lothrop Stoddard's *The Rising Tide of Color Against White World-Supremacy* (1920), these ideas stoked fears that inferior races threatened the extinction of white people. Stoddard made the stakes clear:

> Finally perish! That is the exact alternative which confronts the white race. For white civilization is to-day conterminous with the white race. . . . If white civilization goes down, the white race is irretrievably ruined. It will be swamped by the triumphant colored races, who will obliterate the white man by elimination or absorption. What has taken place in Central Asia, once a white and now a brown or yellow land, will take place in Australasia, Europe, and America. Not to-day, nor yet to-morrow; perhaps not for generations; but surely in the end. If the present drift be not changed, we whites are all ultimately doomed. Unless we set our house in order, the doom will sooner or later overtake us all.

Such fears had led to the rebirth in 1915 of the Ku Klux Klan, which gave voice to a sense of American identity threatened by "internal enemies" who were Black, Catholic, Jewish, immigrant, communist, and in their eyes, morally corrupt. The slogan "100 Percent Americanism"—a country made up of white, native-born men and women dedicated to preserving the institutions, principles, and traditions of America—became a clarion call for many who felt the country slipping away from their fingers.

African Americans fought back. They founded organizations like the National Association of Colored Women's Clubs (NACWC), the National Urban League, and the National Association of Teachers in Colored Schools (NATCS). Some embraced socialism and communism. Others took up the arts and declared the birth of "the New Negro." Marcus Garvey, who founded the Universal Negro Improvement Association (what would become the largest mass movement in Black American history), made his way to the United States from Jamaica in search of Booker T. Washington, the Black leader who stepped into the void left by Douglass's death.

W. E. B. Du Bois, who co-founded the NAACP in 1909 and dared to challenge Washington's accommodationist politics, decried the embrace of white racial superiority as a justification for the plunder of the world and, in response, expressed pride in his own Blackness. He had spent much of his young adult life after graduating as the first African American with a doctoral degree from Harvard—trying to dispel, with the tools of social science and history, the assumptions about Black people that fueled the ugliness of white supremacy. That work helped found the field of American sociology with his classic book *The Philadelphia Negro* (1899), an exhaustive study of the Black community in the Seventh Ward of Philadelphia. By 1920, Du Bois saw the global implications of white supremacy and what it meant for Black people in the United States. He brashly announced in his book *Darkwater: Voices from Within the Veil,* "I hear this mighty cry reverberating through the world, 'I am white!' Well and good, O Prometheus, divine thief! Is not the world wide enough for two colors, for many little shinings of the sun? Why, then devour your own vitals if I answer even as proudly, 'I am black!' "

This was a decidedly different tone from that of his 1903 classic, *The Souls of Black Folk.* Since that book's publication, Du Bois had witnessed not only the ugliness of white supremacy at home but its ghastly horrors around the world. In *Darkwater,* he held up a mirror, questioned the souls of white folk, and found them wanting. Like Douglass, Du Bois would fight for decades, gaining and losing ground, to resolve the split at the heart of the country, only to confront, again and again, the intransigence of America, U.S.A., and the rage that left hearts calloused and so many dead. This was America in the decade that would mark the 150th anniversary of the nation's birth.

Tension; ice-cold ♩ = 80
ppp
p sub.
p nobly
pp nervously
8
3
3
pp
p
pp
mf threatening

CHAPTER FOUR

1926: SESQUICENTENNIAL

The 1926 Sesquicentennial Exposition in Philadelphia was a far cry from the striking success of the Centennial Exposition held in the city fifty years earlier. The beauty of Fairmount Park had given way to the murky swamps of South Philly. City and state bosses like William S. Vare had their fingers all over the celebration, forcing choices in planning and execution that benefited their political machine—even the choice of South Philadelphia reflected Vare's power. Kickbacks and political patronage added millions to the costs of the exposition. Moreover, mass consumption collided with sensibilities that seemed dated. Americans were more interested in what they could buy than in standing starry-eyed before stacked inventions. This was not the nineteenth century. These were the "Roaring Twenties." Modern and slick. The Jazz Age.

The 1876 Centennial Exposition had offered the nation a chance to marvel at its own technological and industrial prowess. It allowed visitors to imagine a sense of national unity in the aftermath of a war that broke the nation in two. By 1926, with world war behind them and talking pictures a commonplace thing, this new fair touting the grandeur of the American project left Americans, well, a bit underwhelmed. It ended up a financial disaster, costing what would amount to an astonishing

$1.44 billion in today's dollars. One symbol can capture the disappointment: a $1,000 Sesquicentennial bond was worth a mere forty dollars by the time the city shuttered the gates of the fair. Over six months, fewer than five million people paid to visit the exposition, half the number of those who attended in 1876.

But the bad attendance, failed finances, and political graft do not tell the entire story of the exposition. The 1926 Sesquicentennial bore the burden of a nation hell-bent on asserting its distinctive national identity. Until this year, the country had maintained an unimpeachable diversity. The sounds of jazz and the American idiom itself—our language and style (the merger of many tongues and regions)—announced that this place was much more than white. And yet, the cultural and political pressures of European immigration had led some Americans to embrace the idea of pure Americanism, where native-born white men and women were considered the true people; the reborn Ku Klux Klan became that idea's most visible defender. Hence, the exposition occasioned a collision of socio-political forces warring over the very idea of who was American.

If that idea was in flux, so was much of American life. Technology, politics, culture—all seemed gripped by rapid and unsettling change. Some took this change as a negative harbinger, questioning whether Americans were still capable of bearing the responsibility democracy demanded. Walter Lippmann, one of the founding editors of *The New Republic,* opined that due to all the distractions of contemporary life, Americans could not achieve the basic knowledge of public affairs necessary to inform their actions as members of a self-governing community. The virtuous citizen whom James Madison had imagined was drowning in a sea of the mundane. Greed and selfishness left Americans bereft of the capacity for self-reflection. Others countered with the old saying that the best cure for the ills of democracy was more democracy, to deepen the responsibility of citizens for self-governance and accountability. But the American philosopher John Dewey insisted that "the old saying . . . is not apt if it means that the evils may be remedied by introducing more machinery of the same kind as that which already exists, or by refining and perfecting that machinery." For Dewey and other progressives, something more transformative needed to happen in the country for democracy to be revitalized. And that effort was bound up with the broader question about American national identity.

The 1926 exposition might have provided the occasion for a new story that made sense of a changing nation—one becoming more diverse, with the consequences of world war and European immigration, and more complicated by mass consumer culture. Here was an opportunity to leave behind the old problems of race. But the exposition failed to do so. This was a profoundly conservative celebration, one that would extend the privilege of being white to European immigrants. The country had already been building toward this for more than a decade, as was made plain in an earlier anniversary event, one that anticipated the exposition.

—

The summer of 1913 marked the 50th anniversary of the Battle of Gettysburg. Over fifty thousand veterans of the Union and Confederate armies attended the event, along with thousands of spectators. The gathering announced the end of "sectionalism." It marked a burying of old enmities, and in framing the war as such, it was steeped in fantasy. Reunion was now complete. The Civil War, it was said, was fought between men of goodwill with good people on both sides. The London *Times* reported that the ceremony and the symbolic significance of the old men in uniform "eradicate[d] forever the scars of the civil war." A reporter from the Louisville *Courier-Journal* couldn't hold back his emotions: "God bless us everyone, alike the Blue and the Gray, the Gray and the Blue! The world ne'er witnessed such a sight as this. Beholding, can we say happy is the nation that hath no history?"

The nation that hath no history. It was a strange question, or perhaps a confession. As the gathering rejoiced in reunion, it disremembered the cause of the war and made invisible the people who suffered the brunt of the forgetfulness. Attendees and commemorators celebrated the courage of past heroes and turned attention away from the challenges of the present. Among the thousands who participated in the 1913 Peace Jubilee, as it was called, Black people, even the living Black Union veterans who had risked their lives for freedom, were wholly absent—rendered invisible during what the historian David Blight called "a Jim Crow reunion" with "white supremacy . . . [as] the silent, invisible master of ceremonies."

Initially, President Wilson, the first Southern president elected since the Civil War—and the man who wrote in *The Atlantic Monthly* in 1901 that Black people were "excited about a freedom they did not understand"—refused to come to Gettysburg. But he ultimately relented, and on July Fourth he took to the stage before a vast crowd of men and women, many of whom dressed in uniforms of Blue and Gray. Wilson immediately ceded the war's moral ground. His aim was not to discuss "how the battle went, how it ended, what it signified!" Slavery and the question of the status of Black people were put aside. Instead, Wilson declared that the fifty years since General Lee's formal surrender "meant peace and union and vigor, and the maturity and might of a nation. . . . How wholesome and healing the peace has been! . . . Our battles long past, the quarrel forgotten." How wholesome. The horrors of Reconstruction; the bonfires of human flesh and the joyous, vengeful rituals surrounding them; the national consumption of popular images that made Black folk "the butt of . . . [a] national joke"; indeed, the very brutal fact of Jim Crow—all of it be damned. The quarrel had been forgotten. Black peopled erased. As if echoing the words of Melville's captain, Amasa Delano, aboard the *Bachelor's Delight,* Wilson basically announced, "The past is passed; why moralize upon it? Forget it."

Just as it happened at the 1876 Centennial Exposition, Black people had to be banished from view as the "Cavalier" and "Puritan" joined at Gettysburg as testament to the power of the Redeemer Nation.

The greatness of America, according to Wilson, had been made possible by the sacrifices of white men. Those who listened at Gettysburg fifty years later were charged with a responsibility for the future of the nation. "We have harder things to do than were done in the heroic days of war," Wilson said to the crowd, "because [it is] harder to see clearly, requiring more vision, more calm balance of judgment, a more candid searching for the very springs of right." America was larger, a more complex society. Capital threatened to overrun everything of value. And the world beyond its shores was no longer this distant place. He asked those in attendance, "Do we deem the Nation complete and finished?" The veterans of Gettysburg had done their task. "Their work is handed on to us, to be done in another way, but not in another spirit."

Wilson's shift from a focus on the past to that of the present allowed him to commend indirectly his progressive agenda. The people who elected him were the people he served. The past mattered, but the present even more so. As president, he was elected to command not the ghostly hosts of those who fought on battlefields long ago. "I have in my mind another host," Wilson said. "That host is the people themselves, the great and the small, without class or difference of kind or race or origin; and undivided in interest, if we have but the vision to guide and direct them and order their lives aright in what we do." And, together, they would strive for "their freedom, their right to lift themselves from day to day and behind the things they hoped for, and so make way for still better days for those whom they love who are to come after them." They would be charged to perfect what those who had sacrificed their lives at Gettysburg had established. Such words strained the ears and the mind, given what was happening to Black people around the nation, and especially in the South, but Wilson's words make sense in light of those who clamored for an unsullied view of American identity as European immigrants flooded into the country.

Many Americans worried about the invading armies of immigrants they viewed as polluting the blood of the nation. Inspired, in part, by the film *The Birth of a Nation,* the Ku Klux Klan reemerged in 1915 as a defender of America; its aim was "to unite white male persons, native-born Gentile citizens of the United States . . . to maintain forever white supremacy . . . and [the] ideals of pure Americanism." The Klan was one among many organizations that took up the cause of "America First" as they wrapped their nativism and hatreds "in Old Glory and the mantle of the Founding Fathers." In Gettysburg, Wilson's passionate embrace of the people, "without class or difference of kind or race or origin," certainly did not include Black Americans, but those Americans weren't his concern. Rather, he sought to hold off those so-called defenders of America who were Jew-haters and who loathed anyone considered foreign.

Wilson had his own suspicions of European immigrants (he worried about the character of some of those who had made their way to America), but at Gettysburg he urged the audience to imagine a more inclusive idea of the white American—to include other white European immigrants, not just those of Nordic stock.

The ghosts of soldiers roaming the battlefield at Gettysburg and Lincoln's powerful words haunted the so-called Peace Jubilee. Lincoln had declared "that we here highly resolve that these dead shall not have died in vain—that this nation, under God, shall have a new birth of freedom—and that government of the people, by the people, for the people, shall not perish from the earth." One even wonders if Lincoln had Black people in mind when he spoke those words. But in one sense, given the state of the nation in 1913, those brave souls did die in vain. For on this day, fifty years later (or even 250 years later), a new birth of freedom could not be celebrated sincerely. The divided soul of the nation remained its greatest danger.

At the end of his Gettysburg speech, President Wilson reached for the future of the American idea. "I would not have you live even today wholly in the past," he said, "but would wish to stand with you in the light that streams upon us now out of that great day gone by." He urged the audience not to fix their gaze on the past, but to understand that American history blessed their efforts to build a better America. Wilson invoked the divine calling of the nation—that feature of America's civil religion—to mobilize a consensus capable of responding to the challenges of the day. "Here is the nation God has builded by our hands," he declared. "What shall we do with it?"

But Wilson's question involved, whether he would admit it or not, reckoning with what Du Bois had declared in *The Souls of Black Folk* a decade earlier: that the problem of the twentieth century would be the problem of the color line. Not the "Negro problem," as Nathaniel Shaler and, later, Lothrop Stoddard saw it, but the problem that white people believed, for whatever reason, that they ought to be valued more than others, and that they alone possessed freedom. Wilson's appeal to America's future was not unusual. When the contradictions or the "internal enemies" threatened to unravel America's way of life, appeals to the future (as well as the need for a scapegoat and the whip) worked to escape what was demanded of Americans in the present. No matter their failings, Americans were always on the road to a more perfect union (a kind of moral holiday, a periodic release from moral constraints that comes with being a divinely chosen nation-state, which absolves the nation of its sins). "More perfect union" talk worked like a ready-made remedy built into the idea of America, U.S.A. It allowed evils to roam, because inevitably, Americans told themselves, the evils would be put to rest. That is the American promise.

—

Three years after President Wilson's speech and his appeal to an idea of "the people" shorn of any concern with race or class or origin, the philosopher Randolph Bourne set out to address the ugly underbelly of 100-percent Americanism. Proponents of this view appealed to the idea of "America first" to cast aside the immigrant German, the Irish, Jew, Slav, and Italian. With the Great War, as more and more European immigrants made their way to the country, nativists like the Klan threw away the idea of the "melting pot" and embraced the fiction of the pure Anglo-Saxon.

Bourne sought to challenge that fiction with an appeal to the future of what he called *a trans-national America.* "Just in so far as our American genius has expressed the pioneer spirit, the adventurous, forward-looking drive of a colonial empire," he wrote, "is it representative of that whole—America of the many races and peoples, and not of any partial or traditional enthusiasm." Bourne's aim was not to reclaim the melting pot. For him, that was a backward-looking imagining of American identity, where American cultural traditions resided in the past and "new" Americans had to somehow claim and conform to them. Instead, Bourne argued that "in the light of our changing ideal of Americanism, we must perpetuate the paradox that our American cultural tradition lies in the future." Who we take ourselves to be as Americans, he suggested, would be the result of our work together in "attacking the future with a new key." In this sense, American nationalism would be different from the nationalisms in Europe that resulted in so much bloodshed—the antithesis of blood and soil.

Bourne understood the attraction of that ugly blood-and-soil nationalism, but he underestimated its power on American shores. For in the United States, the allure of joining the ranks of the white American and accruing their benefits offered a different kind of transformation—one not so much found in the future but rooted in white domination of the world, where the idea of white racial superiority cut across regional and ethnic differences. In the early twentieth century, a more expansive idea of being white began to emerge. Where some would decry the scourge of immigrants, their German-ness, their Italian-ness, Bourne—and Wilson and Theodore Roosevelt, for that matter—insisted on absorbing these internal differences into an idea of the white American. It was this idea that underlaid Roosevelt's rejection of the hyphen and Wilson's invocation of the people "without class or difference of . . . race . . . undivided in interest." And yet this was no neutral absorption—that expanded idea of the white American offered relevance and significance in who remained excluded: Black people and the darker peoples of the world, the people at the bottom of the well.

W. E. B. Du Bois understood this. He argued in "The Souls of White Folk"—an essay originally written in 1910 and substantially revised for *Darkwater* (published the same year as Stoddard's *The Rising Tide of Color Against White World-Supremacy*)—that the idea of white racial superiority was a late-modern invention that justified Europe's and America's belief in "the ownership of the earth forever and ever. Amen!" One could see it at work in the nineteenth-century expansion of European colonialism in Asia and in Africa, and in the declaration that all that was good in the world came from white people. Black and Brown peoples bore the brunt as Europe went to war with itself over the spoils.

America, U.S.A., positioned itself as the peacemaker for the world at war. Du Bois scoffed at this idea. The country was in no position to claim any moral authority in these battles, because it had already declared, in word and deed, "I am white." Du Bois wrote,

> It is curious to see America, the United States, looking on herself, first, as a sort of natural peacemaker, then as a moral protagonist in this terrible time. No nation is less fitted for this role. For two or more centuries America has marched proudly in the van of human hatred,—making bonfires of human flesh and laughing at them hideously, and making the insulting of millions more than a matter of dislike,—rather a great religion, a world war-cry: Up white, down black; to your tents, O white folk, and world war with black and particolored mongrel beasts!

Wilson's imagining of "a new host" at Gettysburg and Bourne's invocation of "a trans-national American identity" failed to acknowledge or make explicit the serpent coiled up in the heart of both views. There, a more expansive idea of the white American resided, in which the differences between white folk receded, yes, but hardened in the confrontation with darker souls. Out of the nettle of vile and stinging nativism, Du Bois suggested, the immigrant, from the moment he landed on these shores, was taught to despise "niggers" and to send that good news back home. Two generations later James Baldwin would refer to that very instruction as "the price of the ticket."

> With a painless change of name, and in the twinkling of an eye, one becomes a white American.

> The price the white American paid for his ticket was to become white—: and, in the main, nothing more than that, or, as he was to insist, nothing less. This incredibly limited not to say dimwitted ambition has choked many a human being to death here. . . . I know very well that my ancestors had no desire to come to this place: but neither did the ancestors of the people who became white and who required of my captivity a song. They require of me a song less to celebrate my captivity than to justify their own.

The 1926 Sesquicentennial was caught between an old, dying world of monarchs and empire and a new, modern one struggling to come into existence—one sanctioned by President Wilson, who appealed to the spirit of American habits in the work to be done on behalf of an American future. The connecting thread was the idea of the white American, but that, too, was evolving. Catholics celebrated mass at the exposition, drawing the largest crowd among all the events held at the fair. Jewish leaders lent their talents and treasure even as they faced the ugliness of antisemitism. And the Ku Klux Klan, with the approval of the mayor of Philadelphia, planned to hold its Klonvocation at the heart of the fair. Burning crosses and declarations of white superiority were to be part of the celebration of the founding of the country.

—

Thirty years after Frederick Douglass's speech in 1894 and Samuel Smith's murder that same year in Greenville, Florida, a fifteen-year-old boy—also named Samuel Smith—was lynched about twenty miles outside of Nashville. A strange repetition. The mob still required its charred bones.

Samuel was accused of robbing a white grocer with his uncle, Jim Smith. Shots were exchanged. The grocer was wounded and so was Samuel Smith. He tried to escape to Nashville but was captured and arrested. The police brought him to the hospital for treatment, but at about midnight, six or seven masked men took him from the hospital at gunpoint. The Nashville *Tennessean* reported, "Within 45 minutes his naked, bullet-mangled body hung from a tree beside the road. . . . Approximately 30 automobiles attended the hanging, and after his body was tied up, shotguns boomed from practically all of them. They then 'disappeared to the four winds of the earth,' according to a mysterious voice that first informed *The Tennessean* of the hanging."

No one was arrested for the murder, though everyone thought the Klan was behind it. The Black community got the message just as they had for the decades since the end of the nineteenth century, as Black people became America's "strange fruit." The act of racial terror was a reminder of the dangers that awaited any Black person who dared believe that they possessed freedom for themselves. The Klan policed those lines with unimaginable cruelty.

It is fascinating to note that the "Roaring Twenties," a time of economic prosperity and consumption, of jazz and the Charleston, was also a period in which the country grappled with the influence of the Ku Klux Klan. Since the fateful 1915 gathering in Stone Mountain, Georgia, where William J. Simmons and fifteen other white men burned a cross and announced the Klan's rebirth, the Klan had grown and come to exercise extraordinary influence over the political and cultural landscape of the country. Its power was on full display ten years later, when, in the nation's capital, over thirty thousand uniformed Klansmen and -women marched sixteen to twenty abreast down Pennsylvania Avenue, toward the grounds of the Washington Monument. They came from Ohio, New Jersey, Pennsylvania, New York, and a few from Florida, Virginia, and North Carolina.

It is important not to reduce the KKK's impact to the violence of lynching and racial intimidation. During the 1920s, the Klan exercised extraordinary influence over the American electoral process. We see its sway at the 1924 Democratic Convention, where, though it probably exaggerated, the organization claimed "that twenty-six governors and 62 percent of Congress were Klansmen. It also took credit for reelecting Calvin Coolidge in 1924." And yet the Klan was most proud of the legislative achievement of the Johnson-Reed Immigration Act, a bill co-sponsored by Klan member Albert Johnson of Washington, who served as chair of the House Committee on Immigration and Naturalization.

On April 27, 1924, Senator David Reed of Pennsylvania, a state that held a Klan membership estimated at 250,000, penned an article for *The New York Times* titled "America of the Melting Pot Comes to an End." Reed made a case for draconian immigration legislation that would "preserve racial type as it exists here today." He concluded that the adoption of the legislation would mean that the "America of our grandchildren will be a vastly better place to live in. It will mean a more homogeneous nation, more self-reliant, more independent, and more closely knit by common purpose and common ideas." These were not the words of a vile Southern politician spouting the claims of Redemption. Reed was from the North.

In the run-up to the passage of the legislation, one witness testified in a hearing before Johnson's Immigration Committee about the nature of the restrictions. "I do not think it would be arbitrary because we have the evidence that they are not fitting into our life. . . . The point is that we may discriminate against them because of our inability to assimilate them," he told the chairman of the committee. In another exchange, one congressman asked, "Are you in favor of a bill which excludes all Africans from this country?" After clarifying that the congressman meant African immigrants, the witness answered, "Yes." The chairman then asked, "What other races would you favor excluding?" The answer: "For the time being, I would not object to the complete suspension of the Japanese, Chinese, Hindu, and other immigration."

After 1924, immigration to the United States was dramatically reduced. National quotas restricted entry into the country from southern, eastern, and central Europe—rejecting "the degraded races of Europe." Immigrants from the Pacific were effectively declared "ineligible to citizenship." (Donald Trump's reference to "shithole countries" has historical precedence after all.) This view shaped American immigration policy until Congress passed the Immigration and Nationality Act of 1965. In fact, though it is rarely explicitly stated, much of the political debate on the right around immigration today concerns repealing that 1965 legislation and returning to what we had in 1924—an immigration policy unquestionably shaped by the Ku Klux Klan.

For the KKK, the un-American menace of unwanted immigrants necessitated a robust response; in their view, the very heart of the country was at stake. The Klan sought to exert its influence, both politically and culturally, across a wide spectrum of American life. Most white Americans were not members of the Klan (although at the height of its power, the organization claimed some four million Americans on its rolls); but the underlying common sense of the nation was amplified and heightened by the Klan. White Americans did not have to wear hoods or join the Invisible Empire to agree with the basic claims that America, U.S.A., was and should always be white, or that "the national origin of an immigrant was a reliable indication of his capacity for Americanization." In this sense, the Klan revealed the bitterness at the bottom of the American cup. They were an exaggerated version of it. No wonder the organization sought to hold its Klonvocation in Philadelphia, at the heart of the nation's remembrance of its founding.

—

In many ways, although the Sesquicentennial paled in comparison to the 1876 Centennial, the fair reproduced some of the same divisions and disappointments. African Americans rejected efforts to marginalize them during the celebration, and were initially excited about the prospect of touting their achievements and contributions to the country. *The Philadelphia Tribune* proudly declared that "this is to be the one big chance for the Philadelphia Negro to prove to the world by deeds well done just how he stands in the outward march of events." Committees were established, announcements made to an audience of Black merchants that the celebration would not be segregated—that "all races will be treated the same." (Add to the ironies that the city of Philadelphia remained fiercely segregated at the time.)

Those pronouncements collided with the actual decisions of the organizers. In the summer before the official opening of the Sesquicentennial, Black leaders in Philadelphia got wind of the decision to allow the Klan to hold its Klonvocation at the exposition. They protested, along with members of the Jewish and Catholic communities. The mayor eventually relented, the Klonvocation was canceled, and he formed an "executive committee of twenty-five prominent Negro residents of Philadelphia to formulate a program showing the development of the Negro along educational lines." But the committee would prove to be powerless, a mere symbolic gesture to quiet discord. The Sesquicentennial officials showed little to no interest in supporting activities proposed by the committee, either by denying their petitions outright or by allocating a pittance in comparison to the requests of others. Appeals to President Calvin Coolidge fell on deaf ears; he was inclined not to intervene in local matters.

Just as had happened in 1876, African Americans were locked out of construction projects and other ways of benefiting from the celebration. The editor in chief of the Associated Negro Press, Nahum Daniel Brascher, echoed the words of the Black resident of Georgia who had visited the Centennial some fifty years earlier: "I saw scores and scores of whites busily engaged in preparations, but not one black face." An uncanny repetition.

In response to the racial animus surrounding the organizing of the Sesquicentennial, a group of leading Black citizens of Philadelphia appealed to the mayor to include a Black speaker. The mayor relented and invited A. Philip Randolph, the head of the Brotherhood of Sleeping Car Porters and the man who would give us the idea of the March on Washington. It was a fascinating choice.

In 1917, Randolph had distinguished himself as the co-editor, with Chandler Owen, of *The Messenger,* a Black socialist publication. They declared, "Our aim is to appeal to reason, to lift our pens above the cringing demagogy of the times, and above the cheap peanut politics of the old reactionary Negro Leaders." Economics and politics centered their efforts, and socialism served as their guiding ideological frame. President Wilson's attorney general, A. Mitchell Palmer, the man responsible for the Palmer Raids during the first Red Scare, labeled Randolph in 1919 the "most dangerous Negro in America." Although much had changed between 1917 and 1926, Randolph still brought the gravitas of his politics to the opening of the Sesquicentennial Exposition on May 31, 1926, though he faced an unfamiliar crowd. The organizers did not list his name among the dignitaries attending the mayor's reception; nor was he included in the printed Opening Day program. Most in attendance had little to no idea who he was.

But Randolph ascended the dais and sought to frame the celebration around the journey of the nation's darker souls. He spoke back to the celebration, invoking the words of the Declaration of Independence—*We hold these truths to be self-evident, that all men are created equal*—as the key to solving what he referred to as "our perplexing problems":

> To Aframericans, the embodiment of this formula of practical, righteous idealism into the warp and woof of American life, its customs, its institutions, its practices, its traditions, its politics, in education and religion, is a consummation devoutly to be wished; for no people on God's green earth have suffered as poignantly as the Negro peoples of the world, on account of the failure of the world to achieve higher reaches of humanity. Thus no group of people in America can have a greater and a more genuine concern in the commemoration and perpetuation of the spirit of the Declaration of Independence on this Sesqui-Centenary than the Negro.

Randolph reached back to the insight of Frederick Douglass, reading the Declaration into America's self-conception and daring to judge the country wanting. No matter what the Klan said or what the organizers of the celebration assumed, he claimed freedom as his own. Randolph went on to say:

> If there are those, either because of ignorance or malice who would challenge the right of Aframericans to share in the glories and achievements of our country, my answer is that of all the Americans, the Negro is, doubtless, the most typically American. He is the incarnation of America. His every pore breathing its

> vital spirit. . . . The insistent cry for freedom on the part of the Negro has kept the American people face to face with the fact that a democracy has not fulfilled its highest mission so long as there are people in the country, black or white who cannot participate in the affairs of government, industry or society generally as free, intelligent human beings.

Whatever else the true American is, or whatever people posit him or her to be, Randolph insisted that Black folk are quintessentially American—that our experience in this country takes one to "the true subject of democracy," which is the ongoing expansion and extension of the democratic process and the principles that make it worth fighting for. In the end, America failed to live up to its promise as long as all of its people were not free. If we are to understand fully the power of the American project, Randolph implied, we must confront those people who put a blue note in the heart of the nation.

Randolph then turned to chronicle the gifts of Black folk, to detail their achievements in history and education, in labor and the arts, as if he were channeling the work of historian Carter G. Woodson—the second Black person to receive a PhD from Harvard University, the co-founder in 1915 of the Association for the Study of Negro Life and History, and the person who started Negro History Week just a few months before the opening of the Sesquicentennial.

Randolph's interjection of African American history and his insistence on the centrality of Black folk to the very idea of America during the opening exercises amounted to a radical interruption of an American fantasy. And, like Frederick Douglass's famous July 5, 1852, oration, Randolph's invocation of Black achievement amid the celebration's ongoing erasure of Black people was a moment where the color line blurred. With thousands listening, white and Black alike heard his words. Even as he spoke, some doubted the veracity of his claims about Black history; others were outraged, including the principal organizer, A. L. Sutton, who passed a note to the mayor to cut Randolph off.

Sutton needn't have worried. Beyond those in the crowd who may have been moved or discomfited, Randolph's words fell on barren soil.

Not much was said about the speech. *The Philadelphia Bulletin* didn't bother to quote from it. And the rest of the Opening Day exercises sought to render the presence of African Americans invisible. Even as some five to six thousand Black people stood in attendance, only two numbered among the hundreds of dignitaries invited. Just as Frederick Douglass found himself denied entry to the exposition in 1876 by a white Philadelphia cop who refused to believe that a "nigger" would be invited to share the stage with President Grant, some fifty years later the president of U.S.-occupied Haiti, Louis Borno, found himself in similar straits when an angry white Philly cop did not believe his driver's claim that he was ferrying a head of state. "I suppose," the officer said, "you'll be telling me that it's General Grant and his wife next." The officer forced the driver to pay two dollars for four tickets. The president of Haiti found himself stranded among the throngs of people, eating a hot dog with his wife and two military aides, when an assistant to the director of the Sesquicentennial recognized him and profusely apologized for the white officer who refused to believe that "niggers" could be that important.

Among the thousands of veterans celebrated for their service and who led the Opening Day parade, not one African American stood among them—despite 350,000 of them having served during World War I. Instead, they were left with "a minstrel mimic laboring under the weight of a massive bass drum." The editor of *The Philadelphia Tribune* was incensed: "We wonder what was in the breast of those black men who fought to make America safe for Democracy and on Monday stood on the sidelines, forgotten, as the Nordic strode by in all his vain pride."

Unlike in 1876, African Americans did manage to complete an exhibit at the Palace of Agriculture. Celebrating the achievements of Black Americans since the centennial, they displayed works of art; offered statistical data about education, entrepreneurship, and homeownership; reveled in the writings of African American authors like W. E. B. Du Bois; and presented publications like the Baltimore *Afro-American* and *The New York Age.* The Women's Committee on Negro Activities staged *Loyalty's Gift: A Historic Pageant in Song,* written by Dora Cole Norman—an epic effort that included "more than a thousand actors" depicting the historic journey of Black folk on American shores. It was a stunning success, drawing praise from reviewers and filling the ten-thousand seat Sesquicentennial Auditorium to capacity. The other pageant, *Ethiopia,* was not as successful—the organizers, headed by A. L. Sutton, who many believed was a member of the Klan, decided to change the date forty-eight hours before the pageant's debut, out of spite, some believed, for the protests against the Klan's Klonvocation.

—

On July 4, a violent storm damaged the buildings at the Sesquicentennial. The next day, President Coolidge spoke. I am sure he had no idea about the significance of the July 5 celebrations among African Americans. His speech, in which he drew on the powerful incantations of America's civil religion, suggested as much.

Coolidge wasn't considered a dynamic personality. H. L. Mencken, the American journalist and satirist, described him as "pretty and dull." He was nicknamed "Silent Cal" because of his reticence and dry sense of humor. But Coolidge brought to the Sesquicentennial the full weight of his conservative views of the American project, and this situates his speech as an important moment in American politics. Unlike President Wilson's effort to urge Americans to look to the present and the future during the 50th anniversary of Gettysburg, Coolidge offered an account of the past that secured the promise of America's divine mission in its 150th year. In moments of crisis or conflict, he commended, the nation need only remember its founding—its history and the sacred values enshrined in its founding documents. Of course, this invocation of the past was a storybook version of the country that erased the presence of Black people. Coolidge told the audience, "It was not only the principles declared, but the fact that therewith a new nation was born which was to be founded upon those principles and which from that time forth in its development has actually maintained those principles, that makes this pronouncement an incomparable event in the history of government." Slavery did not matter. Jim Crow in the South and racial pogroms in American cities were of little concern. Those enduring principles still animated American life. No need to talk about perfecting the Union, Coolidge seemed to suggest. The promise of America had already been secured with the founding of the country itself.

Coolidge's main goal was to sanctify American history. Philadelphia, he told the crowd, was a "holy shrine," Independence Hall "hallowed ground." He drew powerful focus back to the founders and the founding documents, investing them with the qualities of religious scrolls. "Amid all the clash of conflicting interests," Coolidge declared, "amid all the welter of partisan politics, every American can turn for solace and consolation to the Declaration of Independence and the Constitution of the United States with the assurance that those two great charters of freedom and justice remain firm and unshaken." Those documents were the products of what he called "a spiritual event"; and the events that made them possible, "through use for a righteous purpose[,] . . . have become sanctified." This was the "tricky magic" of using consensus to conceal the panic of a country still divided and deeply distrustful of government and politicians. In the end, Coolidge set out to establish the spiritual basis of the American project. The principles informing the Declaration of Independence were not just drawn out of a hat. They reflected a grand religious tradition embodied in the Puritans and the New England saints, not in the deism of Jefferson. As he put it, "Democracy is Christ's government in Church and State."

What makes America special, Coolidge argued, was that it was a nation created on the basis of religious principles. "These were the doctrine that all men are created equal, that they are endowed with certain inalienable rights, and that therefore the source of the just powers of government must be derived from the consent of the governed." The fact that these principles animated the very idea of government made the founding of the country "an incomparable event in the history of government." To ignore or deny the religious underpinnings of America, Coolidge maintained, was to imperil the nation. "We cannot continue to enjoy the result if we neglect and abandon the cause." These principles were enduring truths not subject to the whims of men.

The principle of equality—that, as John Wise preached in 1710, "Every man must be acknowledged equal to every man"—set the American nation apart. And that principle was not the result of revolutions but, rather, was the insight of an ancient wisdom. For Coolidge, then, the creation of the American project was not the result of a radical movement or rebellion; nor was it a blueprint for repeated revolutions. "It was conservative," an affirmation of Christian truths that were final and fixed.

With this formulation, Coolidge was warning those who looked to the Russian revolution or stoked labor unrest—those who clamored for radical change. He insisted, sounding like the originalists of our times, that we understand the conclusions of the founders and that "we must go back and review the course which they followed. We must think the thoughts which they thought." Their spiritual power, rightly understood, would become our own. Our task was simply to remember and to restore. As he said, in the end,

> We must not sink into a pagan materialism. We must cultivate the reverence which [the founders] had for the things that are holy. We must follow the spiritual and moral leadership which they showed. We must keep replenished, that they may glow with a more compelling flame, the altar fires before which they worshiped.

In short, only one revolution was needed. And, when America loses its way, the country must simply return, as Dos Passos wrote, to the "clean words of the founders." This view of American history would be given an evangelical twist by MAGA Republicans one hundred years later.

In the full light of all the bloodlust of the plague years, Coolidge declared that "in the development of its institutions America can fairly claim that it has remained true to the principles which were declared 150 years ago. In all the essentials we have achieved an equality which was never possessed by any other people." His words were shadowed by the ten million or so Black folk whose captivity still required a song.

I can imagine the faces of those darker souls in attendance. They who bore the brunt of the whip and lived amid the wild beasts knew that the president was not thinking of them. His vision of America required their erasure. Their cries muted. Their presence dutifully ignored. The hypocrisy Frederick Douglass identified in American Christendom found its way into the heart of America's civil religion on this day of celebration: the nation could not disentangle its faith from the evil of those who believed, still, in the legacy of the auction block. That was the point. In fact, the invocation of that spiritual consensus—of the Christian underpinnings of the American idea—was an indication of the chaos roaring underneath it all. This was America, U.S.A.

—

A month or so before the opening of the Sesquicentennial, the Imperial Wizard of the Ku Klux Klan, Hiram Wesley Evans, published an article in *The North American Review* entitled "The Klan's Fight for Americanism." Given the standing judgment that the Klan's views were too extreme, the essay sought to rebrand the organization. They weren't domestic terrorists or corrupt opportunists, he argued, but rather defenders of "the idea of preserving and developing America first and chiefly for the benefit of the children of the pioneers who made America, and only and definitely along the lines of the purpose and spirit of those pioneers." Like Coolidge, Evans insisted on the Christian significance and power of the founders or pioneers. For the Klan, these men were of Nordic stock, white men who understood the hierarchy of races and the import of the American experiment. Evans declared that the Klan had "enlisted our racial instincts for the work of preserving and developing our American traditions and customs," and that involved an unshakable loyalty to the nation, understood as white, and to Protestantism. What followed was a screed about the dangers of immigrants, particularly Catholics, and an attempt to render "the imperious urge of superior heredity" in a way consonant with American patriotism.

To read Evans is to see the blueprint for the transformation of right-wing extremism into something more palatable and mainstream. He maps the Klan's hatreds onto the everyday fears of working white Americans: people who simply want to take care of their own, make a better future for their children, and secure the values that define the community and nation they so love. At one point in the essay, he even laments the fact that white people cannot control what their own kids learn in school. The similarity to our own time, in sentiment, in the language, is haunting. We see how the ugliness represented by the Klan can morph into the alt-right with its screeds about immigration and wokeness, and how the alt-right can infuse the MAGA movement and take over government. The bitterness at the bottom of the American cup.

In 1926, Evans wrapped his hatred in the winding sheet of American patriotism. America, for him, was a spiritual matter, too. His version of Americanism was inextricably bound to a particular understanding of American Protestantism. The dangers of the alien immigrant, especially those obligated to the Pope, threatened the sanctity of those of Nordic stock, the true inheritors of the old pioneers. And liberalism, for Evans, just as it is for so many today, "is charged in the mind of most Americans with nothing less than national, racial, and spiritual treason." These people would give away the country for identity politics and their virtue signaling. Given the dangers, he argued, the nation needed protection if it was to survive. True Americans needed protection from those who they believed had betrayed their trust and who endangered *them.* "We believe, in short, that we have the right to make America *American* and for Americans." To those who accused the Klan of hatred and prejudice, Evans was quite clear: "The hatred and prejudice are . . . displayed by our enemies and not by us."

As for Black people, Evans was succinct and direct. We were the special problem and duty of white America. The violence of redemption had successfully put us in our place, and what was left for white America was merely a charitable gesture—an echo of the sentiment expressed by Nathaniel Shaler some forty years earlier—and a warning. "[The Negro] is among us through no wish of his," Evans wrote. "We owe it to him and to ourselves to give him full protection and opportunity. But his limitations are evident; we will not permit him to gain sufficient power to control our civilization. Neither will we delude him with promises of social equality which we know can never be realized." In short, we must remember our place. Sentimentality in the form of paternalism could in the blink of an eye turn into utter brutality.

The editors of *The North American Review* invited a fascinating group of writers to respond to Evans. They ranged from a professor of politics at Princeton to a professor at the College of St. Francis Xavier in New York and an emeritus rabbi at Temple Emanu-El. W. E. B. Du Bois was included among the contributors. His article "The Shape of Fear" strikes at the heart of what he takes to be the sinister meaning of the Klan's existence. He sees the Klan as part of a broader global consequence of the First World War. The wages of war are hate, he claimed, and "the End, and indeed the Beginning, of Hate is Fear." The world and this country, Du Bois argued, are desperately afraid and refuse to understand rationally the source of their fears. Instead, they retreat into the comforts of the mob:

> Before the wide eyes of the mob is ever the Shape of Fear. Back of the writing, yelling, cruel-eyed daemons who break, destroy, maim and lynch and burn at the stake is a knot, large or small, of normal human beings and these human beings at heart are desperately afraid of something. Of what?

People are afraid of losing their homes, their status, of becoming lost in the whip of the whirlwind of modern industrial society. The flotsam and jetsam of modern life have overrun the ground beneath their feet. This is the impetus—the source—of the intensity of the mob. And, for Du Bois, the Klan, no matter the sanitizing efforts of Evans, exploited this fear with lies and innuendo, with whispers and "methods of the night," and with the hooded mask. As he put it,

> Here were white men afraid of degradation; here were white men afraid of hunger; here were black men afraid of hunger and black men afraid of death. And here were secret midnight oath and murder seeking to right it all.
>
> Such were the elements that make for secret mob law: economic rivalry, race hatred, class hatred, sex rivalry, religious dogmatism, and before all the Shape of Fear.

Reason and argument fail in the face of such things. And the Klan exploits it.

But Du Bois also made a broader point. He refused to allow the nation to pass its sins off onto the Klan (just as it continues to do with the South). The Klan made explicit the bitterness that soaks much of American life. As Du Bois wrote, "The danger and shame are not in the movement itself, so much as in the wide tolerance and sympathy which its methods evoke among educated and decent Americans. These people see in the Ku Klux Klan a way of doing and saying that which they themselves are ashamed to do and say." The danger resides in the secrets buried in the hearts of most white American men and women. Klan members are sworn to lie; they hide in plain sight. But "the conscious surrender of the Truth" is not theirs alone. Americans generally lie to themselves, and those lies manage the fears that threaten to overwhelm everything. "Of all the dangerous weapons that civilized man has attempted to use in order to advance human culture," Du Bois wrote, "the secret mass lie is the most dangerous and the most apt to prove a boomerang."

Du Bois knew intimately of the horrors perpetuated by those who hid their faces behind hoods. And he warned the nation in 1926, in its 150th year, not to succumb to Evans's lies. "This is the real thing that we are to fear in the Ku Klux Klan. We need not fear its logic. It has no logic." It is the mass of lies that presents the existential danger.

—

The Sesquicentennial Exposition closed in November 1926. By any measure, it had failed. But as the celebration ended in a whimper, the nation moved toward the tumultuous days ahead. Economic collapse and war on a scale that would transform the country's global standing awaited the inheritors of the old pioneers. The plague years gave way to promise as America, U.S.A., positioned itself as the defender of democracy against fascism.

The Klan's influence would be felt in U.S. immigration policy even as graft, hypocrisy, and murder robbed the organization of any hint of respectability and national influence. Hitler looked to the United States for models and support for his own cruelty. By the late 1930s and '40s, the

Klan dropped its assault on Catholics and embraced the virulent anti-semitism of Father Charles Coughlin. The idea of the white American now included European ethnics, and the Klan "shifted toward a simpler, purer racial system, with two categories: white and not white." And no matter its collapse, the organization gave voice to the sensibility that has shaped, or distorted, American identity from the beginning.

With the mania of MAGA and Donald Trump in the White House, the Klan's and Coolidge's version of Americanism still shadows our days. Immigration, questions of American identity, how we ought to view American history, and who can lay claim to the country drive our current politics. As do the fear and the mass of lies. On the 250th anniversary of the nation, the country drowns in lies.

p
p biting
3
mf

mf

INTERLUDE

THE AMERICAN CENTURY

The so-called Roaring Twenties gave way to unprecedented economic depression. Banks failed. Factories shuttered their doors. Unemployment peaked around 25 percent. Farms and houses were foreclosed on. People struggled to eat. And the tragic choice—expressed in the symbols, rituals, and actions of the Klan and in the way most white Americans lived their lives—made matters worse. The likes of Charles Lindbergh and Father Coughlin touted "America first" with racist venom. The contradictions were glaring.

Twenty thousand white men and women gathered on the evening of February 20, 1939, at New York's Madison Square Garden on the birthday of George Washington—"America's first fascist," the organizers claimed. A thirty-foot-tall banner of Washington's image hung between American flags and swastikas as the speakers proclaimed the greatness of the United States and insisted that "the spirit which opened the West and built our country is the spirit of the militant white man." They mimicked the words of Adolf Hitler himself, who wrote in *Mein Kampf*:

> There is currently one state in which one can observe at least weak beginnings of a better conception. This is of course not our exemplary German Republic, but the American Union, in which an

> effort is being made to consider the dictates of reason to at least some extent. The American Union categorically refuses the immigration of physically unhealthy elements, and simply excludes the immigration of certain races. In these respects, America already pays obeisance, at least in tentative first steps, to the characteristic *völkisch* conception of the state.

It is remarkable how the example for Hitler and his minions was not racial segregation in the South, the region that often bore the burdens of the country's sins, but rather the imagining of America, U.S.A., with its immigration laws, as a *white* Republic. Even as the country mobilized to defeat Hitler and fascism in World War II, fashioned itself as the defender of democracy and freedom around the globe, and experienced postwar prosperity, deep-seated racial hatreds remained, and, in some places, intensified. The divided soul of America endured.

This is not to deny the fundamental shifts that occurred in the postwar period. While the Federal Housing Administration continued to enforce segregationist policies, and Black people were still routinely denied the right to register to vote, we saw positive developments in employment and education. Civil rights organizations had been successful in the courts with the *Smith v. Allwright* decision in 1944, which outlawed all-white primaries, and the *Shelley v. Kraemer* decision in 1948, which declared restrictive covenants unenforceable. Economic gains were also substantial. "The median Black income had risen from 41 percent of the white median in 1939 to 60 percent in 1950; the percentage of male black workers in white-collar and professional jobs had risen from 5.6 in 1940 to 7.2 in 1950, and that of craftsmen and operatives from 16.6 percent of the total in 1940 to 28.8 percent in 1950." And this was part of a broader development. The country experienced a postwar boom that led to the creation of the vaunted American middle class. Henry Luce, the owner of *Time* and *Life* magazines, proclaimed that, despite the deadly reality of the atomic age, this was "the American Century." The American experiment worked. The evidence was clear in the might of the American consumer and the enduring power of American ideals.

The country had defeated fascism, and in the postwar period it took on another threat: communism. American Cold War nationalism can be understood through Arthur Schlesinger's concept of a "vital center" that must hold between the *equal* threats from the left and the right. To hold that center, the Red Scare returned, bigger and stronger, and democracy suffered because of it. Under a cloud of suspicion, the government targeted civil rights and labor organizing, and silenced criticism of racial injustice.

The McCarthy era cast dark shadows over democratic principles. White Americans, especially in the South, doubled down on the world they had created from the ashes of Reconstruction as others embraced the new world that World War II made possible. At the same time, mainstream American historians reached for a story of American identity, of national character, that buried the regional differences in an idea of the country that was remarkably homogeneous and decidedly white.

Ideological consensus, they suggested, defined the American project. A country made up of "undifferentiated" men and women did not suffer from the pangs that convulsed Europe; instead, ours was a nation motivated not by invidious social and class distinctions, but by the power of a practical disposition that flowed from the founding principles. America, U.S.A., was a beacon of freedom. Echoing in some ways the words delivered by President Coolidge at the Sesquicentennial in 1926, where he insisted that the American Revolution "was in no sense a rising of the oppressed and downtrodden"—rather, it "represented the informed and mature convictions of a great mass of independent, liberty loving, God-fearing people who knew their rights"—these historians emphasized the continuity of "the American experience" and the reservoir of wisdom given to us by the founding fathers. As Richard Hofstadter famously put it, "It has been our fate as a nation not to have ideologies *but to be one.*"

The late historian John Higham powerfully described the consequences of this embrace of consensus. It required, in effect, a view of the American project that conceded what Coolidge argued: that America was not a nation pursuing its ideals, but was an example of freedom by virtue of its very existence. After the war, "when the liberal ideology lost its cutting edge" by insisting on consensus and conformity while downplaying conflict, "conservatives ceased to require an ideological shield," Higham wrote.

> At this point a historiography that was conservative, without passing as such, won out. Instead of upholding the role of the right in America, it merges the left with the right. It argues that America has ordinarily fused a conservative temper with a liberal state of mind. It displays, therefore, the homogeneity and the continuity of American culture.

Both fascism and communism could be held at bay by the power of the American idea. But storybook America required a willful blindness. These white men had to ignore the serpent coiled up in the nation's bosom.

—

By the 1950s the country was poised to explode, as those darker souls, many of whom had risked their lives for freedom in the Great War and who raised their children with pride and dignity in the plague years, decided to confront the nation's demons and to demand freedom on their own terms. Violent reactions to the Supreme Court order to desegregate public schools in the *Brown v. Board of Education* decision, and the brutal lynching of Emmett Till, along with the images of his battered body published in *Ebony* magazine, exposed the hypocrisy of the nation representing itself as the last line of defense of freedom against the Soviet threat. Mamie Till-Mobley's decision to publish the images of her child's corpse was a refusal. America, U.S.A., could not hide from itself anymore. From 1954 through the 1960s, the country convulsed as it grappled explicitly with the contradiction at its heart. Freedom seekers pursued what historians describe as a "Second Reconstruction" hell-bent on fulfilling the broken promises of the first. Boycotts, sit-ins, and massive acts of civil disobedience were met with lynchings, the brutality of sheriffs, the violence of the Klan, and "respectable" White Citizens'

Councils. The power of a dream foretold, expressed in 1963 at the Lincoln Memorial, and the promise of civil rights legislation were both devastated by the shock of assassinations. Desperate riots in cities followed, as did the anguish of Vietnam. The heady times included calls for Black Power, the demands of the "forgotten American," and the political corruption unmasked by Watergate. Roiling conflicts shook the foundations of America's self-conception. How could the country imagine itself in such times? How did it remember or disremember against the backdrop of a chorus of demands to be free, an insistence on the continuity of the American experience, and the mounting evidence that we were not who we said we were? The way America's leaders answered these questions in real time revealed the core truths of the country and how they were hidden by a storybook version of itself.

—

In 1957, the year nine Black teenagers attempted to desegregate Little Rock's Central High School, the federal government created the Civil War Centennial Commission. The idea was to use the anniversary of the Civil War "to promote patriotic instruction." Ulysses S. Grant III, the grandson of President Grant, was chosen to chair the commission, and he was explicit in his aim. "Our children and their parents will be inspired by a better knowledge of what Americans have done for the principles they held dear," Grant declared. "We are confident that the results will lead to a better understanding of America's day of greatness, and a more unified country."

The commemorations hoped to fortify an ideological consensus throughout the nation. Members of the commission understood that they could not do this by way of some centralized effort. Television and mass media made it possible to decentralize the commemorations. States and local groups were tasked with developing programs of all kinds. As such, the organizers did not aim to control the activities across the country but to infuse them with the American idea and national unity. These values were expressed in the events that officially launched the centennial celebration—the simultaneous tributes to President Grant at his tomb in

New York and General Lee at his crypt in Lexington, Virginia, in 1961. Both, by this point, were heroes and examples of national unity. Occasions for disremembering.

In late 1961, Ulysses S. Grant III was replaced as chairman of the commission by the historian Allan Nevins, who insisted on balance in the commemorations throughout the country. As the civil rights movement heated up, regional tensions ran high. Those tensions pressed the need for cohesion rather than conflict. As Nevins put it, "Above all our central theme will be unity, not division. When we finally reach the commemoration of Appomattox, we shall treat it not as a victory or defeat, but as a beginning of a century of increasing concord, mutual understanding, and fraternal affection among all the sections and social groups." In this, Nevins and the commission were in lockstep with consensus historians. The challenge, of course, involved how, if at all, a celebration of "increasing concord, mutual understanding, and fraternal affection" would recognize the place of slavery and race, and the role of African Americans, in the Civil War—especially against the backdrop of what was, by all intents and purposes, a social revolution. Nevins washed it over. "A host of white northerners died for what they held a sacred duty," he said, and "a host of Negroes died, many in the uniform of the United States, for the achievement of freedom and human equality. We must honor them all."

Despite Nevins's words, the Civil War celebrations across the country reflected, and in some cases reenacted, the deep divisions at the heart of the war. How could it be otherwise? At the very moment in which the nation sought to commemorate the Civil War, the country was in the middle of its latest battle over the issue of race. The Civil War had never ended.

The dramatic tension of the moment was not lost on the Kentucky-born, Pulitzer Prize–winning poet and novelist Robert Penn Warren. As the Black freedom movement intensified with the sit-ins in 1960 and 1961, Warren was invited by the editors of *Life* magazine to reflect on the centennial of the American Civil War. The result was his important book *The Legacy of the Civil War,* an impassioned meditation on the ways the war "grows in [America's] consciousness," and how a confrontation with its legacies affords a different way of imaging what the United States might be as a nation. Warren declared that "to be American is not . . . a matter of blood; it is a matter of an idea—and history is the image of that idea." He tried to locate the root of Americans' increasing return to the war:

> No, simply piety and blood connection do not account for the appeal, and certainly not for the fact that the popular interest has been steadily rising, and rising for nearly twenty years before the natural stir about the approaching centennial. . . .
>
> The turning to the Civil War is, however, a more significant matter than the manipulations of propaganda specialists, and their sometimes unhistorical history. When a people enters upon a period of crisis it is only natural that they look back upon their past and try to find therein some clue to their nature and their destiny.

Warren called for an unflinching encounter with the past and the present. Such a confrontation meant discarding the crutches of both the Southern "Great Alibi"—the notion that all the region's problems resided with the intrusions of the hypocritical North—and the Northern "Treasury of Virtue": the idea that the North's fight to end slavery absolved it of its own sins. In a way, Warren was asking what happens when the nation's double consciousness is transformed into a kind of double vision with which one could "see the problems and values of [the past] and those of our own, set against each other in mutual criticism and clarification." History then becomes a reservoir of funded experience that enables us to better face the future.

The Civil War, for Warren, presented America, U.S.A., with its deepest questions about our fate as individuals and as a nation. It is tragedy, he suggested, the story of "our monstrous inhumanity," of American men and women ensnared in a kind of vindictiveness that twists and perverts virtue, "of a climax drenched with blood but with nobility gleaming ironically, and redeemingly, through the murk; of a conclusion which, for the participants at least, there is a reconciliation of human recognition." We all suffered from the closing of the eyes at the cruel business of slavery, he believed.

But the Civil War offered the possibility of escape from what Warren described as "the common tragic entrapment"—the idea that somehow the hundreds of thousands of lives lost, the bloodshed that soaked the soil of the country, amounted to a ritual sacrifice that could release Americans into a different way of being together. He invokes Lincoln at Gettysburg and turns to Melville's poems of the Civil War: "Let us pray that the terrible historic tragedy of our time may not have been enacted without instructing our whole beloved country through pity and terror."

Warren argues that we were not fundamentally transformed by the sacrificial blood of the war. Justice and a true sense of community were not achieved. The tumultuous days of the Second Reconstruction proved as much. Yet his faith in the power of humility and in human beings leads him to "affirm for us the possibility of the dignity of life" and to assume that, if we stand in right relation to the story of the Civil War, and to the American story more generally, we may yet reach the other side. But here Warren forgets a fundamental insight he himself makes about America, U.S.A.:

> Righteous is our first refuge and our strength—even when we have acted on the grounds of calculated self-interest, and have got caught red-handed, and have to admit . . . to a great bumbling horse-apple of a lie. In such a case, the effect of the conviction of virtue is to make us lie automatically and awkwardly, with no élan of artistry and no forethought; and then in trying to justify the lie, lie to ourselves and transmute the lie into a kind of superior truth.

To escape the trap and to learn the lessons of tragedy, we must be honest enough to tell ourselves the truth about why the country fell into civil war in the first place. But all too often, as was the case when Warren wrote *The Legacy of the Civil War,* Americans retreat into the comfort of lies—that the war was really about states' rights, for example—and deny that "piety and blood," the superiority of white people, matters after all.

—

The centennial of Gettysburg was commemorated with a three-day celebration in July 1963. A large parade marched through the small Pennsylvania town with Civil War regiments from the North and the South. On the third day, the organizers staged a dramatic reenactment of Confederate General George Edward Pickett's charge. I imagine the man in Pickett's role yelled, "Up, men, and to your posts! Let no man forget today that you are from Old Virginia." Over forty thousand people watched the reenactment. But one hundred years later there was no defeat or victory on the battlefield. No staging of the carnage with six thousand Confederate and fifteen hundred Union casualties. Instead, this battle ended with reunion, "in the joining of both sides on the field for a flag salute and the singing of patriotic songs." Just as it was in 1913, there were no signs of Black Union soldiers. No mention of slavery. On the eve of the March on Washington and Dr. Martin Luther King Jr.'s historic "I Have a Dream" speech, the erasure of Black people was deemed necessary for the illusion of a national unity.

One event stands out among the Civil War commemorations for its address of the issue of slavery and freedom directly: the centennial of the Emancipation Proclamation. Of course, there was debate and resistance to the idea of celebrating it at all, especially among Southern delegates and state commissions, but on September 22, 1962, the Centennial Commission sponsored an event at the Lincoln Memorial to mark one hundred years since President Lincoln had issued the proclamation. The program focused primarily on Lincoln as a symbol of national unity. Again, the aim was to smooth over divisions and conflict and reach for consensus. The tumult of the civil rights movement was left aside. Mahalia Jackson sang "The Battle Hymn of the Republic." Governor Nelson Rockefeller of New York presented an original draft of the document to the Library of Congress. But President Kennedy declined to attend for fear of offending Southern voters.

Dr. King had approached Kennedy in the Lincoln Room in October 1961 about a radical renewal of the proclamation. "Mr. President," he said, "I'd like to see you stand in this room and sign a Second

Emancipation outlawing segregation, one hundred years after Lincoln's. You could base it on the Fourteenth Amendment." Kennedy seemed open to the idea but ultimately refused to sign such a document, still worried about losing the South in the coming election.

In the end, Kennedy sent a taped recording to the commemorative event at the Lincoln Memorial. At the urging of his advisers, he also invited Black leaders to attend an event celebrating Lincoln at the White House—a nice dinner party for the "who's who" in Black America. Symbol over substance. King asked for a new Emancipation Proclamation and he got a dinner. He and A. Philip Randolph refused to attend. In the recording sent to the commemoration, Kennedy emphasized the importance of patriotism and commended Black people for remaining "loyal to the nation," rejecting "extreme or violent policies," and working for civil rights "within the framework of the American constitution." It amounted to a pat on the head.

A year later, in front of a crowd of approximately 250,000 people and televised across the nation, Dr. King invoked the Emancipation Proclamation as he called the nation to live up to the principles of the Declaration of Independence:

> When the architects of our republic wrote the magnificent words of the Constitution and the Declaration of Independence, they were signing a promissory note to which every American was to fall heir. This note was a promise that all men—yes, Black men as well as white men—would be guaranteed the unalienable rights of life, liberty and the pursuit of happiness.
>
> It is obvious today that America has defaulted on this promissory note insofar as her citizens of color are concerned. Instead of honoring this sacred obligation, America has given the Negro people a bad check, a check which has come back marked insufficient funds.

Despite his appeal to the words of the Constitution and the Declaration of Independence, and his attempt to hold the nation accountable for failing to live up to its sacred ideals, the country refused to resolve the double consciousness at its heart. Dr. King would end up paying the ultimate price for his witness. White rage left him dead on a motel balcony in Memphis, Tennessee, on April 4, 1968. America, U.S.A., was tragically trapped, still.

—

In the bicentennial year of 1976, Gore Vidal published *1876,* the third novel in his Narratives of Empire series. Through the eyes of the protagonist, Charles Schuyler, Vidal renders the political corruption that haunted the centennial year of the country, the crude and crass materialism that animated the Gilded Age and its social worlds, and the dishonest machinations behind the contested Tilden-Hayes election that signaled the formal end of Reconstruction. Vidal delights in scandal and gossip, in the libidinal and the trivial. But there is no real attention to the legacy of slavery that shadowed the year, to the violence surrounding the collapse of Reconstruction, or to the Black people who now stood between a shattered world and a broken promise. Much like the Centennial Exposition, Black people ("negroes" and "darkies") inhabit the novel as servants on the margins or as details that add color to a scene. They never speak and rarely, if ever, act. Schuyler's daughter, Emma, declares as she looks out upon the streets of Washington, D.C.,

> "It is Africa!" she whispered to me in French as we made our way along the uneven brick sidewalk, where scores of blacks sat comfortably as though at home. Some drank, some played at dice, others made mournful music on homemade pipes whilst overall, in the distance, floating like a dream carved in whitest soap, was the Capitol, ringed by boarding houses.

What she describes feels like a scene in a cutout diorama. Flat, stiff characters who don't move and matter little in the grand scheme of things. And this is the longest passage about Black people in the entire novel.

Vidal wrote *1876* as a reminder for the country. The centennial year, he believed, was a "low point in our Republic's history." And as the country reached for historical fantasies in its bicentennial year, Vidal wanted to remind Americans, among other things, that the nation's past carried the stench of its present. No respite could be found there from the tumult of the 1970s, he maintained. Vietnam and the Watergate scandal revealed the rot at the heart of the country. But his relative silence about race in 1876 and 1976 speaks volumes. Black folk remained either invisible or in their place two hundred years after the founding.

The repetition. Generations stacked upon generations navigating and negotiating a refusal that traces back to the founding, a refusal shadowed by the idea that skin color determines a person's value, dictates the substance of freedom, and strengthens the deep tissue of America, U.S.A.—a repetition heard in each of America's anniversaries: that in the invocation of history, fantasy, and promise, America, U.S.A., belongs only to them, forever and always. Amen!

accel. poco a poco
p

CHAPTER FIVE

1976: BICENTENNIAL

Frank Rizzo, the controversial police commissioner of Philadelphia who later became mayor (and whose statue there was removed after George Floyd's murder), adamantly opposed the idea of a convention organized by the Black Panther Party in his city in 1970. He accused the party, without evidence, of contributing to the deaths of four police officers in August of that same year, and suggested the Panthers were seeking to acquire weapons to wage war on the nation. Since the organization's founding in October 1966 in Oakland, California—just a few months after Stokely Carmichael (later known as Kwame Ture) unveiled the slogan "Black Power" in Greenwood, Mississippi, and President Johnson signed a bill creating the American Revolution Bicentennial Commission—the Black Panthers had come to represent for mainstream America a dangerous kind of militancy. The nonviolence of the civil rights movement had not changed the heart of white America. Dr. King's assassination proved that. Even after the passage of the Civil Rights and Voting Rights acts, police in cities throughout the country continued to abuse Black people with impunity. Poverty drowned the dreams of children from the "Black Belt" in the South to Chicago's South Side. And Black people, young people in particular, many of whom were veterans of the nonviolent movement in the South, had had enough.

Gun-toting Panthers directly challenged the legitimacy of the state's use of violence. They painted police as pigs, rejected capitalism, embraced the lumpenproletariat (those who stood in the shadows of the working class), sponsored social programs like free lunch for poor children, and advocated for a socialist revolution. J. Edgar Hoover declared the party "the greatest threat to the internal security of the United States of America." Now this "band of organized revolutionaries" wanted to hold a convention at Temple University in September 1970. The organizers hoped to write a new constitution for the nation.

Commissioner Rizzo was incensed, and he was not alone. Many who lived in and around the city—especially working-class white ethnics—felt that such an unpatriotic gathering should not happen in Philadelphia, the birthplace of the Republic. They had grown tired of the constant demands and the incessant protests of the last decade. They had wearied of being called oppressors given their own struggles to keep their heads above water in an economy that did not leave much for them to pass on to their children. President Johnson's "guns and butter" (the expense of the Vietnam War and the costs for the Great Society) had left U.S. cupboards dry. And Nixon had not improved matters. Who was going to fight for them and for the America the city of Philadelphia represented? These would be the voters who elected Frank Rizzo mayor a year later. In the early fall of 1970, the idea of a convention organized by the Black Panthers, a group that called for the violent overthrow of the government and that clashed with the police, left them enraged and demanding that authorities prohibit the gathering.

A wide cross-section of activists would attend the new constitutional convention. The Students for a Democratic Society, women from the women's liberation movement, the Young Lords, and American Indian Movement had joined together, at the behest of the Black Panther Party, to plan the work. Six years before the bicentennial year, the organizers maintained that the relentless pursuit of profit by corporations, the displacement of Native peoples, and the enslavement of Black people stained the founding documents of the nation, so much so that any appeal to the Constitution to address historical and present harms inevitably fell short. Calling on the nation to live up to its principles was not enough. What was needed, they argued, was revolutionary change along the lines of the revolution that created the country—a revolution that would fundamentally transform America, U.S.A.

Commissioner Rizzo feared what the organizers intended, but U.S. district judge John P. Fullam disagreed. He insisted that Rizzo and the Philadelphia police department could not "violate the Constitutional Rights of the Black Panther Party, four other organizations, and 21 individuals" who helped organize the convention. Judge Fullam offered his decision "not based on the assumptions that violations are likely to occur, but to reassure the plaintiffs that their rights are not being ignored." Police were prohibited from entering homes without warrants or harassing the attendees of the convention. They had to respect the conventioneers' rights as citizens. As an editorial in the *Philadelphia Inquirer* put it, "If they wish to come in peace, convene in peace and go in peace, so be it." Common Pleas Court judge Joseph Sloane threw out a last-minute request for an injunction made by a Philadelphia high school teacher and the head of the Jewish Defense League in the city. Despite the opposition, the convention was going to happen.

According to *The New York Times,* some six thousand people gathered at Temple University with the goal of rewriting the American constitution. Huey P. Newton, co-founder of the Black Panther Party, spoke at the plenary session. In front of a packed auditorium, he riffed on the basic reasons for the Declaration of Independence. Usurpations justified the rebellion of the colonies, and—here, Newton unknowingly rebuked President Coolidge and his talk of only one necessary revolution—encroachments on freedom two hundred years later motivated the call for a new constitution. "Friends and comrades throughout the United States and throughout the world," he said in his high-pitched voice, "we gather here in peace and friendship to claim our inalienable rights, to claim rights bestowed upon us by an unbroken train of abuses and usurpations. . . . We gather to proclaim to the world that for 200 years we have suffered this long train of abuses . . . while holding to the hope that this would pass." What followed was an account of the repeated failures of the country to live up to its promise. Newton maintained that the evolution and development of the nation only deepened its corruption: America, born in the demand for freedom and dedicated to life, liberty, and the pursuit of happiness, had "in its maturity become an imperialist power dedicated to death, oppression and the pursuit of profits."

Newton concluded his remarks by declaring a loss of faith in the country. Unlike Frederick Douglass, his was not an argument over the idea of America. He did not seek to reclaim the foundational principles of the nation. As we have seen in this book, for much of the nation's history, political debate presupposed the basic tenets of American civil religion, centering around whether or not the country lived up to its promise. From the Puritans of New England to Dr. Martin Luther King Jr. on the steps of the Lincoln Memorial, the idea of America as a chosen nation framed the form and content of political criticism. Civil religion offered the terms of judgment when the nation failed to live up to its ideals—calling America back to its founding principles and warning that if the country failed to live up to those principles then the divine experiment in democracy could be lost. A lamentation of sorts. A judgment that the country was backsliding.

Like those Black men who marched with weapons in the Southwark district of Philadelphia in 1804, Newton, and the young activists who stood in solidarity with the Panthers, sat outside this framework. For them, America, U.S.A., was corrupted beyond redemption. Its bones had been fatally compromised by the cancer of greed and racial hatred. And like William Lloyd Garrison before him, Newton believed the Constitution itself reflected that sickness. "Black people and oppressed people in general have lost faith in the leaders of America, and in the very structure of American government—that is the Constitution, its legal foundation," he declared. "This loss of faith is based upon the overwhelming evidence that this government will not live according to that Constitution because the Constitution is not designed for its people." Appealing to the founding documents, especially to the founding fathers, and to national consensus could not save us. For Newton and many of those who attended the convention (a third of whom, according to *The Philadelphia Inquirer,* were white), "the history of the United States as distinguished from the promise of the ideas of the United States leads to the conclusion that our sufferance is a basic functioning of the government of the United States." This was more than hypocrisy. America's failings cut to the marrow of the bone.

Nothing really came of the convention's efforts. A gathering in Washington, D.C., in November failed to make any significant headway in writing a new constitution. But the symbolism of the effort spoke volumes about the temperament of a segment of the country as the nation prepared to celebrate its 200th year. Faith in the American idea had been fundamentally shaken. The social revolutions of the 1960s and '70s exposed the split in the country and the nation's refusal to resolve it. Those revolutions also revealed an ongoing struggle over the role of America's past in addressing the problems of a nation breaking under the weight of its divisions. Newton insisted that Americans look forward to something new—that the country's past only revealed the corruption of the American soul. Others still reached for the past as a pathway to a better America. No matter the differences, however, few believed that appeals to the founding fathers or to a national consensus would settle anything.

—

Division and widespread disillusionment shadowed the American promise in the 1970s. Difficult days cast a dark shadow on the upcoming anniversary of the nation. So many Americans had lost faith in the country, for different reasons, and so quickly. It only took a little more than a decade, with the ugliness of wars and social unrest in between, for what many perceived as the greatest moment in American history—the defense of freedom in World War II and the postwar boom—to come undone. The revolutionary rattle of those long-suffering on the margins of America, U.S.A., now threatened the idea of an alabaster Republic. Optimism drowned in the reality of a dystopian urban landscape and in the false hopes that the civil rights laws of the 1960s had settled the race problem. Cynicism shrouded the idea of national unity. Some slouched toward Bethlehem while others wrapped themselves in Old Glory.

The bicentennial celebrations of 1976 carried the burden, as did previous anniversaries, of asserting the identity of the nation, but did so against the backdrop of what the historian Daniel Rodgers called the Age of Fracture, where previously held assumptions about national consensus, markets, and institutions began to fragment.

The social revolutions of the 1960s disrupted so much of what had been assumed as commonly shared sensibilities. Americans witnessed the assassination of Dr. Martin Luther King Jr. two years before the gathering in Philadelphia. Cities burned. The violence revealed that underneath American politics lurked an unwieldy chaos. Political violence and mob violence were as American as apple pie. In response, many clamored for law and order. They wanted to take back the country from these chaos agents. Commissioner Rizzo and law enforcement around the country answered that call with unparalleled viciousness, and the Panthers often bore the brunt of their panic and terror. Bobby Hutton and Fred Hampton were among its victims.

Race was merely one aspect of many. Women stepped out of the domestic sphere, challenged directly patriarchal norms, and demanded equal rights. Fifty-eight thousand young men had been killed in Vietnam, with hundreds of thousands more injured. Protests over the war intensified. Americans, with hard hats and long hair, clashed in the streets. Watergate shattered trust in government. President Nixon resigned. President Ford pardoned him and distrust deepened.

OPEC's oil embargo drove up the price of gas and resulted in long lines at the pump. Growing economic inequality dispelled the promise of the postwar boom as "stagflation" (rising prices and stagnant growth) strangled the American dream. Manufacturing industries shuttered their doors or moved in search of cheaper labor, leaving rusted cars, broken windows, and once vibrant communities in ruin. The so-called American Century had come to an end. These were the beginning days of the after times—that moment when the nation was poised to live up to its promise and darkness descended instead.

For the first time in nearly two generations, the liberal idea that government bears a responsibility for the most vulnerable among us and for the public good—an idea wrought in the hardships of the Great Depression, in the service and sacrifice of war, and shadowed by the ugliness of race—cracked and crumbled under the weight of those who tired of the policies of the New Deal and the Great Society, who distrusted government and affirmed individual initiative, and who believed that America belonged to them. As Sean Wilentz wrote in *The Age of Reagan,* "Far more conservative presumptions about recovering and expanding the nation's greatness were gathering force, forged by a political movement that stood well to the right of Richard Nixon and Gerald Ford."

As one storm swept through the country, another much stronger one followed in its wake. How might the story of our national inheritance speak to the moment when the country felt like it was being ripped apart at the seams?

—

In 1975, eight years after "Civil Religion in America" first appeared, Robert Bellah published a relatively small book entitled *The Broken Covenant: American Civil Religion in Time of Trial.* The underlying moral consensus Bellah had presupposed in his classic essay now more than ever appeared to his critics as a fool's errand. Americans were at each other's throats. Any talk of moral consensus was, at best, aspirational in the face of the political and cultural tensions that threatened to rend the country.

Bellah had reached for consensus in 1967 by positing a jointly shared set of values that was evidenced in the founding documents of the country and in the ritual practices (e.g., Fourth of July, Memorial Day, etc.) that acknowledged America's unique place among nations. But if the conflicts of the 1960s presumed that the nation could live up to its promise, as Dr. King urged in his "I Have a Dream" speech," then the challenges of the 1970s, like those noted by the Revolutionary People's Constitutional Convention and others who demanded systemic change, called all of that into question. The country's harsh reaction to the social movements of the 1960s led some to conclude that the values all Americans supposedly shared were not the true animating values of the country at all. Power and greed were.

Bellah's critics had accused him of something akin to "national self-worship"—to them, the Declaration of Independence and the Constitution, along with the "founding fathers," had in Bellah's hands become sacred and beyond reproach, in the sense that they reflected unquestioned principles aligned with the purposes of God—an idolatry obscuring the evils of the nation.

Bellah responded to his critics before and in *The Broken Covenant* by insisting that American civil religion characterized not so much an unwavering faith in the American project but, rather, the "subordination of the nation to enduring ethical principles that transcend it and in terms of which it should be judged." Principles like the equality of men, rooted in religious beliefs, weren't reducible to the nation itself but constituted a covenant. When understood in this way, American civil religion, he maintained, did not simply affirm America's sacred mission, but also offered resources to criticize the country. For Bellah, those principles at the heart of the covenant force us to ask ourselves, especially in moments of crises: Are we living up to the promise of the Declaration? Have we made good on the claims of the preamble to the Constitution? The values of our civil religion, he suggested, served as the measure to judge and, if necessary, to find wanting our way of life.

Bellah knew even in 1967 that civil religion could be used to cloak "petty interests and ugly passions." Even so, in formulating his ideas, he appealed to ethical principles to call the nation to repent. In 1967, such things may have seemed possible. But between then and 1975—with the assassination of Dr. King, the betrayal of the public trust with Nixon and Vietnam, and with unbridled greed and selfishness overrunning every other value—a deeper cynicism took root, as if the darker angels of the country had won the battle over the soul of America. From the other side, Bellah argued that the civil religion he believed so central to American life was now "an empty and broken shell." America no longer stood as a New Jerusalem in contrast to Babylon. For far too many, the country had become Babylon, or perhaps always was—just like it had been Egypt for those enslaved souls of the antebellum period. The consensus to which he'd appealed in 1967 no longer proved effective. "What we face today," he wrote,

> is not simply a low ebb in that spiritual rhythm such as we have faced many times before. It is not that our external covenant [in which the mission of the nation is aligned with the work of God on earth] is performing its function while waiting once again to

> be filled with a new measure of devotion. The external covenant has been betrayed by its most responsible servants and, what is worse, some of them, including the highest of all, do not even seem to understand what they have betrayed. Nor can we discount the events that were disclosed in the second presidential term of Richard Nixon as the work of a small band of wicked men. The men in question, it seems, were not notably more wicked than other Americans. When the leaders of a republic no longer understand its principles, it is because of a history of corruption and betrayal that has affected the entire society.

The crisis confronting the nation, Bellah believed, was a consequence of the erosion of basic moral and spiritual values. And that crisis touched us all. The external covenant represented by the Declaration of Independence and the Constitution (those "metaphysical" principles to which President Coolidge appealed in 1926 even as he declared that the "chief business of the American people is business") had been betrayed by a crass materialism and individualism that undermined a sense of obligation to others. Americans were selfish, greedy, and exercised by their hatreds. Markets distorted their moral sense as the unfettered pursuit of profit corrupted republican virtue. What's more, Bellah now argued, this betrayal was present at the founding. "The covenant . . . was broken almost as soon as it was made." In the country's beginnings, commerce and slavery commingled to darken the new nation's soul.

As I have argued, many Americans turned a blind eye to the consequences of the country's divided soul for generations. They created rituals to fortify their willful ignorance, banished the contradictions out of view, and ruthlessly protected, with law and the mob, the idea of America as a white nation. It is a strange and consistent feature of American life that if the incoherence of the nation threatens to overwhelm the country's self-conception (no matter how fantastical), violence becomes a ready-at-hand remedy (what the historian Richard Slotkin refers to as "regeneration through violence"). A brutal discipline was necessary to reassert the lie and bring the country back to equilibrium. The lynch mob is just one obvious example, but the brandishing of the law—like immigration law today and in the 1920s—is another. All aimed at beating back the realization that we are not who we say we are.

When I read Bellah in *The Broken Covenant,* it is clear, at least to me, that he refused the safety and comfort of the lie. He declared in 1975 that "today the broken covenant is visible to all." We carried our sins forward, and the question, in the face of the discord suffocating the nation on the eve of its bicentennial, was whether the country's past, rife with blood, greed, and mourning, offered any resources with which to build for the future. Or had the American past, once and for all, foreclosed on the future and condemned the country to darkness?

Even as his view changed, Bellah did not believe the broken covenant meant that we ought to reject the past completely. We need only accept that "we are not innocent," he claimed. "We are not saviors of mankind, and it is well for us to grow up enough to know that." Unlike Huey Newton, Bellah did not look at the past and find only lies and ruin, or simply toss the past aside for what awaits in a future made possible by revolution. Instead, he reached for those who had tried to live up to the covenant; who, even in the face of betrayal, left "genuine achievements behind." Slavery was no more. Women had the right to vote. He found assurance in the idea of "a more perfect union." Still, the moral principles underlying the sacred documents of the nation had to become more than words on parchment—they needed to be inscribed on the hearts of American men and women. Americans had to live them—we had to become the kinds of people democracy and the covenant required. But greed, hatred, and selfishness kept getting in the way.

Bellah argued that the appeal to the past—to tradition—was necessary if the country was to make it to the other side of its current malaise. Even with a broken covenant, the path to America's future ran through the country's past. That insight took on added meaning in the bicentennial year, where memory and history were called upon to help fortify a sense of national unity in a moment where things had fallen apart. But for Bellah, the turn to the past could not be one drenched in sentimentality or nostalgia, a simple longing for a perfect Eden where the country's sins did not exist. His appeal was not the same as that of President Coolidge. Instead, America would have to confront its ugly underbelly, grapple honestly and earnestly with its "experience of loss" and its defeats. He put it this way: "If we are to free ourselves for the future we must remember what we would rather forget."

That is a hard prescription for a country addicted to unfettered possibility, to constant economic growth no matter the devastation left in its wake, and with an insatiable desire to acquire things. A tragic understanding was required (an echo, perhaps, of Robert Penn Warren): a view from here that could take in the power of the American promise—a genuine embrace of the ethical principles that constitute the covenant of this nation—and an admission of our defeats and of the evils that sully the so-called Redeemer Nation. As he put it, "Only through a sense of tragedy is it possible to be instructed by the past."

In the face of the conflicts that threatened the Republic, Bellah recommended a reclamation of our national myths and the enduring principles that continued to give them life. As the bicentennial approached, he offered another version of American civil religion shaped not only by the ideals of the nation but by its broken promises. His answer to our national malaise: a consensus with lumps and bruises, a consensus that sings the blues.

> We must reaffirm the outward or external covenant and that includes the civil religion in its most classical form. The Declaration of Independence, the Bill of Rights, and the Fourteenth Amendment to the Constitution have never been fully implemented. Certainly the words "with liberty and justice for all" in the Pledge of Allegiance are not factually descriptive. But while I can understand the feeling of a [William Lloyd] Garrison that hypocritically employed documents should be rejected, I would . . . insist that they be fulfilled. If they have never been completely implemented, neither have they been entirely without effect. . . . It is for this reason that the reassertion of constitutional principles in the face of the recent challenge is so essential.

This isn't the revolutionary call of Huey Newton and those young activists at Temple in 1970. They could take the ideals of the Declaration as their own, but those ideals would be given new life in a future made possible by revolution. But, for Bellah, revolution was not the answer either. He would ask of us a confrontation with the past that Coolidge found unnecessary. But the two men were, in a way, in agreement about how the principles underlying the American Revolution made only one revolution necessary. Something essential and complete was right there in the founding. Strange bedfellows. Instead of scrapping the experiment altogether after two hundred years of existence, Bellah urged Americans to live up to the ideals of the Declaration of Independence—which, for me, necessarily entails the rejection of the idea of America as a white Republic. "If the storm wakes us from false innocence," he wrote, "makes us see our world as it is and not as we blindly wished it to be, then it may be the beginning of liberation." The bicentennial offered Americans the opportunity to do just that. Once again, the nation's anniversary carried the burden of the question *Who do we take ourselves to be?* Or, better, the anniversary provided an occasion where we might finally discover who we really are.

But one wonders about Bellah's faith, not so much in the power of the Declaration's principles—they, like the Gospels, when sincerely embraced, can offer light in darkness—but in the willingness of white men and women in this country to live up to them. For two hundred years, most white Americans waxed and waned when it came to matters of race and democracy, but never fully rejected the white Republic. Black people found themselves caught up in the whirlwind of the country's ambivalence and periodic rage. Piecemeal responses, and alms based in charity and sentimentality instead of justice, contributed to a kind of melancholy rooted in accumulated disappointment and heartbreak. A blues-soaked people.

The nation says we are free, or that we are full-fledged citizens, but the bloodshot eyes of the people forced to accept it all, with clenched teeth and tight lips, reveal revolt simmering under compliant silence. The country says one thing and snatches it back in the blink of an eye—making this place and the white people in it untrustworthy. It is not enough to say, with Bellah, that we must recognize the evils of the American past—

that we were once monstrous. That past lives in the present. The evils do not simply reside in history, as so many would have us believe. They live in the hearts of countless white Americans. We've had to bury many of our dead because of it, and watch eyes dim as dreams shatter in ghettos and in backwoods. We have had to do everything in our power to raise our children not to believe what this world says about them. We've had to prove ourselves worthy over and over again, knowing in our gut that none of this ugliness had anything to do with us. "Beneath this bland, this conqueror-image, a great many unadmitted despairs and confusions, and anguish and unadmitted crimes and failures hide," Baldwin wrote in 1960, when he still held a cautious faith that the country might change. "Before we can do very much in the way of clear thinking or clear doing as it relates to the minorities in this country, we must first crack the American image and find out and deal with what it hides."

Perhaps this change is what Bellah meant by the storm that may wake us from a false innocence. But the appeal to the power of enduring principles—the clawing need for consensus—often fortifies that image rather than cracks it open. We become trapped in the idea of America as if in a hall of mirrors, trapped in the insistence that no matter what we have done or how bloody the hands or corrupted the soul, America is always on the road to a more perfect union. The problem, of course, is that this journey is a lie, one that covers cycles of violence and betrayal—the whip of the whirlwind. White America refuses to give up the idea that this place is a white Republic. Appealing to the power of enduring principles of the American covenant, or the wisdom of the founding fathers, will not resolve this problem. This is not the lesson of tragedy or the blues, because the story that tells us to return to the founding is, more often than not, a lie.

—

In 1975, white America was in full retreat from the gains and promises of the civil rights movement. Proponents of Black Power and activist groups had concluded that the country refused to change—that it could not change without revolution. Loud and angry countervoices shouted,

"How much more do these people want?" Reactionary forces mobilized to take back their country, empowering police to crack down on radical organizations and activists and politicians, and pressing austerity efforts aimed at dismantling the Great Society. Others refused the demands of desegregation, especially in schools; they simply packed up and left cities. White flight resulted in a massive defunding of American public life. Many white Americans demanded that their tax dollars no longer support the idea of a racially just society.

What would it mean for Black people, these darker souls, to believe that white America might wake from its false innocence when present experience suggested otherwise? When the historical evidence was clear? For them, faith had been broken not so much with the principles of the Declaration (after all, the Panthers included the words of the preamble to the Declaration in their Ten-Point Program), but with *white* Americans who claimed those principles as *their* possession. We had to live in the gap between the America that belonged to white people and the America purportedly governed by the rule of law and committed to the ideals of the Declaration. We knew intimately of the deadly consequences of this double consciousness, because we lived among the people who suffered from it.

In their song/poem, "Bicentennial Blues," the artists Gil Scott-Heron and Brian Jackson gave expression to the skepticism of Bellah's faith and the fantasy sold by the bicentennial celebrations.

America has got the blues and it's a bicentennial edition
America has got the blues
It's got the blues because of partial deification
Of partial accomplishments
Over partial periods of time
Halfway justice
Halfway liberty
Halfway equality
It's a half-ass year

A powerful incantation. If only the country knew it had the blues.

—

For many Americans, the bicentennial celebration of 1976 afforded the country an opportunity to put aside such weighty questions and doubts and revel in the power of the American idea. The organizers at the federal and local level hoped that the discord of the last decade and a half would give way to "a renewal of American consensus and patriotism." They hoped that the flag would be redeemed; that the nation could find common ground across the differences that had so exercised the country. President Gerald Ford announced his faith at a naturalization ceremony held at Monticello on July 5, 1976: "After two centuries, there is still something wonderful about being an American. If we cannot express it, we know what it is. You know what it is. . . . Why not just call it patriotism."

The American Revolution Bicentennial Commission (ARBC) set out to deepen that sense of attachment to the idea of America by way of three programs that occasioned reflection on the country's past, present, and future—what it called Heritage '76, Festival USA, and Horizons '76. When President Johnson authorized the ARBC in 1966, he announced to Congress that "the commission would recall to the nation and to the world the 'majestic significance of the Revolution.'" This was not the encounter with tragedy that Bellah commended, but instead a declaration and commemoration of the unique mission of America, U.S.A., set against the backdrop of a country in turmoil.

The ARBC was born the same year as the Black Panther Party, a year after the Watts riots in Los Angeles, and a year before Bellah published "Civil Religion in America." Its planning phase began before the explosions in cities across the nation and the assassination of Dr. King; before Watergate, Nixon's resignation, and the dramatic images of the fall of Saigon. The ten-year gestation process of the bicentennial celebration unfolded as America was coming apart at the seams. The conflicts of the next decade would make the success of the ARBC's mission damn near impossible.

If Americans had entered a period of deep doubts about the trustworthiness of their public institutions, the ARBC's own problems did little to ameliorate those doubts. Initially, the commission imagined a large international exposition in Philadelphia, just like organizers had planned in 1876 and 1926. But the potential $1.5 billion price tag was prohibitive. Another idea involved a Bicentennial Park "that would provide cultural and recreational opportunities in each of the fifty states." This would have been just as costly as the exposition idea in Philadelphia. Nothing came of either idea. Both seemed far-fetched and a bit callous in light of the economic pressures that gripped the nation.

The commission also came under intense scrutiny after it was revealed that the organization engaged in political dealing, leveraging the bicentennial for the benefit of the Nixon administration. On August 14, 1972, *The Washington Post* published a front-page story about the affair. "The documents show that the bicentennial leadership has become deeply involved in political deals with congressmen of both parties who are seeking special treatment and sometimes jobs for relatives or associates," the *Post* reported. The article revealed efforts to sponsor programs to attract women for electoral benefit and disclosed the appointment of civil rights activist and Georgia state legislator Julian Bond's uncle, Max Bond, a Republican who worked for the State Department, who they believed could "help Blacks better understand and relate to the Republican Party." The celebration that aimed to bring the nation together in the aftermath of mass marches, riots, and government corruption was now mired in corruption.

By 1974, the ARBC had been replaced by the American Revolution Bicentennial Administration (ARBA), which was newly charged with "seeing that the federal government and the states cooperate in a common effort and that each individual should have a right to participate." The new organizers immediately concluded that holding the celebration in one city was not feasible and did not best represent the diversity of the country. Unlike the centennial and sesquicentennial expositions, the 1976 Bicentennial was not held in Philadelphia, or in any one central location. Activities were decentralized so as to encourage broad participation across the country. One catalyst was technology; television now allowed for a certain kind of imagined community in ways that had been impossible in 1876 and 1926. Whether you lived in Washington, D.C., or Los Angeles, or in my small town on the coast of Mississippi, the bicentennial celebration found its way into your living room. The entertaining national programming was complemented by local activities centered around the commission's three themes: America past, present, and future. Sixteen hours of programing, with shows featuring the likes of Bob Hope and the Mormon Tabernacle Choir, offered "an exposition of the nation itself." All with the aim of deepening local attachments to the nation.

The ARBA also sought to incorporate more diverse voices in its decision-making and representations of the past by establishing an advisory board that included Alex Haley and Betty Shabazz, the widow of Malcolm X. Over twelve thousand "bicentennial communities" were designated, as Americans from all backgrounds and races were urged to get involved and celebrate the birth of the nation together. Activities ranged from Operation Sail 1976, which brought sixteen tall sailing ships from around the world into New York Harbor, to the Bicentennial Wagon Train Pilgrimage to Pennsylvania, to the Smithsonian's Festival of American Folklife, which included exhibits of folk songs and dances from a variety of ethnic backgrounds. Each event affirmed national unity and common purpose.

Even though the organizers were mindful of the deep divisions in the country, and in some ways tried to celebrate the diversity of the nation as a response to those divisions, they still relied on a storybook version of America. A devout piety for the past combined with celebrations of American achievement that opened up an unbounded future. This appeal to an open-ended future was critical given the feeling that there was no exit from the morass that engulfed the country. People were still in the streets demanding a more substantive reckoning with the country's past and present. They challenged storybook America. But for organizers of bicentennial celebrations across the country, the American past was not a repository for a broken covenant or even simply the period when the country made a tragic choice. Instead, history and memory called forth reverence and respect in these irreverent times. As the narrator of the ARBA's promotional video, "Bicentennial, USA" made clear: "*Heritage '76 reminds us of our freedoms.*" Bicentennial celebrations drew, then, on a triumphant story about the nation's past and, in doing so, aimed to heal the scars of the last decade with a story that guaranteed a future animated by the country's founding principles. Tragedy played no role here. Consensus was implied.

Much of this was funded by private/public partnerships that invited a tidal wave of commercialization. The celebration would not just be televised—it would be sold. Big business subsidized events and hawked its wares. *Time* magazine reported that "like a sudden swarm of 200-year locusts, commemorative kitsch is appearing everywhere." Star-spangled whoopee cushions; patriotic toilet seats; Liberty hamburgers; red, white, and blue beer cans. In the special bicentennial issue of *Ebony* magazine, a United Airlines ad urged readers to "Celebrate Yesterday's Heroes. Save with United's Bicentennial Fare" with an image of the country overlaid with representations of heroic Black figures in every region. Yale University's Bicentennial Schlock collection, which started as a class project for Jesse Lemisch's American studies course at SUNY Buffalo in the spring of 1976, contains a lot of this kitsch: from bicentennial plates to stuffed bicentennial mice. I believe I even wore a pair of red, white, and blue bicentennial pants as an eight-year-old. Taken together, a kind of crass consumerism attended the celebration of the nation alongside the solemnity of events.

President Ford spoke at the Bicentennial ceremony at the National Archives on July 2, declaring the Declaration of Independence to be the "fixed star of freedom" for the nation:

> I am standing here before the great charters of American liberty under law. Millions of Americans, before me and after me, will have looked and lingered over these priceless documents that have guided our 200 years of high adventure as "a new nation, conceived in Liberty, and dedicated to the proposition that all men are created equal." Those were Lincoln's words as he looked to the Declaration of Independence for guidance when a raging storm obscured the Constitution. We are gathered here tonight to honor both.

It was a familiar, and by now traditional, refrain: that the country was birthed in freedom. And like Lincoln and Frederick Douglass before him, President Ford sought to read the Declaration as the foundation of America's constitutional order and insisted that its moral insights demand "far more than the patriot sacrifices of the American Revolution, more than the legal stabilizer of the Constitution." More than buying things. He spoke of the power of a lasting truth that "we are all born free in the eyes of God." Just as President Coolidge argued fifty years earlier, that truth was not reducible to political matters. Americans simply needed to live up to it.

> That eternal truth is the great promise of the Declaration, but it certainly was not self-evident to most of mankind in 1776. I regret to say it is not universally accepted in 1976. Yet the American adventure not only proclaimed it; for 200 years we have consistently sought to prove it true. The Declaration is the promise of freedom; the Constitution continuously seeks the fulfillment of freedom. The Constitution was created and continues—as its preamble states—"to secure the Blessings of Liberty to ourselves and our Posterity."

President Ford appealed to America's civil religion as a way to resolve the discord of the period, with only a slight nod to the country's failures. Tragedy gave way to the storybook version of America's promise. He didn't talk of "a more perfect union," but President Ford acknowledged that the principles and eternal truth of the Declaration of Independence were "not universally accepted." Unlike the conclusions of those who attended the convention at Temple in 1970, he insisted that our task was not to cast away the promise of America, but to "join with those brave and farsighted Americans of 1776" and pledge our lives to the enduring principles of the Declaration, "with the firm reliance on the protection of divine providence."

No matter the power of the diverse appeals, the patriotism of the bicentennial celebrations could not silence the deep divisions in the country. The appeal to consensus had lost its power by 1976, and the divisions were not mere abstractions; rather, they reflected the lived experiences of many on the margins of American society and revealed the contradictions at the heart of the Republic. Freedom, in many ways that mattered to people's quality of life, from education to jobs, remained the white man's gift, ever elusive. Conservative voices like William F. Buckley Jr. denied the legitimacy of those experiences. They cringed under the weight of identity politics and the cries of victimization. Amid the celebration of the nation, the question arose: Did the country belong to all of its people or only to those who considered themselves, in the language of the Klan of the 1920s, "true Americans"?

—

In previous major anniversary celebrations, a counternarrative emerged from Black people who were rendered invisible or pushed to the margins of the American story. July 5 events or invocations of Black history called attention to the practices that contradicted the storybook version of the nation. But during the bicentennial, that counternarrative also came from white Americans. Jeremy Rifkin, a seasoned anti-war activist, along with other activists who participated in New Left movements, helped organize the People's Bicentennial Commission (PBC) in 1971. They were responsible, in part, for leaking the documents to *The Washington Post* about the ARBC.

The PBC understood the history of the country as a key battlefield in the war for the country's soul, and sought to use the bicentennial celebration not as an occasion to appeal to consensus—and therefore fortify the status quo—but to tell a different story of the nation that made the radical movements of the mid-twentieth century examples of true patriotism. Activists who challenged the country were not anti-American, according to the PBC. A better story of our beginnings revealed that they were, in fact, the custodians of America's promise. The bicentennial celebration was not a time for "grandiose display[s] of chauvinism," Rifkin declared, "but rather a time for the reaffirmation of the principles of democracy and equity for all." Corporations and greed had hijacked the principles of the Declaration and the country. All the cheap bicentennial trinkets made in Japan and China proved the point. The PBC offered a counter vision—especially in the moment of commemoration. In an interview in *The New York Times* in 1975, Rifkin explained what motivated his view:

> We have a great revolution to look back on. Sam Adams was a true revolutionary. Tom Paine was a true revolutionary. The artisans of Boston were revolutionaries. And they won. With that kind of tradition to build on, we can organize a whole new radical movement in this country with which ordinary Americans can identify. We can take patriotism from the D.A.R. [Daughters of the American Revolution] and the American Legion. We'll call it the Red, White, and Blue.

For Rifkin, patriotism and America's civil religion were not the sole possession of conservative forces. Neither was the history of the country, especially the American Revolution. In fact, that history, rightly understood, contained resources to imagine the country anew. And it was on these grounds that the PBC marshalled an all-out campaign that involved marches, protests, and taking out large ads in *The New York Times* condemning big business for hijacking the American Revolution. They even mailed "cassette tapes to the wives of Fortune 500 executives asking the women to interrogate their husbands" about their participation in corporate corruption. The PBC set out not only to claim the bicentennial but, in their criticisms of big business and its capture of government, to reclaim the country. At its height the organization claimed local chapters in "the majority of states" and "a paid membership of over 10,000."

As with all of these celebrations, the battle over the past was not about the past at all. It involved a struggle over the present and its meanings for Americans. The past was needed to make sense of economic and political upheavals and to account for culture and the values that shaped the country's way of life. Appeals were made either to justify the order of things or to disrupt that order. This orientation to the past has been a perennial preoccupation in America, U.S.A.: What is our relation to the

Old World? How are we to think of ourselves here—with Native peoples and with those snatched to clear the land and the swamps, to plant rice and indigo, and to harvest the cotton? All of which was often denied for the comfort of the fantasy of a lily-white America.

—

"Who controls the past controls the future; who controls the present controls the past," O'Brien tells Winston in George Orwell's *1984*. This was the opening line to a J. Anthony Lukas feature in *The New York Times,* "Who Owns 1776?" Lukas would go on to publish the Pulitzer Prize–winning book *Common Ground,* about the battles over busing in Boston, seen through the lives of three families. But in May 1975, he set out to think about the contested character of the bicentennial celebration in the historic city of Boston, where the stories of the Boston Massacre, the Tea Party, Paul Revere, and the Battle of Bunker Hill clashed with the pressing reality of a city at war over enforced busing and school desegregation.

Lukas brilliantly contrasted the different appeals to that history by various actors who laid claim to the past to justify their present actions. Anti-busing activists in East and South Boston likened their experience of being told which school their children would attend to the oppression faced by the American colonists in the 1770s; they claimed "to be fighting for the same right to control their own lives." The PBC also embraced the legacy of that historic revolutionary moment, organizing a massive rally in Concord and staging a midnight ride during which participants shouted, "Big Business is coming." Black Bostonians, among those who chose to participate in the bicentennial celebrations, noted the sacrifice of Crispus Attucks ("the first blood spilled for American liberty") and called attention to the abolition movement of the nineteenth century, which held meetings at, among other places, historic Faneuil Hall, where Frederick Douglass spoke in 1849.

President Ford joined this motley crew all claiming some sense of possession of the country. Lukas described the conflict between these forces as Ford spoke at a commemorative event at the Old North Bridge on April 19, 1975. With thirty thousand young people gathered under the banner of the People's Bicentennial "on a hillside overlooking the Concord River, where the Minutemen had rallied 200 years ago," the president sought to give voice to the power of the American idea. With each word he spoke, according to Lukas, boos rang out, along with shouts from the young activists in attendance of the 200-year-old slogan "Don't Tread on Me" and cries of "No More War!" They dared to claim the American Revolution as their own as they rejected Ford's appeal to a storybook America.

In the background of this confrontation over the meaning of history and what it suggested about the country lay the brewing tensions of the battle over busing and the desegregation of schools in cities like Boston. Lukas interviewed several of the activists involved with the anti-busing group Restore Our Alienated Rights (ROAR), many of whom believed forced busing to be an outrage that precluded the celebration of the bicentennial in Boston. "How can we celebrate our country's history when we are being denied the very rights we fought for in the Revolution?" wondered an activist named Nancy Yotts. Echoing the sentiment of Hiram Evans in 1926, Yotts likened the white communities of East and South Boston to the colonists. "We're a colony demanding our independence," she said. With this analogy, the judge who issued the busing decree functioned like King George, and the politicians who supported it were considered Tories. The irony, of course, is that many of these people were the children and grandchildren of the European immigrants once viewed in the 1920s as a dangerous infestation, a corruption of true American identity. Now they claimed the mantle of the colonists fighting King George. In response to the analogy, Lukas asked Yotts, "And you're the revolutionaries?" Several women in the interview shouted, "No, no. We're not revolutionaries. We're conservatives." The revolutionaries were those who embraced that "People's Bicentennial thing." "We're conservatives. We want to go back to the old way."

A fascinating moment. The women activists imagined themselves as the victims of the tyranny of big government. And yet they invoked the Revolution not as a period of upheaval, but as the moment when the basic values of American life were made clear—values that had now been upended by those who wanted to socially engineer a more equitable society with little to no regard for the cultural institutions (e.g., South Boston High School) of their community. The anti-busing activists believed that they were, in effect, unfree. Here race, class, and ethnicity collided, as avatars of "reactionary populism" voiced fierce resentments toward white elites who cared little about working-class white folk and held deep-seated fears about Black people, whose presence threatened to upend their way of life. As Ronald P. Formisano argues in his important book *Boston Against Busing,* this moment in the city of Boston cannot be reduced simply to racism, although "racism added an ugly, frenetic charge of ferocity and violence to many antibusing protests." Class and status resentments were also powerful forces.

The bicentennial did go on in Boston. And yet Stanley Forman's Pulitzer Prize–winning photograph *The Soiling of Old Glory,* taken on April 5, 1976, amid the city's celebration, solidified Boston as the symbol of the white backlash: Nixon's "silent majority"—those hardworking, patriotic, and trustworthy white folk—were no longer going to stand idly by as Black people and their allies in big government threatened to destroy all that they cherished in the name of some specious idea of racial equality. The image of a young white teenager, Joseph Rakes, attacking a well-dressed Black man, Ted Landsmark, with a staff bearing the American flag during an anti-busing protest ran on the front page of the *Boston Herald* and announced to the country, to the world, that race still haunted the United States—and that some white people had had enough.

That day, two hundred students from South Boston and Charleston had assembled to march to City Hall Plaza to protest forced busing. Some carried signs that said RESIST. Rakes grabbed his family's flag and joined them. Most of these protesters saw themselves as patriots "defending their liberty against a judge run amok." When the students and a few adults arrived at City Hall, city council president Louise Day Hicks, who vehemently opposed busing and helped found ROAR, invited them into the council chamber. It was a demonstration of solidarity. Everyone stood proudly to say the Pledge of Allegiance. When the students left the building, they encountered a group of Black students touring the area. Words were exchanged. Tempers flared. The battle was engaged.

Ted Landsmark, who was rushing to a meeting at City Hall, found himself in the wrong place at the wrong time, walking straight toward the white students protesting. They turned on him. Words rang out: "Get that nigger." They kicked and punched him. Broke his nose. Joseph Rakes, with the American flag in hand, turned around and started to swing the flag at Landsmark. The police stepped in. Others came to help. Landsmark escaped. He later told one reporter, "I was just out there walking to City Hall in my three-piece suit. I was anyone." And suddenly, someone tried "to kill me with the American flag." Class did not matter. The fact that Landsmark was a lawyer did not protect him. As he told one writer, "I couldn't put my Yale degree in front of me to protect myself." In the furious eyes of those who wanted to save their community, he was "a nigger they were trying to kill." Not everything is about race in America, U.S.A., yet so much is.

Against the backdrop of the Old State House, and among the shadows cast by the place where Crispus Attucks, a fugitive slave who stole his freedom, died, Stanley Forman's startling image captured the contradiction at the heart of the Republic in its bicentennial year. The American flag was used as a weapon to assault a Black man. A layered symbol of the history of race in the country, if ever there was one. No matter the particulars—that the white man grabbing Landsmark in the photograph was actually trying to save him—the image affirmed what many believed to be true: that America, U.S.A., on the eve of its bicentennial, had no real place for Black people. One letter to *The Boston Globe* announced, "The black people of Boston have very little reason to celebrate the Bicentennial, for they still are not free to safely walk the streets of this city."

By 1976, the image counted among a vast archive of photographs and film footage of white violence. The nation had witnessed so much over the last decades. Brutal lynchings. Mobs attacking children. Police battering skulls. And though the symbolism of *The Soiling of Old Glory* shocked aesthetic tastes, the image simply took its place among a host of others. Susan Sontag would write just a year later, in her book *On Photography,* about "the lowering of the threshold of what is terrible." People get accustomed to what once upset their stomachs, and compassion fatigue sets in, especially when it feels as if you are losing your own footing. But as Sontag wrote, "Our ability to stomach . . . rising grotesqueness in images (moving and still) and in print has a stiff price."

> In the long run, it works out not as a liberation of but as a subtraction from the self: a pseudo-familiarity with the horrible reinforces alienation, making one less able to react in real life. . . . The point is not to be upset, to be able to confront the horrible with equanimity.

Or, perhaps, the point is to confront and see the horrible as nevertheless just: in that way, the image neither liberates nor subtracts from the self, but rather confirms it. Finally, the "silent majority," with the American flag in hand, was fighting back.

Black America understood that the celebration of the country's 200th birthday occurred against the backdrop of freedom-snatching expressions of white rage. *The Soiling of Old Glory* was a perfect image. When it came to Black people, the country had failed to make good on the promises of the Declaration of Independence, and the nation had tired, once again, of demands for racial justice. Just as in 1876 and 1926, violence shadowed the days, creating a profound ambivalence among Black Americans regarding 1976. While the Afro-American Bicentennial Corporation, one of the organizations that grew out of the attempt to engage more diverse voices in the celebration, insisted that Black history sites be a part of the celebration, many African Americans resisted the bicentennial. When Lukas interviewed Byron Rushing, director of Boston's Museum of Afro-American History, for his *New York Times* piece, Rushing was direct and clear: "Blacks don't respond much to all this Bicentennial talk. That may be because we've always taken the original documents more seriously than whites." Rushing went on to say that "we couldn't get any solace from our experience in the real world, so we fell back on the Bible and the Constitution. They told us what was right and good. They told us the promise. But we did that for so long I'm afraid the documents have lost their magic now. We're not looking for promises now." A bicentennial blues indeed.

—

In the August 1975 special bicentennial issue of *Ebony* magazine, the founder and publisher John H. Johnson expressed his own ambivalence toward the commemoration. "We present here, not a celebration of the Bicentennial but an assessment of 200 years of black history." White America could celebrate, he wrote, but Black America had to call attention to "200 years of slavery, servitude, segregation, discrimination, poverty and even death and destruction." Black America had to point to the ugly underbelly of America, U.S.A., at the very moment in which the nation appealed to consensus.

The special issue offered a sweeping account of Black history and politics, with articles written by Black scholars on issues ranging from the role of African Americans in the Revolutionary War to the place of Black humor in American life. Extended pieces on Black women, electoral politics, business, working-class movements, culture, and education gave *Ebony*'s readers a sense of the progress of the race and the challenges they still faced, and exposed the rank hypocrisy of the country's celebration.

One article, "Martyrs for Black Freedom," was accompanied by images of the dead and posed a searing question: "A nation celebrates 200 years of its history, but how many honors will there be for the black men and women—for Nat Turner and the unnamed victims of lynchers, for Malcolm X and Martin Luther King Jr., for Medgar Evers, George Jackson, Fred Hampton and Lamar Smith—who are martyrs of the virulent notion that black men who refuse to bow must then die?" The images stare back from the page. Some smiling. All dead. Dr. King's hands wave at the crowd at the March on Washington. A broken promise. The glaring eyes of white men, standing over a brutal triple lynching in Marion, Indiana, cover almost half a page. The exposed torsos, the lynching rope, twisted necks of two Black men on a pole, and one body face down beneath their dangling bare feet center the eye. A tall white man on the left with his hat slightly to the side smirks at the camera. He is proud of his work. The script underneath the image reminds the reader of the brutality of "the early 1920s in Ku Klux Klan–infested Marion, Ind." An echo. How, *Ebony*'s editors wondered, do we commemorate their sacrifice?

The question of whether African Americans should celebrate the bicentennial frames the entire issue. The editors invited Joseph H. Jackson, president of the National Baptist Convention, U.S.A., and pastor of Olivet Baptist Church in Chicago; Vernon Jordan, then the executive director of the National Urban League; and historian Lerone Bennett Jr., author of *Before the Mayflower* and, at the time, senior editor of *Ebony*, to respond. Their pieces offered a broad range of perspectives.

Jackson enthusiastically argued that African Americans should celebrate the bicentennial. In celebrating the country, he argued, we celebrate its values and its aspirations. We "re-commit ourselves to the unfinished task that remains before us." His was not an ambivalent embrace, but one qualified by the ongoing work to perfect the Union. "We can rejoice, we do rejoice, that our nation has put aside many of the evils of segregation and discrimination and we believe she will yet subdue them and fulfill herself and her mission in a world of imperfect human beings." In a way, Jackson embraced America's civil religion and those enduring principles that set the nation apart from others in the world, even as he acknowledged the reality of racism. During this historic celebration, he insisted, Black people had to lay claim to the country and to the cause of freedom that it represents.

Vernon Jordan was more ambivalent. Black people, he wrote, should participate in the bicentennial celebrations only "to remind a forgetting nation of the vitally important role blacks have played in it since the days when the wilderness reached to the very shores of the Atlantic." He warned of reducing the complexity of the country to "homogenized myths" that projected consensus and blinded white America to its failures. Jordan then reached for the lasting power of the Declaration of Independence. Its revolutionary ideals remained relevant to the needs and aspirations of Black people and the nation. In this sense, the celebration of the bicentennial required our presence, he argued, "to ensure that what might otherwise be a meaningless, commercialized celebration of mythology becomes a look backward to the past for insights and ideals that can be brought to bear on present problems."

Lerone Bennett disagreed. His was not a qualified or ambivalent embrace. He rejected the idea of celebrating the nation. Pure and simple: America had failed to live up to its promise. The country had failed Black people; as a social historian, he said this with the authority of the American historical archive. In 1975, he maintained, we were still not free:

> Two hundred years of evasion of the central mandate of our revolutionary birth, two hundred years of slavery, segregation, inequality, unemployment, racism, and poverty, two hundred years of Little Rocks and Little Big Horns and Scottsboros and South Bostons have brought us to the brink of national disaster. Our economy is in shambles. Our political institutions are in disarray. Our spiritual temperature is at an all-time low. And grown men are dressed up in ridiculous costumes, playing freedom games with rusty muskets on astroturf.
>
> This spectacle is an affront to truth and freedom. It is a desecration of the ideal. It is a mirage, an illusion, designed, at least in part, to divert attention away from our failure to create a human environment not only for blacks but also for whites and reds.

Invoking Frederick Douglass's July 5, 1852, address, Bennett declared the celebration "a sham" and urged Americans to seize the opportunity to remind the country—to remind white America—of its sins. Repentance was needed; freedom must be demanded. For Bennett, the embrace of freedom involved a collective decision of the nation to finally live up to the "Old Declaration of Independence." America must declare a renewed commitment to the genuine flourishing of each of its citizens regardless of the color of their skin; it must legitimately live the idea that all people are created equal. For this to become a reality in the country, Bennett believed, Americans had "to make the American Revolution, which was betrayed in the hour of its birth." He was not advocating for the kind of revolution Newton called for, but something more akin to what Bellah commended. America had to rid itself, finally, of the double consciousness that was the source of our national misery. And here he turned to the poet Langston Hughes:

O, let America be America again—
The land that never has been yet—
And yet must be—the land where every *man is free.*

No matter their disagreements, all three respondees insisted on the importance of Black history to the nation's self-understanding. By 1976, any celebration of America required an acknowledgment of our role in its journey. Unlike 1876 and 1926, where Frederick Douglass sat mute and A. Philip Randolph was summarily dismissed, in the bicentennial year, in the aftermath of the Black freedom struggle, the role and place of Black people in American history could be ignored only at great peril, for the embers in America's cities were still glowing. In 1976 that history came out of the darkness and was embraced by many as a critical part of the diverse heritage of the nation. The ripping tide of America's diversity was not denied.

But embracing that diversity was not the same as confronting the past or reckoning with the incessant demands for a more just America. Instead, for those who clamored for the comfort of consensus, the discordant elements of the country were "harmonized into a nonthreatening spectacle, one that allowed Americans to feel connected and detached at the same time."

In 1975, for example, President Ford did something no previous president had done. He issued a message on the observance of Black History Week. Of course, underneath it lay a political calculus: that perhaps he could attract more Black people to the Republican Party. Despite his motivation, the message marked a critical moment in the country. "With the growth of the civil rights movement," Ford said,

> has come a healthy awareness on the part of all of us of achievements that have too long been obscured and unsung. Emphasis on these achievements in our schools and colleges and in daily community life places in timely perspective the benefits of working together as brothers and sisters regardless of race, religion or national origin for the general well-being of all our society.
>
> In this spirit, I urge my fellow citizens to be mindful of the valuable message conveyed to us during the celebration of this week.

These were the initial steps in yoking the story of Black people to the American idea. Ford made no attempt to beat back the diversity of the nation or to render Black people invisible, as had happened in speeches in 1876 and 1926. But rather than press for the confrontation with history that Robert Penn Warren had recommended, Ford tried instead to conscript it, to draft the journey of Black Americans into the service of an overarching story about the grandness of the American experiment and the power of American patriotism. He was folding Black experience into the consensus myth in a way that would keep it from threatening the Republic. Read this way, Black history would not expose the lies at the heart of the country, but instead affirm its progress toward a more perfect union.

In 1976, the Association for the Study of African American Life and History—the organization Carter G. Woodson had co-founded in 1915, and that gave us Negro History Week in the sesquicentennial year—urged President Ford to issue a proclamation recognizing the expansion of

Black History Week to Black History Month. It was, in a way, an echo of Dr. King's request to President Kennedy to issue a second Emancipation Proclamation. And, like Kennedy, President Ford refused; instead, he offered a message to the nation in which he urged Americans to "seize the opportunity to honor the too-often neglected accomplishments of Black Americans in every area of endeavor throughout our history." Stevie Wonder's classic album *Songs in the Key of Life* would be released the same year with his lyrical rendering of Black history in the track "Black Man." As a child, I memorized the words, and I still remember the segment on the Richard Pryor special where children of different races and backgrounds sing the song and its refrain for a national audience. These words stand out.

For with justice not for all men
History will repeat again
It's time we learned
This world was made for all men

The song was a celebration and a warning: all was not well in the country. A storm was brewing among those who had tired of the demands for racial justice. They—like the children of those European immigrants in 1920s Boston who felt left behind amid the cultural and political revolutions convulsing the nation—would soon seize control of the country, assert the power of America's sustaining myths, ignore the coiled serpent in the bosom of the nation, and declare, "It's morning in America again."

Like a violent circus ♩ = 152
ff
8
p
ff

INTERLUDE

THE AFTER TIMES

Ronald Reagan's election shifted the center of gravity of the country. For many white Americans, especially those conservatives who rejected any talk of American malaise, the divisions and social tumult of the 1970s had to be put aside, and consensus reasserted. Reagan was elected to "make America great again." The sense of dread that enveloped Black communities as he took office was palpable. Reagan would be the cause of World War III, some said. His economic policies—what George H. W. Bush had described while challenging him in the Republican primary as "voodoo economics"—would destroy the country or, at least, erase Black economic gains since the 1960s. These were reasonable concerns. Reagan was not widely considered a friend of Black America. As governor of California, he had distinguished himself among most Black people as a notoriously bigoted politician in the George Wallace mold as he denounced open housing, attacked the state university system, harassed and jailed Black Panthers, and railed against civil rights laws. In what felt like a fit of vengeance against the social movements of the 1960s and '70s, the country had elected this man president.

Conservatives who rejected the basic premises of the civil rights movement, as well as many of those white ethnics in South and East Boston who felt left behind, now had a champion in the White House. And

Reagan did not disappoint them. With remarkable speed and efficiency, he began an assault on the underlying framework of the New Deal and the Great Society. In so many ways, the former B-list actor turned politician stands as the prototype for Donald Trump. He brought the power of celebrity to the White House in the service of a conservative agenda. And, just as the Heritage Foundation would hand Trump the policy blueprint Project 2025, in 1981 that same organization delivered Reagan a *Mandate for Leadership* with over two thousand policy recommendations that would fundamentally change the trajectory of the country.

But Reagan also did something that Trump would show little to no interest in embracing. In 1983, he signed the Martin Luther King Day bill into law. In a somewhat odd and ironic move for a candidate elected to undo the gains of the civil rights movement, Reagan approved a piece of commemorative legislation that made explicit the connection between the experiences of Black people and the history of the nation. What the bicentennial celebration had sought to do—by bringing into the American story a particular version of Black history—Reagan formalized and extended. This legislation was more than President Ford's acknowledgment of the importance of Negro History Week or the formal recognition of Black History Month in 1976. A federal holiday honoring Dr. King went further—it ushered him into the pantheon of the nation's saints. He and the movement he represented now became one of the most important examples in the story of America's ongoing effort to become a more perfect union. In effect, Dr. King and the civil rights movement became a part of America's civil religion, not so much to acknowledge the tragic dimensions of the country's past, but to help obscure American double consciousness by affirming the nation's inherent goodness.

During the signing ceremony in the Rose Garden, Reagan recounted a particular story of the civil rights movement, one that began with Rosa Parks and the March on Washington, and ended with Dr. King's tragic assassination. King's efforts "awakened something strong and true," Reagan declared. He stirred a "sense that true justice must be colorblind, and that among white and black Americans, as he put it, 'Their destiny is tied up with our destiny, and their freedom is inextricably bound to our freedom; we cannot walk alone.' " Here Reagan drafted King's legacy and the civil rights movement into the storybook version of America. In this telling, King did not introduce anything new into American political discourse—he simply appealed to the ethical principles of fairness and equality that were there since the founding. "He awakened something true." But, in Reagan's twist, those principles and the sense of justice they undergirded had been undermined by race-talk that distracted from individual merit.

Reagan would use this strong misreading of King to attack affirmative action and eviscerate the Equal Employment Opportunity Commission and the U.S. Commission on Civil Rights—all in an effort, much like the one Trump would undertake decades later, to abolish decades of government practices in the area of civil rights. The country, Reagan insisted, should cast race-talk aside and embrace the value of color blindness—rid itself of quotas, clamp down on governmental excess with its "entitlement programs" (a reminder of Frederick Douglass's insight about the power of naming the problem), emphasize personal responsibility, and take a tough stance on crime and punishment. Here a version of the story of the civil rights movement and of Dr. King served to justify a politics based on a context-free, race-blind notion of fairness aimed at stoking white resentments and ending a form of liberalism held hostage by white guilt. It also perversely enabled white families who rejected busing to appeal to Dr. King and the civil rights movement as they claimed to be victims of government overreach. In fact, the framing used by Dr. King to demand freedom could now be used by white Americans who saw themselves as the victims of reverse discrimination, because any use of race to remedy historic harms ended up discriminating against white people.

As Reagan celebrated King in the Rose Garden, he acknowledged that the country had yet to fulfill its promise. "The traces of bigotry still mar America," he told the crowd in attendance.

> So, each year on Martin Luther King Day, let us not only recall Dr. King, but rededicate ourselves to the Commandments he believed in and sought to live every day: Thou shall love thy God with all thy heart, and thou shall love thy neighbor as thyself. And

> I just have to believe that all of us—if all of us, young and old, Republicans and Democrats, do all we can to live up to those Commandments, then we will see the day when Dr. King's dream comes true, and in his words, "All of God's children will be able to sing with new meaning . . . land where my fathers died, land of the pilgrim's pride, from every mountainside, let freedom ring."

With savvy sleight of hand, the president located the power of King's witness in the enduring metaphysical truths evidenced in the Commandments; the same truths that, according to Calvin Coolidge over six decades earlier, shaped the Declaration and the Constitution. It was those fixed religious principles, Reagan believed, that ought to frame our pursuits of justice, not the wrongheaded efforts of big government at social engineering or the 1970s' radical demands for wholesale revolution. The Golden Rule is the best remedy for historic and structural harms. And, like President Lyndon Johnson, who drew on the language of the civil rights movement during his March 15, 1965, speech with the words "we shall overcome," Reagan conscripted "let freedom ring" for his own conservative ends: a colorblind society that refused to tolerate a politics daring to question the underlying consensus myth that made America, U.S.A., possible. Those who did were the enemies, the villains who threatened the Redeemer Nation.

Reagan's effort was the culmination of the intense resistance to the Black freedom struggle. That struggle—the Second Reconstruction—sought to fulfill the broken promises of the first Reconstruction. But by 1980, with the ascent of the Age of Reagan, the movement's vision of America was under full assault. The bicentennial celebrations less than a decade earlier had accelerated a debate over the role of the Black freedom struggle in the overall American story. The issue was no longer one of fighting erasure, but of the form of inclusion. What Black experiences could be included in the storybook version of America, U.S.A., and how might those experiences be used for political ends? What Reagan and others saw was the hunger to resolve the Black freedom struggle into the consensus narrative, and that its inclusion in that story could bolster the idea of the country as a divinely sanctioned project. But doing so meant stripping away most of the parts of the story that challenged the storybook version of America, U.S.A.

Reagan's reluctant embrace of Dr. King required a selective reading of his journey: one in which King's dream emphasized the content of one's character, not the color of one's skin. Race gummed up the basic principles of the country, and the best approach, Reagan and conservatives argued, would be to rid our language and public policy of all such talk. In fact, they suggested, that's what Dr. King was saying.

The Democratic Party, especially under Bill Clinton, invoked a similar story of Dr. King and the civil rights movement, though with different political ends in mind. Democrats absorbed King into a particular version of liberalism, in which the movement could be used to narrow the range of legitimate forms of Black political dissent. The crucial story was Dr. King, the March on Washington, or the Selma Marches—not the breakfast program of the Black Panther Party or the various forms of Black Power. The Black radical political tradition had to be denied, because it fundamentally called into question the storybook version of America and the consensus it presupposed. It asked the hard and rude question of whether Black people could ever be free in this country. Those moments represented radical breaks with the American project. They were unassimilable.

For both Republicans and Democrats, admission of the history of racism was thought to be enough for absolution. No need for further race-specific remedies. No need to further alienate white voters. Republicans called for colorblind policy; Democrats addressed race through broad-based policies that would "lift all boats." And, ironically, the story of Black people in America, U.S.A., justified both approaches.

—

I have always been struck by the parallel between Ronald Reagan's reluctant embrace of Dr. King in the Rose Garden in 1983, with his invocation of King's words "let freedom ring," and President Barack Obama's remarks three decades later at the Let Freedom Ring ceremony commemorating the 50th anniversary of the March on Washington. The echo of the language is obvious, but what struck me then, and remains particularly salient now, was the way Obama, the first African American president in the country's history, tied America's past, present, and future to a certain version of that historic moment on the Mall. Standing in the same spot in which Dr. King spoke in 1963, with the Lincoln Memorial casting a grand backdrop, President Obama told a story of the nation through the experiences of Black people demanding freedom.

> Five decades ago today, Americans came to this honored place to lay claim to a promise made at our founding: "We hold these truths to be self-evident, that all men are created equal, that they are endowed by their Creator with certain inalienable rights, that among these are Life, Liberty and the pursuit of Happiness.

The failed promises of the Declaration of Independence, he proposed, framed the demands of ordinary Americans who, in the face of unimaginable hatred and violence, risked everything to petition for their dignity and rights. From here, Obama shifted the audience's attention from Dr. King to the power of everyday people who learned through hard experience what Frederick Douglass once taught—that "freedom is not given, it must be won, through struggle and discipline, persistence and faith."

Theirs was a story of moral resilience—in the face of hatred and violence, these people "stood up and sat in, with the moral force of nonviolence. Willingly, they went to jail to protest unjust laws, their cells swelling with the sound of freedom songs." It was a strange echo of John F. Kennedy's taped remarks at the celebration of the 100th anniversary of the signing of the Emancipation Proclamation, when he commended Black people for remaining "loyal to the nation" and for rejecting "extreme or violent policies." Nonviolent struggle set these particular Black Americans apart and made their efforts quintessentially American; they did not seek to destroy the country, but to force it to live up to its ideals.

Obama narrated the movement's successes. The March on Washington became a symbol of all the efforts that led to change in American society, changes that touched not just the lives of Black people but every aspect of American life—changes that had made it possible for him to occupy the White House. But, like Reagan, Obama had to acknowledge that even with these victories, the country still had work to do. Just a month earlier, George Zimmerman had been acquitted for killing Trayvon Martin. The Black Lives Matter movement was beginning to challenge the country directly around the police killings of Black people. "The arc of the moral universe may bend towards justice, but it doesn't bend on its own," Obama said. "To secure the gains this country has made requires constant vigilance, not complacency. . . . And we'll suffer the occasional setback. But we will win these fights. This country has changed too much." It is hard to read this today. But with this move, the speech begins to expand the narrative in a way that the civil rights movement became coextensive with the broader agenda of the Democratic Party and its efforts around economic opportunity, education, and social security. Told in this way, the sacrifices of those patriots who participated in the nonviolent civil rights movement in 1963 were not simply for the benefit of Black people, but for all Americans. Their story becomes the nation's promise.

Greed, selfishness, and hatred still stood in the way, but as Obama acknowledged this reality he made a curious move, one that revealed the price of inclusion in the American story. "If we're honest with ourselves," he said,

> we'll admit that during the course of 50 years there were times when some of us claiming to push for change lost our way. The anguish of assassinations set off self-defeating riots. Legitimate grievances against police brutality tipped into excuse-making for criminal behavior. Racial politics could cut both ways, as the transformative message of unity and brotherhood was drowned out by the language of recrimination. And what had once been a call for equality of opportunity, the chance for all Americans to work hard and get ahead, was too often framed as a mere desire for governmental support—as if we had no agency in our own liberation, as if poverty was an excuse for not raising your child, and the bigotry of others was reason to give up on yourself.
>
> All of that history is how progress stalled. That's how hope was diverted. It's how our country remained divided.

Suddenly, Obama was sounding a lot like Reagan. Here was the first Black president suggesting that, alongside the shifts in the economy and politicians trafficking in white grievance, the political and personal choices of some Black people had played just as critical a role in derailing progress. Anger over assassinations, bad racial politics, and a refusal to accept personal responsibility helped bring the country to a moment where "progress stalled." This moment in the speech had little to do with the actual historical facts of the movement and its eventual demise. Rather, it amounted to a dog whistle to white America from the country's first Black president that he was—indeed, that Black history was—safe for the country.

In Obama's hands, the arc of the civil rights story had to be a triumphant one if it was to be yoked to the American story. Black history could no longer function as the mirror that reflected the divided soul of America. It had to affirm America's promise, not deny it or unmask its lies.

Here, the stories of the movement that informed Reagan's and Obama's embrace of Black history overlap. Our story, as it is, remains one about the ongoing effort to perfect the Union. To be anything else would force a different kind of account of the country's failure to live up to the promise of the Declaration of Independence. In Obama's speech, the failures of the moment are placed not in the calloused heart of America, U.S.A., but at the feet of those Black folk who "lost their way." Forms of Black politics that force a confrontation exposing that calloused heart—Black Power in the 1960s, or the angry protests in Ferguson of the 2010s—are made to be the villain, saddled with the weight of the country's failures around race. This would be the price of the ticket.

Bill Clinton made a gesture similar to Obama's during his eulogy of John Lewis at Atlanta's Ebenezer Baptist Church in July 2020, just two months after the murder of George Floyd and in the middle of nationwide protests. Clinton described three significant moments that shaped the character of John Lewis. One was his defeat by Stokely Carmichael (Kwame Ture)—the man to whom many attributed the phrase "Black Power"—as chair of the Student Nonviolent Coordinating Committee in 1966. Lewis himself had recounted that moment as "a coup." Clinton used the story to illustrate the character of Lewis, but he added these words: "I say there were two or three years there, where the movement went a little bit too far towards Stokely, but in the end, John Lewis prevailed." Hushed gasps spread across the church.

For both Clinton and Obama, the embrace of the Black freedom movement required holding at arm's length the movement's more radical energies. Both also seemed to rap the knuckles of those who were protesting in the streets as they spoke. John Lewis's call to get into "good trouble" did not occasion the kind of self-examination that Stokely or Malcolm X or organizations like the Black Panther Party required. America could still be on the road to a greater perfection with Lewis's call for good trouble. Its double consciousness could remain intact even with the admission of a past rife with wrongdoing. Not with Carmichael or Malcolm. For them, at a certain point, the country was irredeemable. The other forms of Black politics, which carried forward the idea of Black men marching with weapons on July Fourth down the streets of the Old City in Philadelphia, threatening white people and invoking the revolution of San Domingo, had to be derided and dismissed altogether.

—

Over the last decade, the role of race in American history has been a vexed issue for the country. The defense of Confederate monuments during the Black Lives Matter movement; the outcry over the 1619 Project and its version of the American story; the insistence that our schools teach nothing of the past that reflects badly on the country; and the question of whether Juneteenth, a day that recognizes the end of slavery, should be a federal holiday—all of this comprises an all-out assault by the Trump administration on the gains of the civil rights era. History remains a key battleground in the struggle for the soul of the nation.

Scholars and critics may not treat Joseph Biden kindly given his decision to run for a second term. But that takes nothing away from the fact that, despite his racial gaffes, Biden was the vice president of the first Black president, the first president with a Black woman as his vice president, and the first to appoint a Black woman to the Supreme Court. One of the fascinating features of Biden's presidency involved the way he embraced Black history quite differently from Presidents Clinton and Obama in his effort to tell a *different* story about America. In certain moments, Biden sought to do exactly what Robert Bellah urged the country to do in *The Broken Covenant.* On the eve of the bicentennial year, Bellah had insisted on a reclamation of America's national myths and the enduring principles that gave them life; but that reclamation, he argued, had to be done without a hint of sentimentality. Americans had to confront honestly their sins and their defeats. Consensus, if it was to be had at all, could not rely on a version of Black history that ultimately affirmed America's inherent goodness. It had to emerge from the blue note in the soul of the nation.

Biden's remarks at the 100th anniversary of the Tulsa Race Massacre in June 2021 closely approximated what Bellah called for. He was the first president to ever come to Tulsa, Oklahoma, and acknowledge the evil done on the day that left nearly three hundred Black people dead. Between May 31 and June 1, 1921, a Memorial Day weekend, a bloodthirsty mob of white residents attacked the Greenwood district in Tulsa after hearing that a Black teenager had assaulted a white woman. The young man was arrested and threatened with lynching as a thousand white men outside the jail demanded his release into their custody. Seventy-five Black men, some of whom were armed, showed up to protect the young man. The sheriff convinced the parties to return home. A conflict broke out as one elderly white man demanded that a Black man hand over his pistol. A gunshot went off during the dispute, and "literal hell was unleashed."

Biden recounted the violence that ensued. "Through the night and into the morning, the mob terrorized Greenwood," he said as the cameras televised his remarks for millions of Americans.

> Torches and guns. Shooting at will. A mob tied a Black man by the waist to the back of their truck with his head banging along the pavement as they drove off. A murdered Black family draped over the fence of their home outside. An elderly couple, knelt by their bed, praying to God with their heart and their soul, when they were shot in the back of their heads.

> Private planes—private planes—dropping explosives—the first and only domestic aerial assault of its kind on an American city here in Tulsa.

Biden's unadorned sentences offered a straightforward description of hate-motivated rage. What happened in Tulsa—the violence, the death, the unmarked mass graves—could never be easily assimilated into a triumphant American story. Biden cited a poem by A. J. Smitherman, the publisher of *The Tulsa Star,* a Greenwood newspaper, recalling what he heard and felt that night. "Kill them, burn them, set the pace . . . teach them how to keep their place. Reign of murder, theft, and plunder was the order of the night." The charred bones of burnt-out buildings and the rank smell of the dead were left in the wake of unadulterated white rage.

"As soon as it happened," Biden reminded the audience, "there was a clear effort to erase it from our memory—our collective memories—from the news and everyday conversations. For a long time, schools in Tulsa didn't even teach it, let alone schools elsewhere." But Biden was not content to simply surface the horror of the past. Instead, he moved to show the audience the redemptive power of confronting what the nation would rather forget. He reminded them of the influence of the Klan during the 1920s—their presence in government at the local, state, and federal levels. He explained that people like himself—Irish, Catholic, Polish, Italian—who came to the United States after World War I, bore the brunt of the Klan's hatreds. The Klan's hate, he declared, "became embedded systematically . . . in our laws and our culture. We do ourselves no favors by pretending none of this ever happened or that it doesn't impact us today, because it does still impact us today."

For Biden, the broad democratic crisis the country faced was steeped in the history the nation actively avoided. Hatred and grievance had the country by the throat. Double consciousness had driven us all mad. Picking and choosing what to learn and what to know, and leaving aside the darker elements of the past, would only seal the country's fate. "The only way to build a common ground," the president suggested, "is to truly repair and to rebuild. I come here to help fill the silence, because in silence, wounds deepen. . . . For too long, we've allowed a narrowed, cramped view of the promise of this nation to fester—the view that America is a zero-sum game where there is only one winner."

Biden went on to discuss his administration's efforts to shift the nation's center of gravity on race. Unfortunately, the proposals did not match the rhetoric; much of it reflected the same cautious approach of the Clinton and Obama administrations, driven by the same fear that remedying historic racial harms would alienate white voters. But on this one critical point—the framing of what ailed the nation—Biden stood apart: he sought to leave behind American innocence. The story of Tulsa refused and refuted the lie.

—

In 1983, as President Reagan prepared to sign Martin Luther King Jr. Day into law, he reached for the words of the poet John Greenleaf Whittier, one of the Fireside poets, who were often read in front of hearths on cold winter days to produce a patriotic feeling among the young. A sentimental image.

President Biden, at the end of his speech in Tulsa, quoted from a decidedly different kind of poem. *The Cure at Troy*, by the Irish poet Seamus Heaney, struck a contrasting tone and timbre. Heaney knew intimately of the Troubles.

History says, Don't hope
On this side of the grave.
But then, once in a lifetime
The longed-for tidal wave
Of justice can rise up,
And hope and history rhyme.

Hope for America's future, Biden seemed to suggest, rested with the country's willingness to tell itself an honest story and to accept responsibility for who and what it is. Only then might Americans live with the possibility of changing it.

Three years and a week or so after Biden delivered his remarks in

Tulsa, the Oklahoma Supreme Court issued an 8–1 ruling in *Randle v. City of Tulsa,* dismissing a case arguing that the massacre's last two living survivors, Lessie Benningfield Randle and Viola Fletcher, should be awarded reparations. The court concluded that the 1921 massacre did not constitute a public nuisance under Oklahoma law, and that the city of Tulsa did not benefit from the events over those two harrowing days. History be damned. Donald Trump and the MAGA faithful agreed. Just a few months later Trump would be inaugurated, again, as the president of America, U.S.A.

ff
molto rall.
mf
p
mf
pp

CHAPTER SIX

2026: SEMIQUINCENTENNIAL

To kick off a yearlong celebration of America's 250th anniversary, President Donald Trump spoke at a rally in Iowa on July 3, 2025. He was especially excited. Congress had just passed the so-called One Big Beautiful Bill, a sweeping piece of legislation that cut Medicaid and food stamps in order to extend tax cuts for the wealthiest Americans. The Congressional Budget Office estimated that the bill would add $3.4 trillion to federal deficits over the next decade while leaving millions of Americans without health insurance. None of this mattered, at least not to Trump. The Republican Congress had passed his signature piece of legislation. And, because of it, the ideals that shaped the role and responsibilities of government—ideals that had once led to the New Deal and the Great Society—had been effectively tossed into the trash bin. A "new golden age of America," Trump believed, had begun.

Trump reveled in it all. Monica Crowley, the United States chief of protocol, spoke to the largely white crowd ahead of his remarks. She looked out on a sea of red, white, and blue—people wearing ultra-MAGA T-shirts, red U.S.A. baseball caps, waving flags and signs that screamed their dedication to Trump and country. "This majestic celebration is about our exceptional history and the start of a new era of American greatness," Crowley told the cheering crowd. "Today we launch the next

250 years of American freedom, strength, dynamism, leadership, and pride." President Trump was central to this story. He was, Crowley said, "a direct inheritor of the founders' heroic character. A profoundly brave man, driven by the noble fight for American freedom, guided by the hand of God." A fight including enemies at home.

Those in attendance were urged to see themselves, like the members of ROAR in Boston had seen themselves some fifty years previously, as "the natural successors to the Revolutionary War generation. Fearlessly independent, ruggedly individualist, faithful to God and country, with a white-hot love of liberty and a unique and enduring spirit." The stage had been set. These were Trump's people—*true* Americans, as Hiram Wesley Evans described them in 1926. And for these Americans, the celebration of 250 years of American exceptionalism required a celebration of Donald Trump himself. The country and the man had become indistinguishable.

As Trump walked onstage to Lee Greenwood's "God Bless the U.S.A.," the kickoff celebration of the 250th anniversary felt more like a MAGA political rally than a nonpartisan, taxpayer-funded effort to commemorate the country's independence. Trump rambled for a little over an hour. He declared independence from national decline and overregulation. He lied about the 2020 election, about the monstrous murderers ICE was supposedly deporting in its sweeps across the country, and about the economic benefits of the One Big Beautiful Bill. He told the crowd that Democrats did not vote for the bill because they hate him. "But I hate them too," he said to a raucous roar. "You know that. So, it's sort of, I hate, I really do. I hate them. I cannot stand them because I really believe they hate our country." This was the rally to kick off the celebration of the nation. The so-called Golden Age of America.

—

In the country's 250th year, we bear witness to an ugliness reborn. Trump and his supporters instinctively disentangle the American story from any history that questions its innocence, as though enforcing a storybook account of the country might relieve the pressures of the past as a source of suffering—an escape hatch from the American nightmare of history. They long for an immigration policy that embraces an idea of the country imagined by the Ku Klux Klan of the 1920s. They reassert a consensus that takes the white American as its moral center of gravity. And they try to hide their hands with talk of merit and colorblind equality, draping it all in American exceptionalism and the glory of the flag. This storybook version of America, U.S.A., requires, as it did in 1876 and 1926, that Black people be made to play a minor role, if any, in the history of the country. And Donald Trump aims to deliver on that demand.

One way in which he intends this can be found in his takeover of the preparations to celebrate America's 250th anniversary. Ten years prior, in 2016, under President Obama, Congress established the U.S. Semiquincentennial Commission to oversee the planning. The commission included eight members of Congress, four from each chamber and each party; heads of major federal agencies; and private citizens appointed to the commission by both Democrats and Republicans. Along with its private, nonprofit partner, America250, the idea was to plan a nonpartisan celebration of the nation that would, in some ways, follow the lead of the bicentennial commemoration. Ideally, the 250th would be driven by local interests, and the goal, as stated by the commission, would be to make the semiquincentennial "the most inclusive commemoration in our nation's history."

Such an ambition ran smack into the country's vexed politics of memory and history as sentimentality began to give way to rage—as Barack Obama's presidency ended and Donald Trump's began. Years after the killings of Trayvon Martin and Michael Brown, protests and efforts to reckon with the country's racist past and present continued. But segments of the American public were becoming increasingly restless and resentful. *What else might these people want?*, they seemed to say. A familiar question.

During Donald Trump's first term in the White House, intense debate about the role of American history convulsed the nation. When, in August 2019, *The New York Times*'s 1619 Project called the standard story of America's founding into question, Arkansas senator Tom Cotton, who sat on the Semiquincentennial Commission, introduced legislation to ban the teaching of the 1619 Project in schools. Moms for Liberty challenged school curricula around the country and urged the banning of books from local school libraries. Christopher Rufo of the Manhattan Institute described "bad American history" as the result of "critical race theory" (CRT). He claimed that CRT taught that "the United States is a nation founded on white supremacy and oppression" and that "all white people are racists." Just as the Grand Wizard of the Klan had complained in 1926 that white Americans were denied the right to have a say in what their children were being taught in schools, his inheritors echoed the same complaint, railing against what they took to be attempts to socialize their children into believing they were inherently racist.

These battles grew even more heated after the George Floyd protests in 2020. Headlines in *The New York Times* like "The Battle for 1776" (echoing J. Anthony Lukas's piece from half a century before), or "Planners Battle over Marking U.S. 250th Anniversary" in *The Wall Street Journal,* signaled the intensity of the history wars. President Trump intervened directly, establishing the 1776 Commission to counter those who taught what he called "a twisted web of lies." With Executive Order 13958, issued on November 2, 2020, just days before voters threw him out of office, Trump insisted that the 1776 Commission, which had already released its final report and disbanded, "advise and offer recommendations to the president and the United States Semiquincentennial Commission regarding the federal government's plans to celebrate the 250th anniversary of American independence and coordinate with relevant external stakeholders on their plans." President Biden rescinded the order on his first day in office.

What was increasingly clear during Biden's term was that many white Americans in the country no longer had an appetite for critical assessments of its past and present, even if those assessments ultimately affirmed the country's inherent goodness. "Diversity" was fast becoming a bad word.

In some ways, the issue of America's diversity had come to reflect the chaos that threatened the Republic from the beginning: the idea that the realities of the New World and the language and culture that emerged from it confounded every effort to define this place as a white Republic.

The country lacked cohesion. For some, that sense was exacerbated by Obama's presidency. The fact of a Black family in the White House angered a lot of white Americans while simultaneously allowing them to point to Obama as proof that the country was not racist. But increasingly, so-called true Americans felt they could no longer claim the country as their own. They had been displaced by a radical cabal of "woke," educated elites, who did not share their basic moral values and who were more interested in "other people." With Trump's reelection, any pretense of consensus shattered.

As in the 1970s and the 1870s, the country remains deeply divided. Those divisions map onto old splits with new cracks and crevices: South and North, rural and urban, Republican and Democrat, white and Black (and anyone else considered other). Today, these political differences have become fundamental indicators of personal identity, bound up with who people take themselves to be. The divisions cut deeper than mere disagreement about political matters or ideological polarization. They have "calcified" as part of people's racial and religious identities, hardening political loyalties, intensifying the stakes of elections, and making any hope for consensus rooted in national identity damn near impossible. Political opponents are often held in contempt, because their positions, for the people who disagree with them, reveal that they are not decent people. Instead of disagreeing civilly, Americans end up seeing each other as enemies across hard battle lines, some of which were drawn generations ago with the debate over slavery and with the Civil War. In so many ways, the moral choice at the founding of the country still haunts. Americans find themselves trapped in the badlands between what often feels like two nations finding it increasingly difficult to pretend to be one.

With Trump, Americans feel and live the maddening split in every moment double ideals, dueling struggles that threaten to rip apart the nation, at once a beacon of freedom for all and a country for white people only. Fear and panic overwhelm people when the dramatic tension between the two visions of the country becomes unbearable. (Especially when freedom must be reconciled with babies crying in the cages of immigrant detention centers, or with prisons like Alligator Alcatraz, or with sweeping declarations that blame DEI for sixty-seven dead in a plane crash.) It is in this context of fear, as in the past, that some Americans reach for an idea of the country where white racial superiority trumps all other differences. They choose the white Republic—and others, who may even disagree, capitulate to that choice. The incoherence of America, U.S.A., is painted over in myth and legend, and in hatred directed toward those who expose the divided soul of America.

We saw this in 1876 as Reconstruction brutally collapsed and the nation first reached for a vision of national unity rooted in an idea of racial hierarchy. That unity required Black people to be relegated to the bottom rung of American life as the marker of how far not to fall. The contrast gave white racial superiority meaning. We saw it in 1926 as the country grappled with European immigration, where the idea of the white American evolved to include formerly excluded others, and the Ku Klux Klan gave voice to a certain vision of America, U.S.A. President Coolidge offered a conservative appropriation of the American Revolution that, once again, required Black people to be erased. And we saw the struggle over the meaning of American identity in 1976, as any longing for consensus collapsed in the aftermath of the social revolutions of the mid-twentieth century and with the backlash from those white Americans who felt left behind.

Like Ronald Reagan, Trump claimed to represent them, and he sought to ensure that the story of the country's founding in its 250th year did as well. Upon his return to the White House in 2025, Trump issued an executive order creating Task Force 250, housed in the Department of Defense and with no obligation under law to be nonpartisan. He made himself and Vice President J. D. Vance chair and vice chair, with the clear intent of influencing and directing the celebration of the nation's 250th anniversary. Meanwhile, MAGA loyalists and veterans of Trump's political circle began to transform America250. Representative Bonnie Watson Coleman of New Jersey, who sits on the Semiquincentennial Commission, told me that it felt like "he was hijacking the branding of A250 for his own purposes." Amanda Moore and Dan Friedman reported in *Mother Jones* that "what was once planned as a unifying celebration for all Americans . . . morphed into a militarized exaltation of Donald Trump—[with America250's] website trumpeting a photo of

Trump's head alongside the presidents on Mount Rushmore." Ariel Abergel, a twenty-five-year-old former producer for *Fox & Friends* who served as Melania Trump's deputy director of communications, was appointed executive director of the nonprofit. (He would be fired in September 2025 for "breaches of authority and trust.") And, as of this writing, Brad Parscale, a familiar face from all three of Donald Trump's presidential races, and his company, Campaign Nucleus, handles the organization's media operation. At every turn, Trump put in place people who support him and his agenda as the driving force behind the semiquincentennial, in order to tell a storybook version of America that has established him as its standard bearer.

—

No wonder the rally on July 3, 2025, felt like a political event. With every word spoken and with every chant, Trump and country blurred together as an expression of American patriotism. Trump aimed to use the 250th "to create this sense of goodness about the country as a distraction," Rep. Watson Coleman said, "while he continues his power grab." And, in the process, the original goal of "the most inclusive commemoration in the nation's history" got tossed into the trash bin. The celebration became decidedly white and "some strange Christian thing," a MAGA/evangelical version of America's civil religion.

The Iowa rally crowd that reveled in Trump's words and the event's symbolism, on the day the One Big Beautiful Bill was passed by Congress, had given themselves over to it all. As they cheered and applauded Trump's ramblings, something akin to the fervor of religious feeling took over. They allowed his words to stand in for their own, to vindicate their indifference and fears, and to hold back God's judgment of them. They soaked in the hatred and condemnation and became, if just for a moment, the whip of the whirlwind "where no cry or lament or song or hope [could] disentangle itself from the roar." In a blink of an eye, these people could become a mob fueled by terror and a desperate need for absolution. A strange American melancholy, baptized in fire, on full display.

About thirty minutes into the speech at the Iowa State Fairgrounds,

Trump turned his attention to the official launch of America250: "It's really a celebration of our flag, our great American flag, and our glorious American freedom." That celebration, he told the audience, would involve "the Great American State Fair" and culminate in "a patriotic festival next summer on the National Mall featuring exhibits from all 50 states"—a combination of the decentralized efforts of the bicentennial celebration and the expositions of the centennial and sesquicentennial in Philadelphia.

None of this was set in stone, but Trump did not care. He mentioned that America250 would host the Patriot Games, a nationally televised competition among the country's best high school athletes; and, perhaps, a UFC title fight on the grounds of the White House. The commemoration, he declared, would officially open the National Garden of American Heroes, "a vast outdoor park featuring statues of the greatest Americans." This came with a rant about the assault on public monuments during the Black Lives Matter movement, particularly the threats against the Jefferson Memorial. *The Washington Post* reported later that day that the National Garden of American Heroes might not be completed until 2029.

The aim of all the programs and events, Trump declared, was "to renew our national pride" and beat back those ideologies that threatened America's freedom. In the face of the cultural and political divisions that imperiled the country, the commemoration would assert a much narrower view of consensus.

As has been the case historically, appeals to consensus are most intense in those moments when the incoherence of the nation is deeply felt. Today Americans are, politically and culturally, at each other's throats. But Trump's remarks revealed that he was less interested in national unity in the face of such divisions ("I hate them because they hate our country") than in consolidating ownership of the American idea for himself and his supporters. For him, as for the Klan in the 1920s, the appeal to consensus distinguished true Americans from the "un-American menace of unwanted immigrants" and from those who failed to demonstrate the requisite gratitude and fidelity to the country—which, at this point, meant the requisite gratitude and fidelity to him.

Amid the political rants and his calls for adoration, Trump drew on the basic tropes of American exceptionalism and civil religion. "In everything we do, we're once again defending the values, traditions, and beliefs that made every generation before us so very proud to be American. . . . We believe that America is an exceptional nation, blessed by God." Trump set the frame for the 250th commemoration—one that doesn't seek to confront or even remember the conflicts and contradictions that stand alongside the triumphs and achievements of American history. Instead, the country's past is invoked to affirm that it was, and remains, a divinely sanctioned project; its founding stands outside of history, its truths enduring and unchanging. Trump cast himself and his MAGA supporters as extensions of the revolutionary moment that occasioned the birth of the nation. They were called to remember and to conserve only the promise of America—in effect, to submit to the past.

The White House reinforced this approach to American history by creating a series of video lectures that told the story of the founding of the "greatest republic to ever exist." To do so, they partnered with Hillsdale College, a conservative Christian liberal arts school in Michigan. The choice of partner spoke volumes. At this moment, Trump was engaged in an all-out assault on American higher education. The administration claimed that universities like Columbia and Harvard had been overrun with antisemitism and "woke culture"—that the radical left had taken over these campuses and were indoctrinating students in critical race theory and post-colonial studies. That DEI programs and policies broke anti-discrimination laws and violated the rights of white and Asian students, and that during protests over the war in Gaza these schools had not done enough to combat antisemitism. He withheld billions of dollars in federal funding because of it.

Hillsdale College, in the eyes of the Trump administration, was different. The college refused federal monies and defended true American values. Hillsdale was also committed to teaching American history without the burden of political correctness. One of its course offerings on the U.S. Constitution covers topics ranging from "the natural rights theory of the founding," to "the meaning of the Declaration and the Constitution," to the "Progressive rejection of the founding." When asked about the partnership with the college, White House spokesperson Anna Kelly said, "President Trump feels strongly about honoring our nation's heritage, and his America250 Task Force is bringing American history to life with its 'Story of America' video series."

The series, formally titled "The White House Presents: The Story of America," includes an introductory video featuring Hillsdale president Larry P. Arnn, who has noted elsewhere that Hillsdale "has always been broadly partisan on behalf of freedom." The video opens with voiceover narration that begins with the first lines of the Gettysburg Address and a fast-moving montage of images, including the Declaration of Independence, a painting of George Washington crossing the Delaware, the Lincoln Memorial, and a photo of a young Asian boy holding the American flag as his diverse classmates, hands over their hearts, recite the Pledge of Allegiance. The iconography signals the expansiveness of the American project, its diversity, and its power. Arnn, shown seated in the Indian Treaty Room of the Eisenhower Executive Office Building, declares that President Trump wishes to celebrate the 250th anniversary of the Declaration of Independence "with an open heart." Hillsdale was proud to join in the celebration, he said, because it "loves the Declaration of Independence."

Early in the video, Arnn invokes Hillsdale's second president, Edmund Burke Fairfield, who, in his dedication of the oldest building on campus in 1853, said that "freedom and learning go together" and that "ignorance and slavery go together." But there is sleight of hand at work here. The images and the words do not quite match up. Fairfield spoke out strongly against chattel slavery, but Arnn seems to use his words to suggest that ignorance leads to some undefined form of slavery. "One of the things we must do to commemorate anything—commemorate is just to remember together," notes Arnn. "First, we have to know the thing. We can't remember it very well, if we don't know it very well. And, so, part of the purpose of this series of lectures is to remember." He doesn't build on Fairfield's comments about ignorance and slavery. For Arnn, slavery could just as easily refer to a kind of mental bondage that comes with willful ignorance, and not necessarily to the enslavement of Black people. Instead he insists on a clear-eyed understanding of the founding without the burden of its wrongheaded critics. We must know it, he insists, so that we might remember it appropriately in our current days.

Arnn then talks about Donald Trump and what motivates the president's effort to the tell the story of America's founding:

> President Trump does this in part, I think—I don't speak for him—but the word *again* is important to him. He has a famous slogan that I will not repeat here . . . and it ends with the word *again.* He wants us to do something *again.* Something already been done. He wants to see it happen *again.* This places him somewhere near the politics of Abraham Lincoln, I think. George Washington did something for the first time—extremely honorable, including the defense of the Declaration of Independence on battlefields. Abraham Lincoln comes along later and he wants to restore all of that. He took the view that that was a very hard thing to do, but it wasn't a new thing to do. It was something we should remember and commemorate.

As Arnn repeats the word *again,* we see images of Americana—of the founders, of the early railroads and the Wright brothers' airplane, the iconic image of eleven ironworkers sitting on a steel beam of the RCA Building, of a sailor kissing his love, of soldiers raising the flag at Iwo Jima—and then Arnn pauses for video footage of Americans making their way to the Lincoln Memorial to the sound of "We Shall Overcome."

With these images of America's greatness as his frame, Arnn likens Trump's political ambition to that of Abraham Lincoln. Trump aims to remember and restore. Of course, there's no mention of slavery. No mention of the second founding or the Civil War amendments. Instead, Arnn insists that what Lincoln did (and I suppose he means the ending of slavery, although I am not entirely sure what he means) was not a revolutionary act. That revolution had already happened—it only had to happen once to be eternal. Lincoln's aim, he claims, was to remember and restore—"to declare the right, so that the enforcement of it might follow as fast as the circumstances should permit." In this we hear echoes of

Ronald Reagan's language—"to awaken something strong and true" that is already there—or Calvin Coolidge's in 1926, for whom the aim was "to go back and review the course which [the founders] followed. We must think the thoughts which they thought." Americans must remember rightly. For Trump and Hillsdale, that did not involve excoriating the founders for slavery or even mentioning the very contradiction of their being enslavers, never mind questioning the Constitution as a slaveholding document. Instead, Americans' primary historical endeavor must be to remember and commemorate. For Arnn, the perfection of the nation can be found in its beginnings—in those enduring principles that make America a beacon of freedom to the world, even when it was a slaveholding society.

In fact, for Arnn and those who agree with him, those principles and the endurance of slavery beyond the Declaration do not require resolution. They do not speak to a double consciousness. In their view, the principles set the path for the end of slavery in the United States. The 1776 Commission wrote in its response to the claims of the 1619 Project that the compromises around slavery at the founding, given the various factions, made the Republic possible. Theirs was not a tragic choice; it was a practical one. "No durable union could have been formed without a compromise among the states on the issue of slavery." But the language of the Declaration itself, the commission noted, was clear: "We hold these truths to be self-evident, that all men are created equal." According to the 1776 Commission, and Arnn would agree, the founders knew that slavery was incompatible with that truth and, as such, "the foundation of our Republic planted the seeds of the death of slavery in America. The Declaration . . . set the stage for abolition," even as abolitionists suffered the violence of pro-slavery advocates who vehemently disagreed with them and all endured a war that left over 600,000 people dead.

A rather smug way of absolving the nation of its sins. There is no need to single out the story of Black people, especially as a basis for criticism of the Republic. In this reading of American history, the grandness of the American experiment in democracy made Black people's freedom possible. And Donald Trump's effort to "Make America Great Again" ought to be read as contiguous with the enduring principles that set all of that in motion.

In Iowa, Trump reached for the wisdom of those principles as he cast himself as the defender of the values and traditions "that made every generation before us so very proud to be American." But those words were accompanied by a familiar ugliness: the move to push the descendants of former slaves to the margins of the story. Indeed, it takes Trump just a sentence to jump from the wisdom of the founders to the dangers of DEI:

> We believe in the wisdom of our founders who declared that our rights do not come from bureaucrats in Washington, our rights come from our Creator in Heaven. That's where our rights come from. And we reject government discrimination and so-called diversity, equity, and inclusion mandates. They're just about washed out the window, actually. . . . Our country is now a country based on merit.

It is an odd shift, even for the "free-wheeling approach" that defines Trump's political speeches. The wisdom of the founders is an ancient wisdom, rooted in enduring metaphysical principles that cannot be regulated by nondescript bureaucrats. Enlightenment philosophy be damned. And with that ancient wisdom, Trump rejects extending those principles to any idea of racial justice that would lead Americans to question the sacredness of the American idea, or to feel guilty about their past:

> We take pride in our heritage, and we want it in a beautiful heritage that we have, and we teach our children to love our country, honor our history, always respect our great American flag. You have to respect our flag. From Philadelphia to Phoenix, from Gettysburg to the Golden Gate Bridge, and from factories of Detroit to the fairgrounds of Des Moines, we stand on the shoulders of heroes and legends who crossed the oceans, blazed the trails, tamed the wilderness, settled the continent, raised up those beautiful skyscrapers, and stood tall and defiant in the face of tyranny and death.

This is Trump's American story, one of triumph after triumph. This is MAGA's evangelical version of American civil religion: an unbendable national pride, precisely because "we are Americans and our hearts bleed red, white, and blue."

Unlike that of the bicentennial celebration, this story makes no pretense to acknowledge the pitfalls of America's racial past. Trump does not feel the need to say, like Reagan or Obama, that "traces of bigotry still mar America." On his first day in office, which ironically coincided with Martin Luther King Jr. Day, Trump issued an executive order ending diversity, equity, and inclusion programs within the federal government. Agencies immediately began to cancel activities associated with MLK Day, Black History Month, Juneteenth, and other celebrations of America's diversity. The Justice Department sent a memo to its staff declaring that "these programs divided Americans by race, wasted taxpayer dollars, and resulted in shameful discrimination" against white Americans. That order was then followed by another one that moved to end affirmative action in federal contracting and placed all federal DEI staff on paid leave. Websites were scrubbed of any hint of DEI, which remains a catch-all term for race and diversity in the country. Military academies were ordered to review books in their libraries that dealt with anti-racism and gender. My own book, *Democracy in Black,* was among those removed from the U.S. Naval Academy.

And yet, even as this unfolded, Trump followed the tradition inaugurated by President Ford in 1976 and issued a presidential proclamation on Black History Month. He acknowledged that the achievements of African Americans, "which have monumentally advanced the tradition of equality under the law in our great country, continue to serve as an inspiration for all Americans." He used the occasion to express his gratitude to those African Americans who helped pave the way for America "to enter a historic Golden Age" with his administration.

The framing of his entire argument is telling, as it follows along the very lines we've been discussing: Black history "advanced the tradition of equality under the law"—African Americans' efforts helped awaken *what was already there.* Black people did not force this equality into being. They simply revealed it. And so there's no need to talk about "a more perfect union" or "tragic history." As C. J. Pearson, a national co-chair of the Republican National Committee's Youth Advisory Council, who is African American, put it, "Black History is American history. And similar to the story of our nation, it is a story of strength, resilience, and dogged perseverance." Instead of Black history being drafted into a story about America's ongoing quest for a more perfect union, that history confirms the greatness—dare I say, the perfection—evident in America's founding. All the while, Trump's administration pursues an agenda—from the assault on DEI, to the ending of affirmative action, to the repeal of consent decrees with police departments around the country found to engage in discriminatory policing, to the legal attacks on the Voting Rights Act—that aims to dismantle the entire infrastructure of civil rights in this country, allowing the tide of the country's ugly past to wash away all that our strength, resilience, and dogged perseverance have accomplished.

—

In March 2025, the president issued an executive order entitled "Restoring Truth and Sanity to American History." It made explicit the approach that would shape the telling of America's founding:

> Over the past decade, Americans have witnessed a concerted and widespread effort to rewrite our Nation's history, replacing objective facts with a distorted narrative driven by ideology rather than truth. This revisionist movement seeks to undermine the remarkable achievements of the United States by casting its founding principles and historical milestones in a negative light. Under this historical revision, our Nation's unparalleled legacy of advancing liberty, individual rights and human happiness is reconstructed as inherently racist, sexist, oppressive, or otherwise irredeemably flawed. Rather than fostering unity and a deeper understanding of our shared past, the widespread effort to rewrite history deepens societal divides and fosters a sense of national shame, disregarding the progress America has made and the ideals that continue to inspire millions around the globe.

The executive order recounts what it takes to be egregious efforts to undermine the cohesiveness of the American polity (or, perhaps more accurately, a cohesiveness among white Americans). Without a coherent national story, they believe, one that affirms the ideals and basic values of the country, America risks losing sight of its divine mission as the Redeemer Nation. From this view, Bellah's consensus, with its lumps and bruises, amounts to betrayal, as it refuses to acknowledge that the victory of America was secured in its beginnings. Any mention of the actual history of racism in the country—of the horrors of slavery, or reasons for the Civil War, or the Tulsa Race Massacre, or historical examples of the country failing to live up to its stated ideals and values—amounts to an assault on America as a symbol of inspiration and greatness. And any such assault on America is felt as a personal attack on those who believe in the storybook version of the country. To remember appropriately, to use the president of Hillsdale College's words, is effectively to disremember.

As such, President Trump set out to restore the "truth" of American history, which involved ordering an assessment of all public monuments, memorials, statues—markers within the Department of Interior's jurisdiction—to ensure "they do not contain descriptions, depictions, or other content *that inappropriately disparage Americans past or living* (including persons living in colonial times), and instead focus on the greatness of the achievements and progress of the American people" [emphasis added]. Even Edgar Allan Poe's home came under scrutiny, because the historical markers mentioned that he was against abolition and trafficked in racist stereotypes. History be damned. This is the stuff of fantasy and romance.

I cannot help but think that Donald Trump and his supporters believe, in some way, that his election amounts to the end of American history. Not so much the end that Francis Fukuyama argued for in *The End of History and the Last Man*—that of the triumph of liberal democracies and free-market capitalism—but rather the triumph of freedom itself without the lies and illusions of liberalism. With Trump, his followers can dispose of America's racist past and be, without worry or concern, unabashedly white, which, for him, means unashamedly American. Heritage makes it so: a repository of meanings about the past that transforms defeat and sin into triumph and grace; a consensus story offering an understanding of the country that coheres around enduring principles, and a people who see in each other purpose, meaning, and unbounded possibility. This story does not require of Black people like me a song, as in Psalm 137. It already claims the music as its own, just as it does the minstrel's face. The desire is not to make the Black face blank or to make it white, but to rid it of any trace of judgment. To shatter the mirrors. We become flat characters in the background, mute and barely present, like those in Dos Passos's *U.S.A.* trilogy, or in Gore Vidal's *1876*.

The Smithsonian Institution found itself the target of Trump's executive order. Accused of "coming under the influence of a divisive, race-centered ideology," the Smithsonian, according to the Trump administration, "promoted narratives that portray American and Western values as inherently harmful and oppressive." Trump charged Vice President J. D. Vance with overseeing the effort to remove all "improper ideology" from the museums.

But for Lonnie Bunch, the first African American secretary of the Smithsonian, the view held by Trump and his supporters smacks of fear. He told me, "I don't understand and it's hard for me to articulate why a nation that identifies itself as a founding leader is afraid of its own history, terrified. It's a fear that somehow embracing that history means admitting America is a failure rather than a work in progress."

Bunch believes he ended up in the crosshairs of the MAGA world not simply as the first Black secretary of the Smithsonian, but because he challenges directly the MAGA version of American civil religion. He told me that the Smithsonian offers a different narrative than the unquestioning patriotic one Trumpism embraces, or even the critical story "that illuminates the dark corners" of the nation. Instead, he suggested that the Smithsonian offers a third narrative: "that basically America is a work in progress . . . [that] the ideals of Jefferson and Lincoln are extremely valid because it is Black people that made those ideals concrete." In their fight to end slavery, and in their demand for full citizenship rights, Black people forced the nation to expound, expand, and develop its basic principles—to give those ideals meaning beyond philosophical abstraction. And all of this follows from a basic claim: that it is okay to have an argument about America. "That's what the nation is," Bunch claims,

> and what they are doing is trying to silence any discussion about the challenges of the nation, about the debate about what's right or wrong. And I'm arguing that the strength of the nation is when you have that argument, when you allow that to be a part of who you are and to be made better by the success of that argument. Not necessarily resolving it, which is why I go back to the more perfect union. We are never going to get to the promised land of a perfect union, but the notion aspiring to that and arguing about what that could be is really, very powerful, I think.

This argument presupposes the founding language of the nation—the Declaration and the Constitution—as the frame within which the argument happens. And, for Bunch, "it is the argument that has moved the nation forward."

Unlike Coolidge and others who would have us look to the past to chart the future, Secretary Bunch is not urging us to return to the founders—to look back, remember, and restore. Simply reaching back doesn't afford us access to some kind of American gospel. The founders didn't get it right, according to Bunch. In fact, they represent the inauguration of the argument of America, not its resolution. Bunch's approach does not shut down critical work. In fact, he believes it enables a fuller story of the country.

But Trump has no need to acknowledge that America, U.S.A., continues to struggle with racism. He doesn't have to invoke the necessity of the continuing work for "a more perfect union." *The future of America, U.S.A., was present in its beginning.* That is MAGA's evangelical certainty. There is no argument. America's victory is secured. All that is required, in its 250th year, is that Americans remember and restore.

—

On July 5, 2025, two days after Trump's rally at the Iowa State Fairgrounds, Vice President J. D. Vance accepted an award for statesmanship from the Claremont Institute, a right-wing think tank. When reflecting on his remarks alongside President Trump's speech in Iowa, one can get a sense of the way this administration thinks about the meaning of America and the history that shapes it. And given Vance's role on Task Force 250, and his assignment to wipe clean any semblance of "improper ideology" at the Smithsonian, one can anticipate how the president and vice president are approaching America's 250th anniversary.

Vance sets out in the speech to "understand" his political opponents on the so-called far left. "What unites Islamists, gender studies majors, socially liberal white urbanites, and big pharma lobbyists," he argues, "isn't the ideas of Thomas Jefferson or even of Karl Marx. It's hatred." Collapsing these "adversaries" together strains credulity, but here he echoes President Trump, who has stated bluntly that his opponents hate him and the country. Vance believes "they hate the people in this room. They hate the President of the United States. And most of all, they hate the people who voted for that President." This feels more like projection than description. Vance and Trump hate the mirror that reflects their refusal to embrace the diversity of the nation because of their embrace of white superiority. They want to be "the white American," without judgment. Vance expresses little interest in imagining a consensus that would include those with whom he vehemently disagrees. Hatred comes with the calcification of political differences, because opponents have become enemies.

Vance then aims to explain the broader context within which this political hatred thrives and how it threatens America, U.S.A. The very idea of belonging has been shattered by the reality of a society overwhelmed by both its diversity and its markets. Americans are more than consumers and producers, he declares. They are made in the image of God, and because Americans discover their purpose and meaning here, in the land they call home, love attaches to it. But today home looks and feels differently because of dramatic demographic shifts. "Every Western society, as I stand here today, has significant demographic and cultural problems," says Vance.

> There is something about Western liberalism that seems almost suicidal, or at least socially parasitic, that tends to feed off of a healthy host until there's nothing left. That's why the demographic trends across the West are so bad, why so many young people . . . say that they would not die for their country, because something about the liberal project in 2025 is broken.

America is the most diverse it has ever been. And educated elites tout that diversity as an overriding value. And yet Vance claims the pressures of that diversity on America's way of life are destroying the institutions that enable "a common sense of purpose and meaning as Americans." Social bonds, in his view, require living together close to the ground. Living in the same neighborhood, kids going to the same school, people sharing similar values. One wonders what he thinks about historic patterns of residential segregation in the United States that make so many Americans mysteries to one another, or the reality that American schools are as segregated today as they were in 1954, and what that might mean for his claims about social bonds.

But facts aside, Vance claims that the constant influx of immigrants and the raging diversity that clamors for recognition have resulted in a definition of what it means to be America that is, at once, "over-inclusive and under-inclusive." We have come to believe, Vance suggests, that at the heart of what it means to be American is an idea, one rooted in the principles articulated in the Declaration of Independence. A view we associate with Abraham Lincoln and Frederick Douglass as they read the Declaration into the Constitution. But this creedal definition of Americanness, he argues, makes American identity so broad that it loses meaning, or becomes so thin that it fails to produce a sense of cohesiveness among its citizens. Moreover, to understand America "as a purely creedal nation" would lead to the rejection of a lot of people who hold illiberal views about immigration or racial equality, or about Jews "that the ADL [Anti-Defamation League] would label as domestic extremists. Even those very Americans [whose] ancestors [fought] in the Revolutionary War and the Civil War."

It strikes me as an extraordinary moment in American political life—that on the day after the 249th anniversary of the nation, the vice president of the United States rejects the American idea as a basis for American identity.

But in the absence of the American idea and its principles, what makes an American? Here, Vance turns to an idea that he believes ought to be the basis of American national identity—one that would have been right at home in the speech of Hiram Evans in 1926. "I think the people whose ancestors fought in the Civil War have a hell of a lot more claim over America than the people who say they don't belong." What matters for Vance is not what you believe—you can even believe in the rightness of slavery and secession—it is really and quite simply a matter of how long your family has been in America. But, of course, that depends on the color of your skin and how you arrived on these shores. For Vance, there are some white people who arrived here in the 1920s who have more of a claim on the country than African Americans whose families have been here since the 1800s. Here he makes explicit what has been a feature of America, U.S.A., since the founding: American identity is based, in part, on blood and soil. In Vance's hands, America's double consciousness is resolved: the country as a beacon of freedom is not enough; America must be a white Republic. "We're a particular place with a particular people and particular set of beliefs and way of life."

This is not to deny the value of immigration and diversity, Vance argues. But citizenship entails obligations to one's fellows, and those obligations are met in the life lived together. "You cannot swap ten million people from anywhere else in the world and expect for America to remain unchanged."

> The founders of our country understood that perhaps better than anybody. They understood that our shared qualities, our heritage, our values, our manners and customs confer a special and indispensable advantage. . . . Citizenship, true citizenship, is not just about rights . . . , it is also about obligations, including the obligations we have to our fellow countrymen.

This is the view of citizenship and of America that shapes Vance's approach to the semiquincentennial. America is a distinctive place with a distinctive people, and to have a sense of obligation to its people and to your home is to feel a sense of gratitude for the country itself.

You can hear the venom in his tone as he recounts the words from then New York City mayoral candidate Zohran Mamdani. "America is beautiful, contradictory, unfinished," Mamdani said. "I am proud of our country even as we constantly strive to make it better." Where is Mamdani's gratitude? Vance wonders. "He dares on the 249th anniversary to congratulate it by paying homage to its incompleteness and to its . . . contradictions." Here it is made plain: the idea of America as an ongoing experiment, the language of America working toward "a more perfect union," or the admission that "we've allowed a narrowed, cramped view of the promise of this nation to fester"—all this is an affront to Vance, because the people who turned wilderness into the greatest country on earth made Mamdani's life here possible. He "might not be alive were it not for the generosity of a country he dares to insult on its most sacred day? Who the hell does he think he is?"

The arrogance of white men grates on the nerves. Vance expects gratitude, because he believes that freedom is the white man's gift to give. How could someone like me, for example, born on the coast of Mississippi, who attended Morehouse College and received his PhD from Princeton, and who lives a comfortable life refuse to show gratitude to "the settlers who carved a civilization out of the wilderness"—to the country that "made my life possible"?

I could remind him of the wounded souls separated from their lands who felled the trees and cleared the swamps here; of those who saw their children sold off to the highest bidders, whose backs bore the sting of the lash of the whip, who took their last breaths without having known freedom; of those who built schools for their children because the country refused to educate them, who toiled in the homes of white folks, beat back the advances of sexual predators, or surrendered in order to put food on the table. I could tell stories of those who dangled from white oak and poplar trees because they dared to claim freedom as their own; or of my dad and mom, who couldn't eat at the local drive-in because they didn't serve niggers; or the moments when somebody, somewhere in some city wailed because they had to bury their child who was killed by the police. I could go on and on. But Vance and Trump say such talk "inappropriately disparages Americans past and living." Gratitude is demanded, still—especially as the "true Americans" celebrate 250 years of America, U.S.A. They just want us to shut up, smile, be grateful, and disappear.

—

Most Black people know the official story that will be told on July 4, 2026. We know Donald Trump and many Americans will gather and claim the mantle of the Revolution and declare that ours is a nation of freedom and that this moment, his moment, represents a "golden age of American democracy." But we come to this day not to celebrate the founders or the heroes of the Revolution, nor even to remind the nation of what we have achieved, or how we have stood by this experiment at every turn. That we were at Bunker Hill and Red Bank. That we died on the battlefield in Gettysburg and in the bloody siege of Vicksburg. That generations have sacrificed defending freedom at home and abroad, risking our lives to make real the promise that Trump and Vance believe has already been fulfilled. But we know better. We know lies when we hear them.

Ours is a moment of reckoning in this 250th year of America, U.S.A. Once again, we have been reminded that too many white Americans believe that freedom is their possession to give and to take away. Just a few years ago the country struggled with the reality that racism still sat on the throne of this nation, and fortune favored us with a liberal hand. Pronouncements and policies suggested that we might finally turn a corner and imagine ourselves as a truly multiracial democracy. But sentimentality masked the deceit, and the racial habits that shuttered the eyes of generations kicked in. White rage swelled.

We watched the country elect Donald Trump, again. And this second time has been especially painful, not only because of the pace of his effort to dismantle a half century of governance, or his greed and corruption. Instead, it has been the quickness with which sentimentalists who so recently marched and protested—who declared their commitment to social justice and said that Trump posed an existential threat to American democracy—have capitulated to his will. As Frederick Douglass asked in his July 5, 1875, address, as the quarrel of the Civil War ended and "the great white race has renewed its vows of patriotism and flowed back into its accustomed channels . . . What tendencies will spring out of it, and how will they affect us?" Douglass witnessed his so-called friends turn their backs on a just vision of democracy and settle comfortably into a view that American life was for white people only. Jim Crow eventually became the law of the land, the Klan an expression of what millions felt in their hearts.

One hundred and fifty years later, we have witnessed *a great capitulation,* and find ourselves and our children caught in the whip of the whirlwind. Trump has engaged in a systematic dismantling of the country our parents fought for. From college admissions to contracts, from voting rights law to American history itself, this administration has worked tirelessly to undermine any effort to remedy historic racial harms or to tell a fuller story about our past and to build a racially just society. We must, they insist, submit to their story. Wherever *we* are and whatever *we* have achieved, they maintain, it was not because of merit, but because of them! White liberals' misguided attempts at socially engineering American life, MAGA argues, have led to the decline of this great nation. Merit becomes the cudgel used to bludgeon us out of sight and mind. With their mediocrity in full view, they retreat into the safety of illusions and myth, where the past guarantees their lies. The semiquincentennial will be their grand spectacle, an affront to truth and freedom.

On July 4, 2026, I will commemorate the fact that after 250 years of existence, America, U.S.A., still refuses to make real the promise of its own Declaration. Those principles are not lost because of the moral failings of men. They come to us—to our children—on this day as we work hard, and with love, to get our babies to the other side of America's madness. And I claim those principles as my own!

—

In *Begin Again,* I urged the country to do its first works over: to return to its past and confront the tragic choices that frame our national story. In these dark days, I am not so sure the country can still do that work. The past haunts everything, consuming our imaginations and possible futures like an insatiable Leviathan. Trump and his ilk believe the past secures the future of America, U.S.A. Revelation 2:5 isn't applicable here. This is the hubris of desperate men and women full of fear and panic. I know what this country is capable of when it is afraid and doesn't quite know what to do. That is part of the haunting.

But what I also know, and I feel this in the marrow of my bones, is that the past still offers resources for us to freedom-dream. As we confront the latest version of freedom-snatchers, we must be freedom-seekers. We must take hold of the reins of our destiny from those who believe they possess freedom for themselves; we must reject alms and insist on justice. Freedom-seekers aren't bogged down in identity politics or the performance of virtue. They aren't concerned about ideological purity, or always being right, or defining enemies. They aren't consumed with the hatred of others. The relentless pursuit of freedom in a more just world is the fire shut up in the bones. We are released from the categories that close us off from one another and opened to the fullness of what it means to be human beings in community with others, human beings with rich histories and traditions, with tragedies and triumphs—people who carry their dead forward.

I keep thinking about Imani Perry's insistence that we haunt the past: that we refuse to stand passively as the ghosts of the past move us about. Instead, we scour the archive (and not just libraries full of books, but lives teeming with experience) for resources to help us live fully and freely, to tell different stories, and to confront the present fortified by experiences that allow us to recognize the rhyme and rhythm of our current days.

In its 250th year, America, U.S.A., is in deep trouble, and I cannot say with certainty that the country will survive. Some might ask for a blueprint for how we might respond to it all. I have written about the need for a revolution of values. I have called for a Third Founding. These are just two recommendations among countless efforts in the history of this country to push Americans to imagine themselves differently. In some ways, I have become wary of the demand for solutions, which too often works as part of the ritual that leads the country to believe that it is actually *trying* to be more just, to be better. I have no interest, especially now, in playing that game. It is clear, and it has been so since the founding, that we cannot be a white Republic *and* a beacon of freedom. A choice must finally be made. Trump and Vance have made their choice. Now we must make ours. If the country is to survive these troubled times, it will depend on what we do today in defense of democracy, and on whether we are honest enough and courageous enough to admit the duality at the heart of America, U.S.A., that is the source of our madness.

How shall we stand our trial now that the color question has emerged from the shadows? We must *all* be freedom-seekers, haunting the past for resources to live unshackled from the lies that bind our feet, because the country's present and future depend on us.

Prayerfully ♩ = 52
pp
1.
2.
allarg.
a tempo
ff
p
poco rit.
With hope ♩ = 48
molto rall.
Weary ♩ = 32
pp
p
pp
ppp
3
8

CONCLUSION

LOVE AND COUNTRY

While writing this book I taught a seminar on James Baldwin's nonfiction, which, funny enough, was what I was doing in 2016 when Trump won the first time. We began with *Notes of a Native Son,* read closely *Nobody Knows My Name* and *The Fire Next Time,* sat with *No Name in the Street* and *The Devil Finds Work,* and ended with *The Evidence of Things Not Seen.* In between, we read fugitive essays, speeches, and interviews. I've been reading and teaching Baldwin for many years; I know his words like the back of my own hand. But this time, reading them again in this moment, I noticed something different—that a kind of madness shadows the page. Maybe it is the madness in me that led my eye to see it. I had not detected before how hard Baldwin struggles to hold himself together. I am not simply referring to his suicide attempts; that much is evident. Rather, I am talking about his manic efforts to keep himself together in the face of an exasperating world.

When I asked my students to read the essay "Notes of a Native Son," I was prepared to talk about how Baldwin aligns his father's death with the 1943 Harlem riots and the birth of his sister in this marvelous parable about the perils of the nation and the difficulties of self-creation. But what hit me, like a brick, was the prevalence of madness in the piece. It is, in fact, a meditation on madness. There is the madness of the nation that refuses to know itself and shapes the world in such a way as to avoid confrontation with that refusal. The consequences for those who must live in that refusal are brutal. This is the whip of the whirlwind. Baldwin's stepfather illustrates as much. We are forced to live with the idea that, because of the color of our skin and because of the color of yours, somehow *that* says something about *our* value, *our* worth. Your disease becomes our trial. And if we are to live fully, we must move mountains to keep that menacing idea—that virus—from taking hold in our guts.

Eventually, Baldwin's stepfather would be "locked up in his terrors," where "the disease of his mind allowed the disease of his body to destroy him." He believed what the world said about him, and, as result, he "lived and died in an intolerable bitterness of spirit." Baldwin admits, confesses really, that this bitterness had, in fact, become his own. He tells the story of the moment in New Jersey, on Route 1, down the street from Princeton, where, with a friend, he enters a diner for the fourth or fifth time and waits to be served, only to be ignored and finally told, "We don't serve Negroes here." Blind with rage, he hurls a glass at the waitress's head only to see it shatter the mirror behind the bar. This scene is prefaced by a description of his state of mind: "I first contracted some dread, chronic disease, the unfailing symptom of which is a kind of *blind fever,* a pounding in the skull and fire in the bowels" [emphasis added]. This *Künstlerroman* reveals the depth of the madness that consumes, and what is needed to break its fever.

One must let go of the hatred that fuels the rage. As Baldwin prepares to bury his father, the man who caused so much pain and anguish in his life, he confronts the aftermath of the Harlem riots. "That bleakly memorable morning," he writes,

> I hated the unbelievable streets and the Negroes and whites who had, equally, made them that way. But I knew that it was folly [a form of madness], as my father would have said, this bitterness was folly. It was necessary to hold on to the things that mattered. The dead man mattered, the new life mattered, blackness and whiteness did not matter: to believe that they did was to acqui-

esce in one's own destruction. Hatred, which could destroy so much, never failed to destroy the man who hated and this was an immutable law.

For Baldwin, as I read him here, the path to the other side of madness involves *accepting* the world for what it is; to not be naïve about the failings and beauty of men and women; to not fall privy to the sirens who sing of race and its enchanting fantasies—and also to fight with all your strength against the injustices of the world and what that evil has placed inside of you.

Of course, Baldwin's view about surviving madness evolved. He was a young man when he wrote this essay. He had not yet witnessed the murder of Medgar Evers, Malcolm X, and Dr. Martin Luther King Jr. He had not seen the country turn its back on all those young people who risked everything in the bowels of the South to get the country to live up to its promise. But the rage in his blood that he identified in 1955, that *blind fever,* kept coming back until the day he took his last breath. Why? Because the nation, because *these* people, insist on being white.

What might it mean to love amid this madness? Love takes off the mask, Baldwin writes in *The Fire Next Time;* it allows us to see the fragile human being in front of us. He is not being sentimental here. Love demands something from each of us: that we reach outside of ourselves and risk being in right relation with another human being who is also prone to suffering, who feels pain, and who needs love. But what might it mean to love this country, to love people who seem to despise you or, periodically, want to get rid of you? One of my students wrote in her final paper, "There are moments when I feel an overwhelming affection for this country—for its people, its possibility, its diversity. And then, sometimes in the very same breath, I feel anger so sharp I can't speak." A bitterness of spirit. How does love resolve this split, this sense of rage and deep disappointment?

Certainly, by the end of his life, Baldwin felt both rage and disappointment. No matter what he said or did, the country refused to be better. He put his father in the grave. Buried Malcolm X and Dr. King. Saw his friends go mad and jump off bridges because of America, U.S.A.

We can shout to the heavens about what this country has done and continues to do to millions of souls. "It's been said, and it's been said, and it's been said. It's been heard and not heard. You are a broken motor." Repetitions, echoes, and shattered mirrors. What Baldwin said about Ronald Reagan applies equally to Donald Trump—he "represents the justification of their history, their sense of innocence. He means the justification of *Birth of a Nation.* The justification, in short, of being white." This view compromises and, eventually, corrupts "all the American efforts to build a better world—here, there, or anywhere." We cannot love that.

Love and country can come together in a different way: In the loves we experience in the places and with the people who shape how we see the world, how we sense beauty, and how we feel grace. We are more than wreckage and ruin left after the plunder. More than objects of scorn and hate. Love affords us an expansive interior life where dreams, hopes, and ambitions commingle with wound and sorrow. Here, in this place, love fortifies the spirit and the body in a country that repeatedly declares that you are less valued. Baldwin put it powerfully in a passage I repeatedly turn to:

> I have been, as the song says, *'buked and scorned* and I know that I always will be. But, my God, in that darkness, which was the lot of my ancestors and my own state, what a mighty fire burned! In that darkness of rape and degradation, that fine, flying froth and mist of blood, through all that terror and in all that helplessness, a living soul moved and refused to die.

That resilience and grit happened here and was made possible by a thick love that was willing to sacrifice everything so that our babies might survive and flourish. We don't need MAGA to celebrate that. We don't need America to co-opt it to feel good about itself. We know, to reference an old gospel song, how we got over in America, U.S.A.

I love this place, because this is *my* home. It wasn't gifted to me by white folks in Moss Point, Mississippi, or in Washington, D.C., but by the sweat and tears of my parents, my family, and my people, who dared to imagine themselves as more than what this country said they could be.

That is my American inheritance. And with love, as my student taught me in her reading of Baldwin, we can demand that the country strip itself of its illusions; we can pull our loved ones close as white people rage. With love, we claim freedom as our own; and that love can carry the weight of our grief, memory, and anger as we confront a country that refuses to discover who and what it is.

Love can also be the basis for answering the question that the late historian Vincent Harding asked: "Is America Possible?" It is a question that has always been at the heart of our struggle for democracy, and a question that needs to be asked in the country's 250th year. Unlike the certainties invoked by Trump and Vance, for those who have borne the brunt of America's hubris, this country has never been an example of democracy achieved. Its victory was not secured in its beginnings. How could it have been, with those suffering in chains and living unfree? Rather, a tragic course was set for the nation from the start. Is America possible? It is not easily answerable. What is required is an imaginative leap: to look beyond the ugliness of our days, to see past the venom of those who hate, and to reach for the power of the imagination and of what is possible. If not for ourselves, then for the love of our children.

As Secretary Bunch talked about how the argument over America moves the country forward, he told me this:

> It is the voice of W. E. B. Du Bois, it is the voice of Dorothy Height, it is the voice of all those people who have said, as Langston Hughes said, how do I help America be America, how to be the America of our dreams. And it is Black folks who have had that dream. What I love about Black people is this notion of dreaming a world anew, believing in an America that didn't believe in them, believing in an America yet to be. That to me is my North Star.

Vincent Harding makes a similar point when he urges us to scour the past and enter the dreams of those visionaries who have gone before us, "hearing and speaking their words, singing their songs, exploring the hope that moved their lives" and finding connections between then and now that spark our ability to freedom-dream—to be freedom-seekers. To make the point, Harding, like Lerone Bennett in 1976, reached for Langston Hughes's poem, "Let America Be America Again":

O, let America be America again—
The land that never has been yet—
And yet must be—the land where every *man is free.*

America is possible if we imagine it so, if we tell ourselves better stories and follow the signs, like those on the quilts of the enslaved, that direct us to the path of freedom. But Trump and his supporters want to occupy our imaginations. They tell us on this 250th anniversary that there is nothing left for Americans to imagine, because the founding fathers settled it all. Safety found in the certainty of an illusion. But Harding urges us to "hear all the heroic voices of struggle joining Hughes in a common message. It says loudly that the work of discovering, exploring, and developing this true America is our work—we, the people, are in charge."

I must admit, especially as of late, that it is hard to believe this. Secretary Bunch spoke of the attacks and threats he faces every day, of how tired he is—a seventy-two-year-old Black man, fighting this fight as his opponents shout from distant corners that "a nigger should not run the Smithsonian." There it is again. A "nigger" can't be on the dais with President Grant. A "nigger" can't be the head of a country. "Niggers" can't be part of the celebration of the Fourth of July. These people believe that the country belongs to them, and they desperately want to put us in our place. "If I am wrong," Secretary Bunch said to me about his approach to American history, "then it calls into question everything I believe in, everything I've worked my entire career to do." He went on to say that "if that is the case, then this really is simply a white person's country and there's not much we can do about it. That scares me. You know, the one thing I've always had as a historian is that I've always been hopeful. Now . . . I'm not so sure. But, you know, the study of our story continues to give me hope."

The secretary is not alone in his fears and ambivalence. There is this palpable sense throughout the country that everything is collapsing around us—that hatred has overrun basic values and that greed has trumped decency. Hope for a racially just society seems like a fool's desire, because so many white folks—those who can't imagine themselves as anything but white—have lost their damn minds.

But love breaks through. Not some sentimentalized love of country that can easily slip into a kind of idolatry that makes one monstrous, but the love of people close to the ground, who give this place meaning and purpose. The love that motivated slaves to imagine a future as a free people when nothing about their experience suggested that such a future could be possible; the love that announces hatred must never have the last word. The last sentence of my student's final paper about Baldwin's view of love may serve as a balm to Secretary Bunch's fearful conclusion, as it has for me. "What remains," she wrote, "is not hope, but something just as lasting: the insistence on truth, carried by love and lit by rage."

Your country? Your history? No. It is ours. Our sweat and tears have shaped this land. You feel us in the music; our sound rolls off your tongue. Our presence fills your classic literature. Our wails and moans, our joys and laughter, make this place swing. Your country? No. The bars of music that begin each chapter of this book suggest otherwise. And no matter your efforts to make us invisible or to deny the history of the country that unravels your myths and legends, we know America would not be America without us.

The reality is what it is. The country has given us Donald Trump, and we have to deal with this madness again. The pounding in the skull returns as we struggle to beat back the "intolerable bitterness of spirit," because these people have done this shit again in the 250th year of America, U.S.A., a semiquincentennial blues.

AUTHOR'S NOTE

Managing the difficulty of these dark days and the scale of the ambition of this book project has brought me to the brink of despair on several occasions. Thank God for family and friends, and for a fearless and faithful editor. *America, U.S.A.* is an interpretation of the 250-year history of the country. I offer a way of seeing this place and our current moment in the full light of a past that haunts. I rely on the work of historians who have already mined the archive. My task involved stitching together various parts and pieces, drawing on American history, literature, philosophy, music and cultural criticism to tell a story about the madness that rests at the heart of the nation. Think of it as an old quilt. None of the material is new. The worn pieces of fabric, together, make something new.

W. E. B. Du Bois shadows the book. His 1903 classic work, *The Souls of Black Folk,* inaugurated an approach to the study of race, culture, and American democracy. No one disciplinary method captures the vast complexity and chaos of the American experiment. *Souls* consists of sociology, history, cultural criticism, and political commentary. We must be bricoleurs, as the philosopher Jeffrey Stout insisted. Imani Perry's *Black in Blues: How a Color Tells the Story of My People* and *South to America: A Journey Below the Mason-Dixon to Understand the Soul of a*

Nation provided contemporary examples of how I might approach what I wanted to do. I just needed to find the courage to take the plunge.

At the heart of *America, U.S.A.* is a meditation on history and memory. David Blight's classic work, *Race and Reunion: The Civil War in American Memory,* was a key resource. John Bodnar's *Remaking America, Public Memory, Commemoration, and Patriotism in the Twentieth Century,* Michael Kammen's *Mystic Chords of Memory: The Transformation of Tradition in American Culture,* and Thomas Keels's *Sesqui! Greed, Graft, and the Forgotten World's Fair of 1926* provided a treasure trove of material to work with. I returned to Eric Foner's *Reconstruction: America's Unfinished Revolution, 1863–1877,* Ron Chernow's masterful biography *Grant,* Nell Painter's *The History of White People,* Carol Anderson's *White Rage: The Unspoken Truth of Our Racial Divide,* and Andrew Delbanco's *The War Before the War: Fugitive Slaves and the Struggle for America's Soul from the Revolution to the Civil War* and his powerful William E. Massey Sr. lectures, *The Real American Dream: A Meditation on Hope.* Along with *The Souls of Black Folk,* John Hope Franklin's *From Slavery to Freedom: A History of African Americans* is another important work that sits at the heart of my lifelong reading in the field of African American studies, a tradition of writing that has offered a different American story than the standard one.

Since the publication of *Democracy in Black: How Race Still Enslaves the American Soul,* I have been trying to make sense of this fragile experiment—to understand how race has distorted and disfigured this Republic and what needed to be done to imagine the nation anew. With *Begin Again: James Baldwin's America and Its Urgent Lessons for Our Own,* I thought with Baldwin to find resources to help in this regard—to help me find my feet in a moment when the country betrayed its promises. With the last book in the trilogy, *America, U.S.A.: How Race Shadows the Nation's Anniversaries,* and with great pain and terror, I have assessed the history that has brought us to these dark days in which, once again, we stand trial for our sins and wage battles for our future.

ACKNOWLEDGMENTS

This has been one of the most difficult books I have ever written. I am not referring to the subject matter, although reading and thinking about Donald Trump and this perilous moment in the nation's 250th year has brought me to the brink of madness. I am thinking about my mom. She was diagnosed with throat cancer as I set out to write this project. She had major surgery as I wrapped my mind around the argument of the book. My sister, brother, and I rotated trips home to be with her during her radiation treatments. I edited chapters in the early hours of the morning, before she stirred. Honestly, my mind has been elsewhere at times: with her, with family and the people I love. I have mulled over the indifference of time as people who were once indefatigable, whose smile could light up universes, and whose will could conquer any challenge have slowed down and gotten sick. Time Past. Present. Future. Eliot's "Burnt Norton" returns. Thanks to my mom, Juanita Glaude, and dad, Eddie S. Glaude Sr., for their strength and love, and to my sisters, Angela and Bonita Glaude, and my brother, Alvin Jones, for their faith and encouragement. We made it, with grace, to the other side of this particular journey . . . together.

Dr. Winnifred Brown-Glaude has endured, once again, my retreat into what we call "the cave." There I am lost amid papers and books.

Working and writing. This time she worked on her own project, *Neoliberalism in a Small Place.* It is a brilliant book, and I cannot wait for it to enter the world. Our son, Langston, passed the California bar (we are so proud of him!) and got engaged to the young woman he met in his first year at Brown University. Nicole Ubinas has been a gift to our family. Her infectious enthusiasm helped make the world a bit better as I struggled to put words on the page. Thanks to my in-laws, Doreen Brown and Wilfred Brown. When I started thinking about the project, Dad was battling cancer. He is now cancer-free. Grace.

I owe an enormous debt to a community of folk who helped make this book possible. My brilliant writing and conversation partner, Imani Perry, pushed me at a every turn. *South to America* and *Black in Blues* affected me deeply—at the level of ideas and form. I tried my hand at quilting because of her. She read numerous versions of chapters and offered invaluable advice along the way. Cornel West has read every book I have written, and I am thankful for all that he has modeled for me over these many years. I sent him the manuscript, and he called me while I was home with my mom. His words of encouragement brought a much-needed smile to my face. Thanks to the folks at MSNOW—the hosts, the executive and booking producers—who have given me space to think in public with others.

My colleagues in African American studies are the best colleagues in the world: Anna Arabindan-Kesson, Wendy Belcher, Ruha Benjamin, Wallace Best, Reena Goldthree, Joshua Guild, Tera Hunter, Marcus Lee, Khalil Gibran Muhammad, Kinohi Nishikawa, Chika Okeke-Agulu, Lorgia Garcia Pena, and Autumn Womack. Special thanks to Keeanga-Yamahtta and Naomi Murakawa (especially you!) for taking the time to read a draft of the book and to offer words of encouragement. I am grateful for Shelby Sinclair, Melvin Rogers, Jamila Minnicks (thank you for the phrase "freedom snatching"), Kiki Denis, Ishmael Reed, and Jonathan Walton, who read the book and offered insightful suggestions and commentary. The mistakes are my own, but you helped make the book better. Thanks also to Radcliffe Roye and Stanley Forman, who let me use their searing photographs in this book.

I am blessed with close friends whom I have known since my days at Morehouse College. Paul Taylor, Charles McKinney, Ronald Sullivan, and Mark Jefferson are my brothers. Each of you makes this world bearable in your own funny and loving way. Thanks for reading the manuscript—and special thanks to Mark for his helpful and prescient suggestions.

Princeton has been an amazing place to grow as an intellectual. The support of my colleagues and the institution is immeasurable—particularly in this moment of storm and stress. I am thankful for my students over the years, especially those in my James Baldwin seminar. Each year they teach me something not only about the power of Baldwin's writings, but about the persistence of hope. This book basically ends with one of their sentences that helped me keep myself together amid the storms of our days.

Special thanks to my editor, Kevin Doughten. We have a ritual with each book, and it is not easy. He has a way of getting *everything* out of me (no matter the busyness of my life!). Thank you, my friend, for your willingness to help me speak to the country. I could not have written this book without you. I am grateful for Jess Scott and my amazing copy editor, Lawrence Krauser, and production editor Craig Adams and the entire team at Crown for helping bring this book into the world. And I am forever thankful for my agent, Gail Ross.

I can't remember the day, but at about 3:00 A.M., in the witching hour, I suddenly woke up. An idea had grabbed hold of me and would not let go. I thought about music as the epigraph to each chapter, an echo of W. E. B. Du Bois's *The Souls of Black Folk*. I didn't want to use the sorrow songs or blues or hip-hop. I didn't want to juxtapose *our* music with *their* verse. I thought of the work of Joel Thompson. We had met at the Colorado Music Festival in 2021, where he premiered "To Awaken the Sleeper." He asked me to read James Baldwin's words as part of the performance. It was a transformative experience. I wanted to be in conversation with him again, but this time on the page. I sent a text at some God-awful hour, and he responded. I cannot put into words how meaningful this collaboration with Joel is to me. Thank you for saying yes and for pouring so much into the sound that shapes this book. We have offered our gift to America, U.S.A. . . . together.

And to all those people around the country who stop me in airports or take the time to read my Substack, *A Native Son,* or send me notes of affirmation after an appearance on MSNOW, or tell me how proud you are of me, I want you to know that you have poured love into this lil' country boy from Moss Point, Mississippi. You inspire me, and I am so grateful. Grace, still.

NOTES

Introduction: Bitterness at the Bottom of the Cup

1 **"Whoever is part of whatever civilization":** James Baldwin, *No Name in the Street,* in *Collected Essays,* ed. Toni Morrison. New York: Library of America, 1998, p. 474.

2 **"silent hatred of the pale world":** W. E. B. Du Bois, *The Souls of Black Folk,* in *Writings,* ed. Nathan Huggins. New York: Library of America, 1986, p. 364.

4 **"It is a peculiar sensation":** W. E. B. Du Bois, *The Souls of Black Folk,* p. 364.

6 **"we are two nations":** Here is the full quotation:

they have clubbed us off the streets . . .
we are beaten . . .
America our nation has been beaten by strangers who
have turned our language inside out who have taken the
clean words our fathers spoke and made them slimy and foul . . .
all right we are two nations.

John Dos Passos, "Big Money," in *U.S.A.,* eds. Daniel Aaron and Townsend Ludington. New York: Library of America, 1996, p. 1156.

7 **"accept that BLM divided the country":** The exchange with Rufo occurred on X on May 19 and 27, 2025. Pew Research Center data offers a sense of the shift. According to their report, "The Views of Race, Policing, and Black Lives Matter in the 5 Years Since George Floyd's Killing," 49 percent of Americans today doubt that Black people will ever have equal rights to white people. It was 39 percent in 2020. And 72 percent of Americans do not believe that the focus on racial inequality after George Floyd's death changed or improved the lives of Black people in the country. More than half hold the view that the United States remains the same as it was before George Floyd was killed, a third believe it's worse, and only 11 percent say it's better. https://www.pewresearch.org/race-and-ethnicity/2025/05/07/views-of-race-policing-and-black-lives-matter-in-the-5-years-since-george-floyds-killing/.

7 **"The BLM Era is over":** Tragically, the rate of police killings continued to rise after the protests. See Steven Rich, Tim Arango, and Nicholas Bogal-Burroughs, "Since George Floyd's Murder, Police Killings Keep Rising, Not Falling," *New York Times,* May 24, 2025, https://www.nytimes.com/2025/05/24/us/police-killings-george-floyd.html.

8 **Every individual, every community was conscripted:** See Erwin Chemerinsky, *No Democracy Lasts Forever: How the Constitution Threatens the United States.* New York: Liveright, 2024, pp. 7–8.

8 **"wild beasts":** Frederick Douglass, *Autobiographies,* ed. Henry Louis Gates Jr. New York: Library of America, 1994, p. 90.

9 **"midway people in somewhat ambiguous positions":** Lionel Trilling, "The America of John Dos Passos," in *The Moral Obligation to Be Intelligent: Selected Essays.* Evanston: Northwestern University Press, 2000, p. 6.

9 **"Dos Passos is primarily concerned with morality":** Lionel Trilling, "The America of John Dos Passos," p. 7.

10 **"to locate freedom":** John P. Diggins, "Visions of Chaos and Visions of Order: Dos Passos as Historian," *American Literature,* vol. 46, no. 3, November 1974, p. 331.

10 **"We stand on quicksand":** John Dos Passos, *U.S.A.,* p. 893. Also quoted in John P. Diggins, "Visions of Chaos and Visions of Order," p. 331.

11 **the founding fathers set the path:** John P. Diggins, "Visions of Chaos and Visions of Order," p. 338.

11 **"the clean words our fathers spoke":** John Dos Passos, *U.S.A.,* p. 1157.

12 **Out of the bits and pieces of tattered fabric:** See Imani Perry, *Black in Blues: How a Color Tells the Story of My People.* New York: HarperCollins, 2025.

14 **"I refer to the exasperation and bemusement":** Ralph Ellison, "What America Would Be Like Without Blacks," in *The Collected Works of Ralph Ellison,* ed. John F. Callahan. New York: Modern Library, 1995, p. 578.

14 **from schemes during the antebellum period:** Eddie S. Glaude Jr., "The Fantasy of a Lily-White America," *Time,* April 15, 2024, https://time.com/6966768/fantasy-white-america-eddie-glaude/.

15 **"It is like a boil bursting forth":** Ralph Ellison, "What American Would Be Like Without Blacks," p. 577.

16 **"ages become retrospective, building sepulchres":** Ralph Waldo Emerson, "Nature," in *Ralph Waldo Emerson: Essays and Lectures,* ed. Joel Porte. New York: Library of America, 1983, p. 7.

16 **"a set of beliefs, symbols, and rituals":** Robert Bellah, "Civil Religion in America," *Daedalus,* vol. 117, no. 3, Summer 1988, p. 104. Bellah wrote, "Behind the civil religion at every point lie biblical archetypes: Exodus, Chosen People, Promised Land, New Jerusalem, and Sacrificial Death and Rebirth. But it is also genuinely American and genuinely new. It has its own prophets and its own martyrs, its own sacred events and sacred places, its own solemn rituals and symbols. It is concerned that American be a society as perfectly in accord with the will of God as men can make it, and a light to all nations" (p. 115).

17 ***We are a divinely ordained nation:*** See Ernest Tuveson, *Redeemer Nation: The Idea of America's Millennial Role.* Chicago: University of Chicago Press, 1968, and https://www.wilsonquarterly.com/quarterly/_/still-the-redeemer-nation.

17 **"the jangling discord of our nation":** Dr. Martin Luther King Jr., "I Have a Dream," https://www.npr.org/2010/01/18/122701268/i-have-a-dream-speech-in-its-entirety. Also see Richard Slotkin, *A Great Disorder: National Myth and the Battle for America.* Cambridge, MA: Harvard University Press, 2024, p. 13.

18 **"Among democratic nations":** Alexis de Tocqueville, *Democracy in America,* 2 vols., trans. Phillips Bradley. New York: Vintage, 1990, pp. 138–39.

19 **"life every American Negro must live":** W. E. B. Du Bois, *The Souls of Black Folk,* p. 502.

19 **enduring and unchanging principles:** See Andrew Delbanco, *The Real American Dream: A Meditation on Hope.* Cambridge, MA: Harvard University Press, 1999.

19 **"I have always been struck, in America":** James Baldwin, *No Name in the Street,* p. 385.

20 **"history is interior":** Norman Mailer, *The Armies of the Night.* New York: New American Library, 1968, p. 255. Also quoted in Andrew Delbanco, *The Real American Dream,* p. 6.

Chapter One: Freedom Is the White Man's Gift

23 **"drown himself rather than being Sold":** Nicholas Wood, "A 'Class of Citizens': The Earliest Black Petitioners to Congress and Their Quaker Allies," *William and Mary Quarterly,* 3rd ser., vol. 74, no. 1, January 2017, p. 110.

24 **"Let him be a fugitive in a strange land":** Frederick Douglass, *Autobiographies,* ed. Henry Louis Gates Jr. New York: Library of America, 1994, p. 90.

24 **"the contorted sense":** Andrew Delbanco, *The War Before the War: Fugitive Slaves and the Struggle for America's Soul from the Revolution to the Civil War.* New York: Penguin Press, 2018, p. 42.

24 **"masters from liberating their slaves":** Nicholas Wood, "A 'Class of Citizens,'" p. 110.

25 **"divers evil-minded persons":** *A Documentary History of the Negro People in the United States,* vol. 1, ed. Herbert Aptheker. New York: Citadel Press, 1990, p. 39.

25 **"Ten Silver Dollars Reward":** John Parrish, *Remarks on Slavery of the Black People: Addressed to the Citizens of the United States.* Philadelphia, 1806, p. 53; Nicholas Wood, "A 'Class of Citizens,'" p. 109.

26 **"rendition of [their] property":** Andrew Delbanco, *The War Before the War,* p. 20.

26 **"The Declaration of Independence made equality normative":** Ira Berlin, *The Long Emancipation: The Demise of Slavery in the United States.* Cambridge, MA: Harvard University Press, 2015, p. 43.

28 **"To be an Afro-American, or an American black":** James Baldwin, *No Name in the Street,* in *Collected Essays,* p. 474.

28 **"The statue is a deplorable monument":** "City Announces Removal of Rizzo Statue," City of Philadelphia website, June 3, 2020, https://www.phila.gov/2020-06-03-city-announces-removal-of-rizzo-statue/.

28 **Walter was shot fourteen times:** Ellie Rushing, Bethany Ao, Mensah M. Dean, and Dylan Purcell, "Walter Wallace Jr., 27, a 'Family Man with Many Mental Crises and Encounters with the Police," *Philadelphia Inquirer,* October 27, 2020.

29 **Nostalgia was everywhere:** Svetlana Boym, "Nostalgia and Its Discontents," *Hedgehog Review,* The Uses of the Past, Summer 2007, https://hedgehogreview.com/issues/the-uses-of-the-past/articles/nostalgia-and-its-discontents.

30 **"In Pursuit of a More Perfect Union":** See the Philadelphia Visitor Center Corporation's annual report, 2024, p. 6, https://www.visitphilly.com/wp-content/uploads/2025/04/2025.03.18_ANNUAL-REPORT_Digital_Web.pdf.

31 **"hunted day and night, like beasts of the forest":** "The 1797 Petition and Debate," *The Making of African American Identity,* vol. 1, *1500–1865,* National Humanities Center Resource Toolbox, https://nationalhumanitiescenter.org/pds/maai/community/text4/petitioncongress.pdf.

31 **"the solemn compact, the Constitution, was stained":** "A 'Disquieting' Negro Petition to Congress, 1800," in *A Documentary History of the Negro People in the United States: From Colonial Times Through the Civil War,* vol. 1, ed. Herbert Aptheker. New York: Citadel Press, 1979, p. 44.

33 **"I would ask gentlemen":** *Annals of the Congress of the United States: The Debates and Proceedings in the Congress of the United States with an Appendix Containing Important State Papers and Public Documents,* Sixth Congress, p. 230.

33 **it aims to reclaim an American past:** Adam Serwer, "The Great Resegregation," *Atlantic,* February 22, 2025.

"If the Great Resegregation proves successful, it will restore an American past where racial and ethnic minorities were the occasional token presence in an otherwise white-dominated landscape. It would repeal the gains of the civil-rights era in their entirety. What its advocates want is not a restoration of explicit Jim Crow segregation—that would shatter the illusion that their own achievements are based in a colorblind meritocracy. They want an arrangement that perpetuates racial inequality indefinitely while retaining some plausible deniability, a rigged system that maintains a mirage of equal opportunity while maintaining an unofficial racial hierarchy."

35 **"a failure of feeling":** Wallace Stevens, *Collected Poetry and Prose,* eds. Joan Richardson and Frank Kermode. New York: Library of America, 1997, p. 903.

35 **Or, later in the early twentieth century:** William James, *The Principles of Psychology.* New York: Dover, 1950. William James describes a wealthy matron who weeps at the plight of the characters on stage while her servants wait for her in the freezing cold outside. The feelings are paramount, not the social condition or the consequence of direct action.

35 **"The only remedy to racist discrimination":** Ibram X. Kendi, *How to Be an Antiracist.* New York: One World, 2019, p. 19.

36 **"the manner of these declarations":** David Bromwich, "Is America Ungovernable? The Difference Between Protest and Reform," *Harper's,* November 2020.

36 **"the mark of dishonesty, the inability to feel":** James Baldwin, "Everybody's Protest Novel," in *Collected Essays,* p. 12.

36 **the historian Carol Anderson calls "white rage":** Carol Anderson, *White Rage: The Unspoken Truth of Our Racial Divide.* New York: Bloomsbury, 2016.

37 **That deceit became the source of our national suffering:** Fyodor Dostoevsky, "The Grand Inquisitor," in *The Brothers Karamazov,* p. 253: "This deceit will constitute our suffering, for we shall have to lie."

38 **"Since the beginning of the nation":** Ralph Ellison, "What America Would Be Like Without Blacks," p. 583.

39 **"to place the contributions of black Americans":** *The 1619 Project,* https://www.nytimes.com/interactive/2019/08/14/magazine/1619-america-slavery.html.

39 **"by truthfully recounting the aspirations":** The President's Advisory 1776 Commission, *The 1776 Report,* January 2021, https://trumpwhitehouse.archives.gov/wp-content/uploads/2021/01/The-Presidents-Advisory-1776-Commission-Final-Report.pdf.

40 **"As the struggle for universal freedom gained":** Ira Berlin, *The Long Emancipation,* pp. 44–45.

40 **"idolaters of the old":** Ralph Waldo Emerson, "Compensation," in *Essays and Lectures,* ed. Joel Porte. New York: Library of America, 1983, p. 302.

41 **"We cannot stay amid the ruins":** Ralph Waldo Emerson, "Compensation," p. 302.

41 **Where and how we begin our stories:** As the late scholar Edward Said wrote, "The problem of beginning is the beginning of the problem." Said, *Beginnings: Intention and Method.* New York: Columbia University Press, 1985, p. 42.

41 **"fellow-black now confined in the jail of this city":** Nicholas Wood, "A 'Class of Citizens,'" p. 111.

41 **"If, notwithstanding all that has been publicly":** *A Documentary History of the Negro People in the United States,* vol. 1, ed. Herbert Aptheker. New York: Carol Publishing Group, 1990, p. 43.

42 **"We are incited by a sense of Social duty":** *1799 Petition of Absalom Jones, and Others, People of Color, and Freemen Against the Slave Trade to the Coast of Guinea,* National Park Service, https://www.nps.gov/articles/000/inde-1799-12-30-petition-ajones-abolition-guinea.htm.

43 **"When the Congress sat at New York":** *Annals,* p. 230.

43 **"Some of the States would never have adopted":** *Annals,* p. 230.

44 **"was admirable . . . , and well executed":** *Annals,* p. 240.

44 **"I recollect that gentleman in France":** *Annals,* p. 242.

44 **"Runaway slaves and those who pursued them":** *Annals,* p. 100.

45 **"damning the whites":** Gary Nash, *Forging Freedom: The Formation of Philadelphia's Black Community.* Cambridge, MA: Harvard University Press, 1988, p. 176. Also see *Pennsylvania Correspondent,* Doylestown, PA, July 18, 1804.

46 **"Yeah, he was hateful all right":** Toni Morrison, *Beloved.* New York: Vintage, 2004, pp. 83–84.

Chapter Two: What Is the Fourth of July to Us?

49 **"The past is all that makes the present coherent":** James Baldwin, *Collected Essays,* p. 7.

50 **"The Fourth is yours, not mine":** Frederick Douglass, "What to the Slave Is the Fourth of July?," July 5, 1852, National Museum of African American History and Culture, https://nmaahc.si.edu/explore/stories/nations-story-what-slave-fourth-july.

52 **"Time present and time past":** T. S. Eliot, "Burnt Norton," in *Four Quartets,* Boston: Houghton Mifflin Harcourt, 1971, p. 13.

52 **"I know a wind in purpose strong":** Herman Melville, "The Conflict of Convictions," https://poets.org/poem/conflict-convictions.

52 **"See through time in order to see today":** Imani Perry, *Black in Blues,* p. 235.

53 **The statue is a near-replica of the original:** Justin Murphy, "Frederick Douglass Statues to Be Installed Throughout Rochester," *Democrat and Chronicle,* July 17, 2018, https://www.democratandchronicle.com/story/news/2018/07/17/frederick-douglass-statues-rochester-olivia-kim-bicentennial/775231002/.

54 **"the vulgar prejudice of color":** Victoria Sandwick Schmitt, "Rochester's Frederick Douglass: Part One," *Rochester History,* vol. 67, no. 3, Summer 2005, pp.13–14, https://www.libraryweb.org/~rochhist/v67_2005/v67i3.pdf.

54 **He had named his new newspaper *The North Star:*** David Blight, *Frederick Douglass: Prophet of Freedom.* New York: Simon & Schuster, 2018, p. 190.

54 **With its high ceilings and elegant chandeliers:** David Blight, *Frederick Douglass: Prophet of Freedom,* p. 230.

54 **"the most magnificent auditorium":** Emily Morry, "Susan B. Anthony's Rochester," *Rochester Beacon,* February 6, 2020. She cites the *Democrat and Chronicle,* December 3, 1898, p. 11.

56 **"an occasion for consensus":** Lyn Spillman, *Nation and Commemoration: Creating*

National Identities in the United States and Australia. New York: Cambridge University Press, 1997, pp. 23–24. Also see Michael Kammen, *Mystic Chords of Memory: The Transformation of Tradition in American Culture.* New York: Knopf, 1991, p. 49; Charles Warren, "Fourth of July Myths," *William and Mary Quarterly,* vol. 2 (1945), pp. 237–72.

56 **"We have just returned":** *New-York Commercial Advertiser,* July 12, 1834, quoted in John H. Hewitt, "The Sacking of St. Philip's Church, New York," *Historical Magazine of the Protestant Episcopal Church,* vol. 49, no. 1, March 1980, p. 7.

56 **"demanded that white families illuminate":** Eddie S. Glaude Jr., *Exodus! Religion, Race, and Nation in Early Nineteenth-Century Black America.* Chicago: University of Chicago Press, 2000, pp. 107–8.

58 **"The God of Nature has endowed our children":** Nathaniel Paul, "An Address Delivered on the Celebration of the Abolition of Slavery in the State of New York, July 5, 1827," *Freedom's Journal,* August 10, 1827, in *Negro Orators and Their Orations,* ed. Carter G. Woodson. New York: Russell & Russell, 1969, p. 76.

59 **"Like the people of God in Egypt":** *Austin Steward: Twenty-Two Years a Slave and Forty Years a Freeman,* in *Four Fugitive Slave Narratives.* Reading, MA: Addison-Wesley, 1969, p. 96. Also quoted in Glaude, *Exodus!,* p. 98.

60 **"visions of hope":** David Blight, *Frederick Douglass: Prophet of Freedom,* pp. 231–36.

64 **"We see the thief preaching against theft":** Frederick Douglass, *Autobiographies,* p. 19.

64 **These were white Christians who would distort:** Idaho-based pastor Joe Rigney published *The Sin of Empathy* (Canon Press, 2025), where he announced that "the so-called virtue of empathy is the greatest rhetorical tool of manipulation of the 21st century."

66 **"At each of these junctures the American revolution":** Charles Long, "Civil Rights—Civil Religion: Visible People and Invisible Religion," in *American Civil Religion,* eds. Russell E. Richey and Donald G. Jones. New York: Harper & Row, 1974, p. 21.

66 **"We Americans are the peculiar, chosen people":** Herman Melville, *White Jacket, or The World in a Man-of-War.* Evanston, IL: Northwestern University Press, 1970, p. 151.

67 **"As if we had not strained the voting":** Walt Whitman, *Prose Works 1892,* ed. Floyd Stovall, vol. 2. New York: New York University Press, 1964. Also see Paul Outka, "Whitman and Race ('He's Queer, He's Unclear, Get Used to It')," *Journal of American Studies,* vol. 36, no. 2, August 2002, p. 296.

68 **"You had far better all die":** Henry Highland Garnet, *An Address to the Slaves of the United States of America,* April 15, 1848, DigitalCommons@University of Nebraska–Lincoln, https://digitalcommons.unl.edu/cgi/viewcontent.cgi?article=1007&context=etas.

70 **"For decades, Black life has been seen as disposable":** "The Other Kind of Racism in Buffalo, with Evan Osnos," *New Yorker Podcast,* May 19, 2022, https://www.newyorker.com/podcast/politics-and-more/the-other-kind-of-racism-in-buffalo.

70 **"She was the person who held us together":** Testimony of Garnell Whitfield Jr., Senate Judiciary Committee Hearing on "Examining the 'Metastasizing' Domestic Terrorism Threat After the Buffalo Attack," June 7, 2022, https://www.judiciary.senate.gov/imo/media/doc/Testimony%20-%20Whitfield%20-%202022-06-07.pdf.

71 **"It was very difficult":** Author's interview with Garnell Whitfield Jr., September 26, 2022.

71 **"I wish we had a hearing":** "Ted Cruz Slams Democrats' Response to Buffalo Shooting: 'That's Cynical, It's Dishonest,'" June 7, 2022, YouTube, https://www.youtube.com/watch?v=FLvWpPsA-VM.

72 **"America is built on violence":** Author's interview with Garnell Whitefield Jr., September 26, 2022.

73 **"spread awareness to my fellow whites":** "Buffalo Shooter's Manifesto Promotes 'Great Replacement' Theory, Antisemitism and Previous Mass Shooters," ADL, May 14, 2022, https://www.adl.org/resources/blog/buffalo-shooters-manifesto-promotes-great-replacement-theory-antisemitism-and-previous-mass-shooters.

Chapter Three: 1876: Centennial

77 **"endowed with a vast":** Walt Whitman, *Democratic Vistas,* in *The Portable Whitman,* ed. Mark Van Doren. New York: Penguin Books, 1945, p. 326.

78 **"We were unable to find the body":** Ron Chernow, *Grant.* New York: Penguin Press, 2017, p. 759. Also see Nicholas Lehman, *Redemption: The Last Battle of the Civil War.* New York: Farrar, Straus & Giroux, 2007, p. 21.

79 **"enemies of society":** Eric Foner, *Reconstruction: America's Unfinished Revolution, 1863–1877.* New York: Harper Perennial, 1988, p. 517.

79 **the "era of moral politics":** Eric Foner, *Reconstruction,* p. 527; *New York Herald,* October 19, 1874.

80 **"a kind of superior truth":** Robert Penn Warren, *The Legacy of the Civil War.* Lincoln: University of Nebraska Press, 1998, p. 75.

80 **"Armed bodies of men":** Ron Chernow, *Grant,* p. 788.

80 **"Regretting the necessity":** Albert Dorsey Jr., "Vicksburg's Troubles," *Black Participation in the Body Politic and Land Ownership in the Age of Redeemer Violence.* Dissertation, Florida State University, 2012, p. 52.

80 **"I have tried to get troops":** Ron Chernow, *Grant,* p. 788.

81 **"to slaughter whites on the August election day":** Albert Dorsey Jr., "Vicksburg's Troubles," p. 52.

81 **By December 5, armed members:** Ron Chernow, *Grant,* p. 789.

81 **"Mississippi Plan":** Nicholas Lemann, *Redemption: The Last Battle of the Civil War.* See Chapter 5, "The Mississippi Plan," pp. 170–209.

81 **"The whole public are tired out":** Eric Foner, *Reconstruction,* p. 560.

82 **"classical financial liberalism":** David Blight, *Race and Reunion: The Civil War and American Memory.* Cambridge, MA: Belknap Press, 2001, p. 123.

82 **"Reconstruction seems to be morally":** Quoted in David Blight, *Race and Reunion,* p. 123. Also see *Nation,* March 21, 1872, and July 6, 1871.

82 **"Seven years ago these men":** Ron Chernow, *Grant,* p. 784.

82 **"a mass of black barbarism":** Eric Foner, *Reconstruction,* p. 525.

83 **"that there be no further interference":** Ron Chernow, *Grant,* p. 785.

83 **"the Negro votes the republican ticket":** Ron Chernow, *Grant,* p. 786.

83 **"Reconstruction and slavery we have done with":** David Blight, *Race and Reunion,* p. 123.

83 **"the hour that the loyal North":** Frederick Douglass, *The Life and Times of Frederick Douglass, Written by Himself: His Early Life as a Slave, His Escape from Bondage, and His Complete History* (1892). New York: Collier Books, 1962, p. 539.

84 ***Black people were the problem:*** I am reminded of W. E. B. Du Bois. In an essay

he published in *The Atlantic* in August 1897, "Strivings of the Negro People," he wrote:

"Between me and the other world there is ever an unasked question: unasked by some through feelings of delicacy; by others through the difficulty of rightly framing it. All, nevertheless, flutter round it. They approach me in a half-hesitant sort of way, eye me curiously or compassionately, and then, instead of saying directly, How does it feel to be a problem? they say, I know an excellent colored man in my town; or, I fought at Mechanicsville; or, Do not these Southern outrages make your blood boil? At these I smile, or am interested, or reduce the boiling to a simmer, as the occasion may require. *To the real question, How does it feel to be a problem? I answer seldom a word*" [emphasis added].

This essay would be revised and retitled in *The Souls of Black Folk* as "Of Our Spiritual Strivings," https://www.theatlantic.com/magazine/archive/1897/08/strivings-of-the-negro-people/305446.

84 **"Each generation sought to shift":** W. E. B. Du Bois, "The Suppression of the African Slave-Trade," in *Du Bois: Writings,* p. 197.

85 **"mostly used to cover the sleeper":** James Baldwin, "As Much Truth as One Can Bear," in *The Cross of Redemption: Uncollected Writings,* ed. Randall Kenan. New York: Random House, 2010, p. 29.

85 **"destitute of political memory":** David Blight, *Frederick Douglass: Prophet of Freedom,* 2018, p. 530. Also see David Blight, "For Something Beyond the Battlefield: Frederick Douglass and the Struggle for the Memory of the Civil War," *Journal of American History,* March 1989, pp. 1156–78.

86 **"There was scarcely a white man in the South":** W. E. B. Du Bois, *The Souls of Black Folk,* p. 389.

86 **"had done the Negro no good":** David Blight, *Race and Reunion,* p. 138.

86 **The Civil War may have ended:** W. E. B. Du Bois, *The Souls of Black Folk,* p. 389.

86 **"negro will disappear from the field":** See David Blight, *Race and Reunion,* p. 138; *Nation,* April 5, 1877.

86 **"the bottom of the well":** Derrick Bell, *Faces at the Bottom of the Well: The Permanence of Racism.* New York: Basic Books, 2018.

87 **"In the summer of 1875":** David Blight, *Frederick Douglass: Prophet of Freedom,* pp. 556–57.

87 **"observed with fear the unraveling":** David Blight, *Frederick Douglass: Prophet of Freedom,* p. 551.

88 **"pronouncing black suffrage a failure":** Eric Foner, *Reconstruction,* p. 527.

88 **"the alienation between the North and the South":** Richard B. Drake, "Freedman's Aid Societies and Sectional Compromise," *Journal of Southern History,* vol. 29, May 1963, p. 183.

90 **"The fathers of this Republic":** Frederick Douglass, "The Color Question: An Address Delivered in Washington, D.C., on July 5, 1875," Frederick Douglass Papers Project, https://frederickdouglasspapersproject.com/s/digitaledition/item/18187.

91 **Despite the success of the Democrats:** Lyn Spillman, *Nation and Commemoration: Creating National Identities in the United States and Australia.* Cambridge, UK: Cambridge University Press, 1997, p. 45.

91 **"an overgrown and spread-eagle Fourth of July":** Philip Foner, "Black Participation in the Centennial of 1876," *Phylon,* vol. 35, no. 4, Winter 1978, p. 284. Also see *Workingman's Advocate,* Chicago, March 6, 1875.

91 **"bitch-goddess Success" . . . "moral flabbiness":** *The Letters of William James,* vol. 2. Boston: Atlantic Monthly Press, 1920, p. 260.

92 **"To me individually":** Thomas Carlyle, *Shooting Niagara: And After?* London: Chapman & Hall, 1867, p. 46.

95 **"the colored people's desertion of the Republican Party":** David Blight, *Frederick Douglass: Prophet of Freedom,* p. 559.

95 **On May 10, 1876:** Ron Chernow, *Grant,* pp. 828–29.

96 **"We have listened too long":** Ralph Waldo Emerson, "The American Scholar," in *Emerson: Essays and Lectures,* p. 70.

96 **The Philadelphia police refused to admit him:** Philip Foner, "Black Participation in the Centennial of 1876," p. 283.

96 **"It was feared he might have gone":** Philip Foner, "Black Participation in the Centennial of 1876," pp. 283–84.

96 **They marveled at new inventions:** See John Henry Hepp IV, *Mystery and Marvel: Philadelphia's 1876 Centennial Exposition.* Havertown, PA: Brookline Books, 2024.

97 **Reviewing the Centennial Exposition:** William Dean Howells, "A Sennight of the Centennial," *Atlantic,* July 1876, https://www.theatlantic.com/magazine/archive/1876/07/a-sennight-of-the-centennial/631397/.

97 **"argued that the Centennial":** Philip Foner, "Black Participation in the Centennial of 1876," p. 285; *Congressional Record,* 43rd Congress, 1st Session, Appendix, pp. 250–53.

98 **"The policemen sponsoring the event":** Philip Foner, "Black Participation in the Centennial of 1876," p. 288.

98 **"that the great show of the American":** Philip Foner, "Black Participation in the Centennial of 1876," p. 289.

98 **"to read the Emancipation Proclamation":** Philip Foner, "Black Participation in the Centennial of 1876," p. 289.

99 **"*mis*-created or *mal*-created":** James W. C. Pennington, *The Fugitive Blacksmith and Other Essential Writings,* eds. Jan Stievermann, Caitlin Smith, and Eddie S. Glaude Jr. New York: Oxford University Press, 2025.

99 **"What remains certain is that Reconstruction failed":** Eric Foner, *Reconstruction,* p. 604.

Interlude: The Plague Years

103 **The old man fell to his knees:** David Blight, *Frederick Douglass: Prophet of Freedom,* p. 752.

103 **"faith in the nobility of the nation":** Frederick Douglass, "Lessons for the Hour: An Address in Washington, D.C., on January 9, 1894," Frederick Douglass Papers Project, https://frederickdouglasspapersproject.com/s/digitaledition/item/18815.

104 **"the nadir":** Rayford W. Logan, *The Betrayal of the Negro: From Rutherford B. Hayes to Woodrow Wilson.* New York: Hachette Books, 1997.

104 **They even created a national anthem:** See Imani Perry's *May We Forever Stand.* Chapel Hill: University of North Carolina Press, 2018. Also see Michele Mitchell, "Nadir," in *Keywords for African American Studies,* eds. Erica Edwards, Jeffrey O. G. Ogbar, and Roderick Ferguson. New York: New York University Press, 2018.

104 **"bone soldered by coral to bone":** Derek Walcott, "The Sea Is History," https://poets.org/poem/sea-history.

104 **"I cannot shut my eyes to the ugly facts before me":** In his brief preface to Ida B. Wells's *Red Record: Tabulated Statistics and Alleged Causes of Lynching in the United States* (1895), Douglass wrote on "the lynch abomination now generally practiced

against colored people in the South." He said, "It sometimes seems we are deserted by earth and Heaven—yet we must still think, and trust in the power of a merciful God for final deliverance."

105 **"The Negro Problem":** Nathaniel Southgate Shaler, "The Negro Problem," *Atlantic Monthly,* vol. 54 (1884), pp. 698–703.

105 **"excited by a freedom they did not understand":** Woodrow Wilson, "The Reconstruction of the Southern States," *Atlantic Monthly,* January 1901, https://www.theatlantic.com/magazine/archive/1901/01/the-reconstruction-of-the-southern-states/520035/.

106 **"if the negro is *thoughtfully cared for*":** Nathaniel Southgate Shaler, "The Negro Problem," p. 708.

107 **the storming adolescent:** No wonder W. E. B. Du Bois wrote in *The Souls of Black Folk:* "To the real question, How does it feel to be a problem? I answer seldom a word." Or that James Baldwin wrote in "The Artist's Struggle for Integrity": "There is no Negro problem. The problem is that one is still in a kindergarten, an emotional kindergarten, and the Negro in this country operates as some kind of weird gorilla who suddenly is breaking up all the blackboards."

107 **"there is no room for the hyphen in our citizenship":** President Theodore Roosevelt, "An Address to the Knights of Columbus, Carnegie Hall, NYC, October 12, 1915." Roosevelt continued, "This is one of the demands to be made in the name of the spirit of American nationalism. The other is equally important. We must treat every good American of German descent or any other American, without regard to his creed, as on a full and exact equality with every other good American, and set our faces like flint against the creatures who seek to discriminate against such an American, or to hold against him the birthplace of himself or his parents." Obviously, this view did not apply to Black Americans.

108 **"Finally perish!":** Lothrop Stoddard, *The Rising Tide of Color Against White World Supremacy.* New York: Charles Scribner's Sons, 1920, p. 304.

108 **The slogan "100 Percent Americanism":** See Frederick Lewis Allen, *Only Yesterday: An Informal History of the Nineteen Twenties.* New York: Harper Perennial, 2010.

108 **They founded organizations:** Wong Chin Foo established the Chinese Equal Rights League (1892), and Nissim Behar founded the National Liberal Immigration League (1906).

109 **"I hear this mighty cry reverberating":** W. E. B. Du Bois, *Darkwater.* New York: Oxford University Press, 2007, p. 25.

Chapter Four: 1926: Sesquicentennial

111 **an astonishing $1.44 billion in today's dollars:** Thomas H. Keels, *Sesqui!: Greed, Graft, and the Forgotten World's Fair of 1926.* Philadelphia: Temple University Press, 2017, p. x. (This chapter is indebted to Keels's extraordinary work. He dedicates an entire chapter to race and the 150th anniversary of the nation. I rely heavily on his account.)

112 **fewer than five million people:** Thomas H. Keels, *Sesqui!,* p. xii.

112 **Americans could not achieve a basic knowledge:** Walter Lippmann, *Public Opinion.* New York: Warbler Classics, 2024.

112 **"the old saying":** See John Dewey, *The Public and Its Problems: An Essay in Political Enquiry.* Chicago: Gateway Books, 1946.

113 **"eradicate[d] forever the scars" . . . "God bless us everyone":** Quoted in David Blight, *Race and Reunion,* p. 9. Also see *London Times,* July 4, 1913; *Louisville Courier-Journal,* July 4, 1913.

114 **"white supremacy . . . [as] the silent":** Quoted in David Blight, *Race and Reunion,* p. 9. (David Blight's classic sets the frame for how I am thinking about this moment.)

114 **"how the battle went, how it ended, what it signified!":** Wilson's speech at Gettysburg, American Presidency Project, UC Santa Barbara, https://www.presidency.ucsb.edu/documents/address-gettysburg-0.

114 **"the butt of . . . [a] national joke":** Michele Mitchell, "Nadir," in *Keyword for African American Studies,* eds. Erica R. Edwards, Roderick A. Ferguson, and Jeffrey O. G. Ogbar. New York: New York University Press, 2018, p. 118.

115 **"to unite white male persons, native-born Gentile citizens of the United States":** *The Klansman Manual* (1925), https://ehistory.osu.edu/sites/ehistory.osu.edu/files/mmh/clash/Imm_KKK/KKK%20pages/Documents/klanmanual.htm.

115 **"in Old Glory and the mantle of the Founding Fathers":** Frederick Lewis Allen, *Only Yesterday,* p. 51. See also Jon Meacham, *The Soul of America: The Battle for Our Better Angels.* New York: Random House, 2018, p. 113.

117 **"Just in so far as our America":** Randolph S. Bourne, *War and the Intellectuals: Collected Essays, 1915–1919.* New York: Harper & Row, 1964, p. 115.

119 **"It is curious to see America":** W. E. B. Du Bois, *Collected Writings,* p. 937.

119 **"With a painless change of name":** James Baldwin, "The Price of the Ticket," *Collected Essays,* p. 842.

120 **"Within 45 minutes his naked, bullet-mangled body":** *Nashville Tennessean,* December 16, 1924, p. 1.

121 **"that twenty-six governors and 62 percent":** Linda Gordon, *The Second Coming of the KKK: The Ku Klux Klan of the 1920s and the American Political Tradition.* New York: Liveright, 2017, p. 163.

121 **"America of the Melting Pot":** Also see Jill Lepore, *This America: The Case for the Nation.* New York: Liveright, 2019, pp. 87–88.

122 **"I do not think it would be arbitrary":** *Hearings Before the Committee on Immigration and Naturalization; House of Representatives, Sixty-Seventh Congress,* November 21, 1922, https://archive.org/details/analysisofameric00unit/page/n17/mode/2up.

123 **"the national origin of an immigrant":** David M. Chalmers, *Hooded Americanism: The History of the Ku Klux Klan.* New York: Liveright, 2017, p. 283.

123 **"all races will be treated the same":** Thomas H. Keels, *Sesqui!,* p. 208; "Fraternal Flashes: Sesqui-Centennial," *Philadelphia Tribune,* June 18, 1921; "Produce! We Must," editorial, *Philadelphia Tribune,* March 21, 1925.

123 **"executive committee of twenty-five":** Thomas H. Keels, *Sesqui!,* p. 208

124 **"I saw scores and scores of whites":** Thomas H. Keels, *Sesqui!,* p. 211.

124 **In 1917, Randolph had distinguished himself:** Thomas H. Keels, *Sesqui!,* p. 217.

124 **"Our aim is to appeal to reason":** Statement of the Editors for the first publication of *The Messenger,* 1917; https://www.marxists.org/history/usa/pubs/messenger/index.htm.

125 **"To Aframericans, the embodiment of this formula":** A. Philip Randolph, "The Negro Faces the Future," *African American Political Thought, 1890–1930,* ed. Cary D. Wintz. New York: Routledge, 2015, p. 310.

125 **"If there are those":** A. Philip Randolph, "The Negro Faces the Future," p. 310.

126 **"the true subject of democracy":** Ralph Ellison, "What America Would Be Like Without Blacks," p. 582. I amended Ellison's formulation. He wrote: "the extension of the democratic process in the direction of perfecting itself." I am a bit skeptical of that language in the U.S. context. "On the way to a more perfect union" works as a kind of alibi for historic and persistent harms.

126 **Randolph's words fell on barren soil:** See Thomas H. Keels, *Sesqui!,* p. 218.
127 **"I suppose," the officer said:** Thomas H. Keels, *Sesqui!,* p. 223.
127 **"a minstrel mimic laboring":** Thomas H. Keels, *Sesqui!,* p. 218.
127 **"We wonder what was in the breast":** Thomas H. Keels, *Sesqui!,* p. 218; also see *Philadelphia Tribune,* June 5, 1926.
128 **"It was not only the principles declared":** President Calvin Coolidge, *Address at the Celebration of the 150th Anniversary of the Declaration of Independence in Philadelphia, Pennsylvania,* American Presidency Project, https://www.presidency.ucsb.edu/documents/address-the-celebration-the-150th-anniversary-the-declaration-independence-philadelphia.
131 **"the idea of preserving and developing":** Hiram Wesley Evans, "The Klan's Fight for Americanism," *North American Review,* vol. 23, March–May 1926, p. 34.
131 **"enlisted our racial instincts":** Hiram Wesley Evans, "The Klan's Fight for Americanism," p. 35.
132 **"is charged in the mind of most Americans":** Hiram Wesley Evans, "The Klan's Fight for Americanism," p. 42.
133 **"Before the wide eyes of the mob":** W. E. B. Du Bois, "The Shape of Fear," *North American Review,* vol. 223, no. 831, June–August 1926, pp. 291–304, at 294.
133 **"Here were white men afraid of degradation":** W. E. B. Du Bois, "The Shape of Fear," p. 300.
133 **"the danger and shame":** W. E. B. Du Bois, "The Shape of Fear," p. 302.
134 **"Of all the dangerous weapons":** W. E. B. Du Bois, "The Shape of Fear," p. 303.
134 **"shifted toward a simpler, purer racial system":** Linda Gordon, *The Second Coming of the KKK: The Ku Klux Klan of the 1920s and the American Political Tradition.* New York: Liveright, 2017, p. 199.

Interlude: The American Century

137 **"There is currently one state":** Quoted in James Q. Whitman, *Hitler's American Model: The United States and the Making of Nazi Race Law.* Princeton: Princeton University Press, 2017, pp. 45–46.
138 **"The median Black income had risen":** Manning Marable, *Race, Reform, and Rebellion: The Second Reconstruction and Beyond in Black America, 1945–2006.* Jackson: University Press of Mississippi, 2007, p. 15.
139 **The McCarthy era cast dark shadows:** See John Higham, "The Cult of the 'American Consensus': Homogenizing Our History," *Commentary,* February 1959, https://www.commentary.org/articles/john-higham/the-cult-of-the-american-consensushomogenizing-our-history/.
139 **Ideological consensus:** Jill Lepore, *This America,* pp. 100–6.
139 **"It has been our fate as a nation not to have ideologies *but to be one*":** Richard Hofstader, book review of Louis Hartz's *The Liberal Tradition in America: An Interpretation of American Political Thought Since the Revolution, New York Times,* February 27, 1955, https://www.nytimes.com/1955/02/27/archives/without-feudalism-the-liberal-tradition-in-america-an.html; also quoted in Jill Lepore, *This America,* p. 100.
140 **"At this point a historiography":** John Higham, "The Cult of the 'American Consensus,'" p. 13.
141 **"Our children and their parents":** Quoted in John Bodnar, *Remaking America: Public Memory, Commemoration, and Patriotism in the Twentieth Century.* Princeton: Princeton University Press, 1992, p. 207.
142 **"Above all our central theme will be unity":** John Bodnar, *Remaking America,* p. 213.

142 **"A host of white northerners":** Michael Kammen, *Mystic Chords of Memory: The Transformation of Tradition in American Culture.* New York: Vintage, 1993, p. 597.

143 **"To be American is not . . . a matter of blood":** Robert Penn Warren, *The Legacy of the Civil War.* New York: Random House, 1961, p. 79.

143 **"No, simply piety and blood connection":** Robert Penn Warren, *The Legacy of the Civil War,* pp. 78–79.

143 **"of a climax drenched with blood":** Robert Penn Warren, *The Legacy of the Civil War,* p. 103.

144 **"Let us pray that the terrible historic tragedy":** Melville's Supplement to *Battle Pieces,* quoted in Robert Penn Warren, *The Legacy of the Civil War,* p. 107.

144 **"affirm for us the possibility of the dignity of life":** Robert Penn Warren, *The Legacy of the Civil War,* p. 108.

144 **"Righteous is our first refuge and our strength":** Robert Penn Warren, *The Legacy of the Civil War,* p. 75.

145 **"in the joining of both sides on the field":** John Bodner, *Remaking America,* p. 220.

145 **the centennial of the Emancipation Proclamation:** Michael Kammen, *Mystic Chords of Memory,* pp. 598–607.

145 **"I'd like to see you stand in this room and sign":** Taylor Branch, *Parting the Waters: America in the King Years, 1954–1963.* New York: Simon & Schuster, 1988, p. 518.

146 **"within the framework of the American constitution":** John Bodnar, *Remaking America,* p. 211.

146 **"When the architects of our republic wrote":** Dr. Martin Luther King Jr., "I Have a Dream" speech, NPR, https://www.npr.org/2010/01/18/122701268/i-have-a-dream-speech-in-its-entirety.

147 **"It is Africa!":** Gore Vidal, *1876.* New York: Vintage Books, 1976, p. 150.

Chapter Five: 1976: Bicentennial

153 **"violate the Constitutional Rights of the Black Panther Party":** Edward Eisen, "Courts Put Restraints on Police," *Philadelphia Inquirer,* September 5, 1970, p. 1.

153 **some six thousand people gathered:** Paul Delaney, "Panthers Weigh New Convention," *New York Times,* September 7, 1970, p. 13. Also quoted in Robin D. G. Kelley, "Into the Fire," in *To Make Our World Anew: A History of African Americans from 1880,* vol. 2. New York: Oxford University, 2000, p. 266.

153 **"Friends and comrades throughout the United States":** "Huey Newton's Message to the Revolutionary People's Constitutional Convention, Plenary Session, September 5, 1970, Philadelphia, PA," https://freedomarchives.org/Documents/Finder/DOC513_scans/Rev.Convention/513.HueysMessagetothePlenarySession.pdf.

156 **"Far more conservative presumptions":** Sean Wilentz, *The Age of Reagan: A History, 1974–2008.* New York: HarperCollins, 2008, pp. 15–16.

158 **"an empty and broken shell":** Robert Bellah, *The Broken Covenant: American Civil Religion in Time of Trial.* New York: Seabury Press, 1975, p. 142.

158 **". . . is not simply a low ebb":** Robert Bellah, *The Broken Covenant,* pp. 142–43.

159 **"The covenant . . . was broken":** Robert Bellah, *The Broken Covenant,* p. 139.

160 **"today the broken covenant is visible to all":** Robert Bellah, *The Broken Covenant,* p. 139.

160 **"we are not innocent":** Robert Bellah, *The Broken Covenant,* p. 141.
161 **"If we are to free ourselves":** Robert Bellah, *The Broken Covenant,* p. 144.
161 **"Only through a sense of tragedy":** Robert Bellah, *The Broken Covenant,* p. 151.
161 **"We must reaffirm the outward or external covenant":** Robert Bellah, *The Broken Covenant,* p. 151.
162 **"If the storm wakes us from false innocence":** Robert Bellah, *The Broken Covenant,* p. 162.
163 **"Beneath this bland, this conqueror-image":** James Baldwin, "In Search of a Majority," in *Collected Essays,* p. 218.
164 **"Many white Americans demanded":** See Kevin Kruse, *White Flight: Atlanta and the Making of Modern Conservatism.* Princeton: Princeton University Press, 2007.
165 **"a renewal of American consensus and patriotism":** John Bodnar, *Remaking America,* p. 227. (I rely heavily on Bodnar's detailed and insightful account of the Bicentennial celebration.)
165 **"After two centuries":** President Ford's speech at Monticello, July 5, 1976. American Presidency Project, UC Santa Barbara, https://www.presidency.ucsb.edu/documents/remarks-naturalization-ceremonies-monticello-virginia. Also see John Bodnar, *Remaking America,* p. 228.
165 **"the commission would recall to the nation":** John Bodnar, *Remaking America,* p. 229.
166 **"that would provide cultural and recreational":** John Bodnar, *Remaking America,* p. 230.
166 **The commission also came under intense scrutiny:** John Bodnar, *Remaking America,* p. 231.
166 **"help Blacks better understand and relate":** Eugene L. Meyer, "Bicentennial Commission: Deeply Involved in Politics," *Washington Post,* August 14, 1973.
166 **"seeing that the federal government":** John Bodnar, *Remaking America,* p. 232.
167 **"an exposition of the nation itself":** Christopher Capozzola, "It Makes You Want to Believe in the Country: Celebrating the Bicentennial in the Age of Limits," in *America in the Seventies,* eds. Beth Bailey and David Farber. Lawrence: University of Kansas Press, 2004, p. 43.
168 **"like a sudden swarm of 200-year locusts":** "Bucks from the Bicentennial," *Time,* September 9, 1975, p. 73; Christopher Capozzola, "It Makes You Want to Believe," p. 33.
168 **"I am standing here":** President Gerald Ford, "Remarks at National Archives: Friday, July 2, 1976." Ford Library Museum, https://www.fordlibrarymuseum.gov/sites/default/files/pdf_documents/library/document/0122/1252949.pdf.
170 **"grandiose display[s] of chauvinism":** John Bodnar, *Remaking America,* p. 234.
171 **"We have a great revolution to look back on":** J. Anthony Lukas, "Who Owns 1776?," *New York Times,* May 18, 1975, https://www.nytimes.com/1975/05/18/archives/who-owns-1776-the-battle-in-boston-for-control-of-the-american-past.html.
171 **"cassette tapes to the wives of Fortune 500 executives":** John Bodnar, *Remaking America,* p. 236.
172 **"Who Owns 1776?":** J. Anthony Lukas, "Who Owns 1776?"
174 **"reactionary populism":** Ronald P. Formisano, *Boston Against Busing: Race, Class, and Ethnicity in the 1960s and 1970s.* Chapel Hill: University of North Carolina Press, 2004, p. 3.
174 **"racism added an ugly, frenetic charge":** Ronald P. Formisano, *Boston Against Busing,* p. 8.

174 **"defending their liberty against a judge run amok":** Louis P. Masur, *The Soiling of Old Glory: The Story of a Photograph That Shocked America.* Waltham, MA: Brandeis University Press, 2008, p. 2.

175 **"to kill me with the American flag":** Louis P. Masur, *The Soiling of Old Glory,* p. 19.

175 **"The black people of Boston":** Louis P. Masur, *The Soiling of Old Glory,* p. 69.

176 **"In the long run":** Susan Sontag, *Essays of the 1960s and 70s,* ed. David Rieff. New York: Library of America, 2013, pp. 556–57.

177 **"We present here":** John Johnson, "Publisher's Statement," *Ebony,* August 1975, p. 32.

177 **"Martyrs for Black Freedom":** *Ebony,* August 1975, pp. 138–40.

178 **"re-commit ourselves to the unfinished task":** Dr. Joseph H. Jackson, "A Resounding Yes!," *Ebony,* August 1975, p. 36.

178 **"to remind a forgetting nation":** Vernon Jordan Jr., "A Qualified Maybe," *Ebony,* August 1975, pp. 37–38.

179 **"Two hundred years of evasion":** Lerone Bennet Jr., "An Adamant No," *Ebony,* August 1975, pp. 40, 42.

180 **"harmonized into a nonthreatening spectacle":** Christopher Capozzola, "It Makes You Want to Believe," p. 44.

180 **"With the growth of the civil rights movement":** President Gerald Ford, *Message on the Observance of Black History Week,* American Presidency Project, February 3, 1975, https://www.presidency.ucsb.edu/documents/message-the-observance-black-history-week.

181 **"seize the opportunity to honor":** President Gerald Ford, *Message on the Observance of Black History Month,* American Presidency Project, February 10, 1975, https://www.presidency.ucsb.edu/documents/message-the-observance-black-history-month-february-1976.

Interlude: The After Times

186 **"awakened something strong and true":** President Ronald Reagan, "Remarks on Signing the Bill Making the Birthday of Martin Luther King Jr. a National Holiday," Ronald Reagan Presidential Library & Museum, https://www.reaganlibrary.gov/archives/speech/remarks-signing-bill-making-birthday-martin-luther-king-jr-national-holiday.

187 **Reagan would use this strong misreading of King:** Howell Raines, "Reagan Reversing Many U.S. Policies," *New York Times,* July 3, 1981.

190 **"Five decades ago today":** President Barack Obama, "Remarks by the President at the 'Let Freedom Ring' Ceremony Commemorating the 50th Anniversary of the March on Washington," Obama White House, https://obamawhitehouse.archives.gov/the-press-office/2013/08/28/remarks-president-let-freedom-ring-ceremony-commemorating-50th-anniversa.

192 **Bill Clinton made a gesture similar:** President Bill Clinton, "Bill Clinton Eulogy Transcript at John Lewis Funeral, July 30," *Rev,* 2020, https://www.rev.com/transcripts/bill-clinton-eulogy-transcript-at-john-lewis-funeral-july-30.

196 **"President Biden, at the end of his speech in Tulsa":** President Joseph Biden, "Remarks by President Biden Commemorating the 100th Anniversary of the Tulsa Race Massacre," June 1, 2021, Biden White House, https://bidenwhitehouse.archives.gov/briefing room/speeches remarks/2021/06/02/remarks by president-biden-commemorating-the-100th-anniversary-of-the-tulsa-race-massacre/.

197 **"The Oklahoma Supreme Court":** Martha F. Davis, "Oklahoma Supreme Court Rejects Reparations for Tulsa Race Massacre," *State Court Report,* June 21, 2024.

Chapter Six: 2026: Semiquincentennial

199 **"This majestic celebration":** President Donald Trump, "President Trump 'Salute to America' Event in Iowa, One Year to America's 250th Birthday," YouTube, https://www.youtube.com/watch?v=YrrRWx0kwmQ.

200 **"But I hate them too":** President Donald Trump, "Speech: Donald Trump Delivers a Salute to America Speech in Des Moines, Iowa—July 3, 2025," *Roll Call,* https://rollcall.com/factbase/trump/transcript/donald-trump-speech-salute-to-america-des-moines-iowa-july-3-2025/.

201 **"the most inclusive commemoration":** John Garrison Marks, "The 250th Birthday of the U.S. Is Just a Few Years Away. Get Ready for the Controversy," *Time,* March 21, 2022.

202 **What was increasingly clear during Biden's term:** Much of this groundwork had been laid in the 1980s with attacks on affirmative action and declarations about "the closing of the American mind," which railed against the purported capture of American higher education by liberal forces committed to moral relativism.

203 **As in the 1970s and the 1870s . . . "calcified":** John Sides, Chris Tausanovitch, and Lynn Vavreck, *The Bitter End: The 2020 Presidential Campaign and the Challenge to American Democracy.* Princeton: Princeton University Press, 2022.

203 **intensifying the stakes of elections:** Cathleen Kaveny, *Prophecy Without Contempt: Religious Discourse in the Public Square.* Cambridge, MA: Harvard University Press, 2016.

204 **"what was once planned as a unifying celebration":** Amanda Moore and Dan Friedman, "How MAGA Took Over America's 250th Birthday," *Mother Jones,* June 13, 2025, https://www.motherjones.com/politics/2025/06/military-parade-army-trump-american250-a250/.

205 **"some strange Christian thing":** Author's interview with Representative Bonnie Watson Coleman, August 4, 2025.

205 **"where no cry or lament or song or hope":** James Baldwin, "Nothing Personal," in *Collected Essays,* p. 704.

206 **None of this was set in stone:** Janay Kingsberry, "White House Says Garden of American Heroes May Not Be Complete Until 2029," *Washington Post,* July 3, 2025.

208 **"President Trump feels strongly":** Amanda Friedman, "White House Partners with Conservative College for Independence Day Videos," *Politico,* April 23, 2025, https://www.politico.com/news/2025/04/23/trump-hillsdale-college-partnership-00306508.

210 **"No durable union could have been formed":** *The 1776 Report,* President's Advisory 1776 Commission, January 2021, pp. 11–12, https://trumpwhitehouse.archives.gov/wp-content/uploads/2021/01/The-Presidents-Advisory-1776-Commission-Final-Report.pdf.

212 **"which have monumentally advanced the tradition of equality":** *White House: Proclamation from President Donald J. Trump on National Black History Month,* January 31, 2025, https://it.usembassy.gov/white-house-proclamation-from-president-donald-j-trump-on-national-black-history-month/.

213 **"Black History is American history":** Matt Brown and Michelle L. Price, "White House Will Celebrate Black History Month as Some Government Agencies Skip After Anti-DEI Order," Associated Press, February 20, 2025, https://www.whitehouse.gov/presidential-actions/2025/03/restoring-truth-and-sanity-to-american-history/.

213 **"Over the past decade":** "Restoring Truth and Sanity to American History,"

March 27, 2025, White House, https://www.whitehouse.gov/presidential-actions/2025/03/restoring-truth-and-sanity-to-american-history/.

214 **As such, President Trump set out:** Fallon Roth, "Trump Admin Will Review Panels on Edgar Allan Poe's Opposition to the Abolitionist Movement at Philly Site," *Philadelphia Inquirer,* August 4, 2025.

215 **"I don't understand and it's hard for me":** Author's interview with Lonnie Bunch, August 11, 2025.

216 **"and what they are doing is trying to silence":** Author's interview with Lonnie Bunch, August 11, 2025.

217 **"What unites Islamists, gender studies majors, socially liberal white":** "Transcript: JD Vance's Speech at the Claremont Institute's Statesmanship Award Event," July 10, 2025, https://singjupost.com/transcript-jd-vances-speech-at-the-claremont-institutes-statesmanship-award-event/.

Conclusion: Love and Country

228 **"I hated the unbelievable streets":** James Baldwin, *Notes of a Native Son,* in *Collected Essays,* p. 83.

230 **"It's been said, and it's been said":** James Baldwin, *The Last Interview and Other Conversations.* Brooklyn: Melville House, 2014, p. 89.

230 **"represents the justification of their history":** James Baldwin, *The Last Interview and Other Conversations,* p. 115.

230 **"all the American efforts to build a better world":** James Baldwin, *The Fire Next Time,* in *Collected Essays,* p. 345.

230 **"I have been, as the song says":** James Baldwin, "Nothing Personal," in *Collected Essays,* p. 705.

231 **"It is the voice of W. E. B. Du Bois":** Author's interview with Lonnie Bunch, August 11, 2025.

231 **"hearing and speaking their words":** Vincent Harding, "Is America Possible?," *On Being,* November 7, 2016, https://onbeing.org/blog/is-america-possible/.

232 **"If I am wrong":** Author's interview with Lonnie Bunch, August 11, 2025.

233 **Your country? Your history? No. It is ours:** W. E. B. Du Bois asked the question in 1903, "Would America have been American without her Negro people?" *The Souls of Black Folk,* in *Collected Writings,* p. 545.

SELECTED BIBLIOGRAPHY

Allen, Frederick Lewis. *Only Yesterday: An Informal History of the 1920s.* New York: Harper Perennial, 1964.

America's Birthday: A Planning and Activity Guide for Citizens' Participation During the Bicentennial Years. People's Bicentennial Commission. New York: Simon & Schuster, 1970.

Anderson, Carol. *Bourgeois Radicals: The NAACP and the Struggle for Colonial Liberation, 1941–1960.* New York: Cambridge University Press, 2014.

———. *White Rage: The Unspoken Truth of Our Racial Divide.* New York: Bloomsbury, 2017.

Bailey, Beth, and David Farber, eds. *America in the Seventies.* Lawrence: University Press of Kansas, 2004.

Baldwin, James. *Collected Essays,* ed. Toni Morrison. New York: Library of America, 1998.

———. *The Cross of Redemption: Uncollected Writings.* New York: Vintage Books, 2010.

———. *The Last Interview and Other Conversations.* Brooklyn: Melville House, 2014.

Bell, Derrick. *Faces at the Bottom of the Well.* New York: Basic Books, 2018.

Bellah, Robert. *The Broken Covenant: American Civil Religion in Time of Trial.* New York: Seabury Press, 1975.

Bellah, Robert, and Phillip E. Hammond. *Varieties of Civil Religion.* San Francisco: Harper & Row, 1980.

Bercovitch, Sacvan. *The Rites of Assent: Transformations in the Symbolic Construction of America.* London: Routledge, 2014.

Berlin, Ira. *The Long Emancipation: The Demise of Slavery in the United States.* Cambridge, MA: Harvard University Press, 2015.

Blight, David. *Race and Reunion: The Civil War and American Memory.* Cambridge, MA: Belknap Press, 2001.

———. *Frederick Douglass: Prophet of Freedom.* New York: Simon & Schuster, 2018.

Bodnar, John. *Remaking America: Public Memory, Commemoration, and Patriotism in the Twentieth Century.* Princeton: Princeton University Press, 1992.

Bourne, Randolph. *War and the Intellectuals: Collected Essays, 1915–1919.* New York: Harper & Row, 1964.

Bowers, Claude G. *The Tragic Era: The Revolution After Lincoln.* Cambridge, MA: Houghton Mifflin, 1929.
Branch, Taylor. *Parting the Waters: America in the King Years, 1954–1963.* New York: Simon & Schuster, 1988.
Bromwich, David. *Moral Imagination: Essays.* Princeton: Princeton University Press, 2014.
Brundage, William Fitzhugh. *The Southern Past: A Clash of Race and Memory.* Cambridge, MA: Belknap Press, 2005.
Carlyle, Thomas. *Shooting Niagara: And After?* London: Chapman & Hall, 1867.
Cashman, Sean Dennis. *America in the Gilded Age: From the Death of Lincoln to the Rise of Theodore Roosevelt.* 3rd ed. New York: New York University Press, 1993.
Chalmers, David M. *Hooded Americanism: The History of the Ku Klux Klan.* New York: Liveright, 2017.
Chermerinsky, Erwin. *No Democracy Lasts Forever: How the Constitution Threatens the United States.* New York: Liveright, 2024.
Chernow, Ron. *Grant.* New York: Penguin Press, 2017.
Colaiaco, James A. *Frederick Douglass and the Fourth of July.* New York: St. Martin's Griffin, 2006.
Coolidge, Calvin. *The Autobiography of Calvin Coolidge.* New York: Cosmopolitan Book Corporation, 1929.
Delbanco, Andrew. *The Real American Dream: A Meditation on Hope.* Cambridge, MA: Harvard University Press, 1999.
———. *The War Before the War: Fugitive Slaves and the Struggle for America's Soul from the Revolution to the Civil War.* New York: Penguin Press, 2018.
———. *Melville: His World and Work.* New York: Knopf, 2025.
Dewey, John. *The Public and Its Problems: An Essay in Political Enquiry.* Chicago: Gateway Books, 1946.
———. *The Quest for Certainty. Vol. 4: 1929,* ed. Jo Ann Boydston. Carbondale: Southern Illinois University Press, 1988.
Documentary History of the Negro People in the United States, ed. Herbert Aptheker. New York: Citadel Press, 1990.
Dorsey, Leroy G. *We Are All Americans, Pure and Simple: Theodore Roosevelt and the Myth of Americanism.* Tuscaloosa: University of Alabama Press, 2007.
Dos Passos, John. *The Ground We Stand On: Some Examples from the History of a Political Creed.* Boston: Houghton Mifflin, 1941.
———. *U.S.A.,* eds. Daniel Aaron and Townsend Ludington. New York: Library of America, 1996.
Dostoevsky, Fyodor. *The Brothers Karamazov: A Norton Critical Edition.* New York: W. W. Norton, 2011.
Douglass, Frederick. *Autobiographies,* ed. Henry Louis Gates Jr. New York: Library of America, 1994.
Du Bois, W. E. B. *Writings,* ed. Nathan Huggins. New York: Library of America, 1986.
———. *Black Reconstruction in America, 1860–1880.* New York: Free Press, 1998.
Eagleton, Terry. *Tragedy.* New Haven: Yale University Press, 2020.
Edwards, Eric R., Roderick A. Ferguson, and Jeffrey O. G. Ogbar. *Keywords for African American Studies.* New York: New York University Press, 2018.
Egerton, Douglas R. *The Wars of Reconstruction: The Brief, Violent History of America's Most Progressive Era.* New York: Bloomsbury Press, 2014.
Eliot, T. S. *Four Quartets.* Boston: Mariner Books, 1943.
Ellison, Ralph. *The Collected Works of Ralph Ellison,* ed. John F. Callahan. New York: Modern Library, 1995.
Emerson, Ralph Waldo. *Essays and Lectures,* ed. Joel Porte. New York: Library of America, 1983.

Fariello, Griffin. *Red Scare: Memories of the American Inquisition; an Oral History.* New York: Knopf, 2008.
Foner, Eric. *Reconstruction: America's Unfinished Revolution, 1863–1877.* New York: Harper Perennial, 1988.
Formisana, Ronald P. *Boston Against Busing: Race, Class, and Ethnicity in the 1960s and 1970s.* Chapel Hill: University of North Carolina Press, 1991.
Franklin, John Hope. *Race and History: Selected Essays, 1938–1988.* Baton Rouge: Louisiana State University Press, 1989.
Givens, James. *Fugitive Pedagogy: Carter G. Woodson and the Art of Black Teaching.* Cambridge, MA: Harvard University Press, 2021.
Gordon, Linda. *The Second Coming of the KKK: The Ku Klux Klan of the 1920s and the American Political Tradition.* New York: Liveright, 2017.
Harris, Leslie. *The Rhetoric of White Slavery and the Making of National Identity.* Lansing: Michigan State University Press, 2023.
Hepp, John Henry, IV. *Mystery and Marvel: Philadelphia's 1876 Centennial Exposition.* Havertown, PA: Brookline Books, 2024.
Hofstadter, Richard. *The Age of Reform: From Bryan to FDR.* New York: Knopf, 1948.
———. *The Paranoid Style in American Politics, and Other Essays.* New York: Knopf, 1965.
James, William. *The Will to Believe and Other Essays in Popular Philosophy.* New York: Dover, 1956.
Kammen, Michael. *Mystic Chords of Memory: The Transformation of Tradition in American Culture.* New York: Knopf, 1991.
Kaveney, Cathleen. *Prophecy Without Contempt: Religious Discourse in the Public Square.* Cambridge, MA: Harvard University Press, 2016.
Keels, Thomas H. *Sesqui!: Greed, Graft, and the Forgotten World's Fair of 1926.* Philadelphia: Temple University Press, 2017.
Kelley, Robin D. G., and Earl Lewis. *To Make Our World Anew: A History of African Americans from 1980.* New York: Oxford University Press, 2000.
———. *Freedom Dreams: The Black Radical Imagination.* Boston: Beacon Press, 2002.
Kendi, Ibram X. *How to Be an Antiracist.* New York: One World, 2019.
———. *Stamped from the Beginning: The Definitive History of Racist Ideas in America.* New York: Bold Type Books, 2023.
Kruse, Kevin. *White Flight: Atlanta and the Making of Modern Conservativism.* Princeton: Princeton University Press, 2007.
Kruse, Kevin, and Julian E. Zelizer. *Fault Lines: A History of the United States Since 1974.* New York: W. W. Norton, 2020.
Lehman, Nicholas. *Redemption: The Last Battle of the Civil War.* New York: Farrar, Straus & Giroux, 2012.
Lepore, Jill. *These Truths: A History of the United States.* New York: W. W. Norton, 2018.
———. *This America: The Case for the Nation.* New York: Liveright, 2019.
Lowdnes, Joseph E. *From the New Deal to the New Right: Race and the Southern Origins of Modern Conservatism.* New Haven: Yale University Press, 2008.
Madison, James H. *The Ku Klux Klan in the Heartland.* Bloomington: Indiana University Press, 2020.
Mailer, Norman. *The Armies of the Night.* New York: New American Library, 1968.
Marable, Manning. *Race, Reform, and Rebellion: The Second Reconstruction and Beyond in Black America, 1945–2006.* Jackson: University Press of Mississippi, 1984.
Masur, Louis P. *The Soiling of Old Glory: The Story of a Photograph That Shocked America.* Waltham, MA: Brandeis University Press, 2008.

Meacham, Jon. *The Soul of America: The Battle for Our Better Angels.* New York: Random House, 2018.

Melville, Herman. *White Jacket, or The World in a Man-of-War.* Evanston, IL: Northwestern University Press, 1970.

Morrison, Toni. *Beloved.* New York: Vintage Books, 1987.

Nash, Gary. *Forging Freedom: The Formation of Philadelphia's Black Community, 1720–1840.* Cambridge, MA: Harvard University Press, 1988.

Nature of a Humane Society: A Symposium on the Bicentennial of the United States of America, ed. H. Ober Hess. Philadelphia: Fortress Press, 1976.

Negro Orators and Their Orations, ed. Carter G. Woodson. New York: Russell & Russell, 1969.

Painter, Nell. *Creating Black Americans: African-American History and Its Meanings, 1619 to the Present.* New York: Oxford University Press, 2006.

———. *The History of White People.* New York: W. W. Norton, 2010.

Perry, Imani. *May We Forever Stand: A History of the Black National Anthem.* Chapel Hill: University of North Carolina Press, 2021.

———. *South to America: A Journey Below the Mason-Dixon to Understand the Soul of a Nation.* New York: Ecco, 2023.

———. *Black in Blues: How a Color Tells the Story of My People.* New York: Ecco, 2025.

Piereson, James. *Shattered Consensus: The Rise and Decline of America's Postwar Political Order.* New York: Encounter Books, 2015.

Rodgers, Daniel. *The Age of Fracture.* Cambridge, MA: Belknap Press, 2011.

Said, Edward. *Beginnings: Intention and Method.* New York: Columbia University Press, 1985.

Schlesinger, Arthur M., Jr. *The Cycles of American History.* Boston: Houghton Mifflin, 1986.

———. *The Disuniting of America.* New York: W. W. Norton, 1992.

Schulman, Bruce. *Rightward Bound: Making America Conservative in the 1970s.* Cambridge, MA: Harvard University Press, 2008.

Sides, John, Chris Tausanovitch, and Lynn Vavereck. *The Bitter End: The 2020 Presidential Campaign and the Challenge to American Democracy.* Princeton: Princeton University Press, 2022.

Sides, John, Micheal Tesler, and Lynn Vavereck. *Identity Crisis: The 2016 Presidential Campaign and the Battle for the Meaning of America.* Princeton: Princeton University Press, 2019.

Singh, Nikhil Pal. *Black Is a Country: Race and the Unfinished Struggle for Democracy.* Cambridge, MA: Harvard University Press, 2004.

Sinha, Manisha. *The Rise and Fall of the Second American Republic: Reconstruction, 1860–1920.* New York: Liveright, 2025.

Slotkin, Richard. *Regeneration Through Violence: The Mythology of the American Frontier, 1600–1860.* 1973; reprint New York Oxford University Press, 2000.

———. *A Great Disorder: National Myth and the Battle for America.* Cambridge, MA: Harvard University Press, 2024.

Sontag, Susan. *Essays of the 1960s & 70s,* ed. David Rieff. New York: Library of America, 2013.

Spilman, Lyn. *Nation and Commemoration: Creating National Identities in the United States and Australia.* New York: Cambridge University Press, 1997.

Stoddard, Lothrop. *The Rising Tide of Color Against White World Supremacy.* New York: Charles Scribner's Sons, 1920.

Tocqueville, Alexis de. *Democracy in America,* ed. J. P. Mayer. New York: Doubleday, 1969.

Trilling, Lionel. *The Moral Obligation to Be Intelligent: Selected Essays.* Evanston, IL: Northwestern University Press, 2000.

Tuveson, Ernest. *Redeemer Nation: The Idea of America's Millennial Role.* Chicago: University of Chicago Press, 1968.
Vidal, Gore. *1876: A Novel.* New York: Vintage International, 1976.
Walzer, Michael. *What It Means to Be an American.* New York: Marsilio, 1992.
Warren, Robert Penn. *The Legacy of the Civil War.* New York: Random House, 1961.
Whitman, James Q. *Hitler's American Model: The United States and the Making of Nazi Race Law.* Princeton: Princeton University Press, 2017.
Whitman, Walt. *The Portable Whitman,* ed. Mark Van Doren. New York: Penguin Books, 1945.
Wilentz, Sean. *The Age of Reagan: A History, 1974–2008.* New York: Harper, 2008.
Williams, Kidada E. *I Saw Death Coming: A History of Terror and Survival in the War Against Reconstruction.* New York: Bloomsbury, 2023.
Wilson, Charles Reagan. *Baptized in Blood: The Religion of the Lost Cause, 1865–1920.* Athens: University of Georgia Press, 1980.

INDEX

ABOUT THE AUTHOR

EDDIE S. GLAUDE JR. is the James S. McDonnell Distinguished University Professor of African American Studies at Princeton University and author of *New York Times* bestselling *Begin Again* and *Democracy in Black.*